Land Law and Urban Policy in Context

This book is a collection of essays honouring and engaging with the work of the late Professor Patrick McAuslan. It is a collection that narrates, analyses and critiques McAuslan's contributions, as well as offering substantive perspectives on how his work has impacted the legal fields in which he was involved: including those of land law, urban planning law and policy, land use and participation in developing countries, democratic constitutionalism, and legal education. The essays present McAuslan's contributions in the contexts in which they emerged, and according to both the circumstances and motivations that shaped them, as well as the challenges they encountered. It thus provides an ideal point of engagement for scholars, students and policy makers that have already interacted with McAuslan's ideas and work, or who have yet to do so.

Thanos Zartaloudis is based at Kent Law School, University of Kent, UK.

Land Law and Urban Policy in Context

Essays on the contributions of Patrick McAuslan

Edited by
Thanos Zartaloudis

Routledge
Taylor & Francis Group
LONDON AND NEW YORK

First published 2017
by Birkbeck Law Press

2 Park Square, Milton Park, Abingdon, Oxfordshire OX14 4RN
711 Third Avenue, New York, NY 10017

Routledge is an imprint of the Taylor & Francis Group, an informa business

First issued in paperback 2018

British Library Cataloguing in Publication Data
A catalogue record for this book is available from the British Library

Library of Congress Cataloging-in-Publication Data
A catalog record for this title has been requested

ISBN: 978-1-138-66910-9 (hbk)
ISBN: 978-1-138-59082-3 (pbk)

Typeset in New Baskerville
by Fish Books Ltd.

To Fiona McAuslan

Contents

Acknowledgements

The editor would like to thank the School of Law at Birkbeck College (University of London) and Birkbeck Law Press for their support to the publication of this edited collection, as well as Kent Law School (University of Kent) for their funding of the index preparation. The contributors to this volume have enriched this effort in a multiplicity of significant ways and their perseverance and patience with the long process that was required in the making of this collection is most deserving of genuine gratitude. Colin Perrin and the production team have kindly and attentively facilitated this volume (particular thanks are due to Simon Barraclough and Karl Harrington). Valerie Hoare, finally, has been the most generous and caring assistant in the editorial process throughout the various stages of producing this volume and I cannot thank her enough for her dedication, care and collegiality. Above all heartfelt thanks are due to Patrick McAuslan for being a most genuine mentor and friend over the years.

Contributors

Martin Adams has over forty years of experience as an international consultant, now specialising in national land policy and related issues. Over the last 25 years, he has worked with governments and civil society organisations, mainly in eastern and southern Africa. He is a member of Mokoro Ltd, a consultancy firm based in Oxford whose members share a commitment to sustainable international development and poverty reduction.

Antonio Azuela is a researcher at the Instituto de Investigaciones Sociales, Universidad Autònoma de Mèxico in Coyoacan and has acted as Mexico's Federal Attorney for the Environment.

Martin Loughlin is professor of public law at the London School of Economics and Political Science. In 2007–8 he was a Fellow of the Wissenschaftskolleg zu Berlin, and in 2012–13 he held a Law and Public Affairs Fellowship at Princeton University. He is also a Fellow of the British Academy.

Ambreena Manji is professor of land law and development at Cardiff Law School, Cardiff University. She has held academic posts at Keele and Warwick and between 2010 and 2014 was seconded to Nairobi as the director of the British Institute in Eastern Africa.

John McEldowney is professor of law at the University of Warwick. He has held visiting appointments in universities in Japan and France. In 2000 he was the World Bank Visiting Fellow in the Supreme Court in Venezuela. He has given evidence to a number of inquiries held by the House of Lords Select Committee on the Constitution.

Linda Mulcahy is a professor of law at the LSE and director of its PhD academy. Previously she was a professor of law at Birkbeck College, School of Law.

Abdul Paliwala is emeritus professor of law at the School of Law, University of Warwick and a visiting professor at Birkbeck University of London.

Leslie A. Stein was a visiting scholar at the Center for Climate Change Law at Columbia Law School, before becoming a scholar in residence at the Center for Environmental Legal Studies at Pace Law School, New York. He has also taught in England, Canada, and Australia. From 1993 to 2003, Professor Stein served as chief judge of the Town Planning Appeal Tribunal of Western Australia.

William Twining is Emeritus Quain Professor of Jurisprudence at UCL, London and has held chairs in Belfast and Warwick and numerous international visiting appointments.

Liz Alden Wily [PhD] is a political economist specialising in agrarian land tenure, working as both technical adviser and researcher, mainly in Africa. She is a Fellow of the Rights and Resources Initiative (Washington), the Van Vollenhoven Institute of the School of Law in Leiden, and Katiba Institute in Kenya.

Thanos Zartaloudis co-convened Land Law with Patrick McAuslan for a decade at Birkbeck College, School of Law, before being appointed at Kent Law School (University of Kent). He also teaches at the Architectural Association (London).

Preface

Dorrette McAuslan

Following the untimely death of my husband Professor Patrick McAuslan, in January 2014, there came numerous tributes from many who knew him personally, from some who were acquainted with his academic work, and from others who knew him through his involvement in the affairs of many countries.

Several of these tributes commented on the serious and purposeful quality of his thinking, of his warm and supportive nature, of his conversations which were always full of interest and topped with a quizzical sense of humour; all qualities which added value to his distinguished career not only as an academic lawyer but also as a legal consultant to Governments of many countries on issues concerning land use and constitutional affairs, and as a local district councillor in Warwickshire, England.

Patrick, as many knew him, was a very modest man who could not be described as being pretentious in any sense, he listened to the less intellectual with the same degree of interest as he gave to his academic and intellectual colleagues as well as members of governments. Yet in his quiet way he was forceful enough to encourage changes in some traditionally conservative institutions which benefitted some of the most disenfranchised people in our world.

Most of the people who posted comments on the internet, or wrote of him in the obituary columns of papers and professional magazines were highly educated, intellectual and influential in their own spheres.

Missing from among the very public tributes to Patrick (or 'the Prof', as most of these other individuals knew him) were the comments of admiration, messages of sadness, but most strikingly of gratitude from people whose life he, or an element of his work, had touched. Many of these would not have matched the eloquence of other tributes, but the notes, telephone calls and personal messengers reflected another aspect of Patrick's life, known only by his family and in particular myself.

Throughout our lives together, he has always taken a keen interest in my activities in the communities with which I worked – mainly in the more deprived areas of large cities in the UK. It was his strong sense of justice and his inner anger at the plight of many of the people he had come across and helped in various parts of the world that brought us together in the first place.

Early in our married life, this was once demonstrated by his interest in the lives of 18 young women of African Caribbean background with whom I became involved when they were youngsters going through an educational system in which the lack of opportunities to them meant, to quote their then headmistress, 'The best would end up in Tesco's and the rest in the launderette in the south of town in Leamington Spa', which was at that time symbolic of the lack of any achievement whether socially, economically or educationally. I must add that this is no longer the case today as South Leamington Spa is now a successful area of Warwickshire from which a number of local talents frequently emerge.

It was my involvement with these girls and their frustration at not being able to pursue their desires to attain better careers than had their parents that drew Patrick's attention to their dilemma. What dilemma? Being born into a society in which all avenues of progress were blocked to them. This was at a time when Patrick was deep in the throes of writing what has sometimes been described as his masterpiece, otherwise entitled *The Ideologies of Planning Law*.

I knew how important this work was to him (as were most other things he did). He decided to spend the sabbatical at home writing. This he did daily from 8.30 a.m. to 6.30 p.m., with only limited breaks for his meals. And so it was with a degree of trepidation that I suggested to him that the 18 high-spirited and sometimes boisterous girls should meet twice weekly at our home so that I could help them with their studies and at the same time support them in their aspirations. Patrick did not object and expressed surprise that I thought he may have done so. 'Won't that disturb your work', I asked him. And his reply? – 'Someone has to give them a chance'. That was some 40-plus years ago. He helped me open the way for these young people and he watched with me as they grasped the opportunity, that *chance*, which was made available to them through Patrick's commitment to social justice and fairness, and he enjoyed with me the knowledge that all but one had gained better positions in their lives than their parents had. The *chance* had at last come their way.

This experience opened his eyes to forms of deprivation other than those he had observed while living in Nigeria and Tanzania and it consolidated his belief that access to education was the only way out for the many. He noticed when working or travelling in countries in Africa, as well as other parts of the world, that the failed American Dream of George and Lennie, main characters in John Steinbeck's *Of Mice and Men*, was to be repeated time and again. He believed that in many instances the reality of owning that small piece of land with a house and garden, yielding provisions to feed a family, evaded the poor because of the greed of the rich whose rights were enshrined in unfair practices and archaic land laws. It was this that caused him to dedicate a great part of his life and scholarship to bringing about a degree of change wherever he could. Change that motivated some of the individuals who contacted me after his death to credit him with the fact that they now own a place they call their own. 'I am now a land owner! Thanks to McAuslan', said one proud Ugandan woman.

Patrick noticed just how much the lack of books and other materials hindered the progress of some students in countries outside the UK where students and scholars do not have the same access to funds to purchase materials or have the luxury of the use of well stocked libraries. Shortage of funds did not only trouble students in the developing world, but here at home also.

He was visibly angered and distressed when on one occasion I told him about my day in court as a magistrate. A young student, away from home for the first time, had run out of funds before the end of term. For some reason he felt unable to ask his parents who were already strapped for cash, for money. Overcome by hunger, he stole a piece of pork pie from the grocery shop on campus, was apprehended by the store detectives and brought to court. In court were two store detectives, the store manager and the city police officer who was called to the store to arrest and charge the hungry young man – all to hear the young man plead guilty to stealing a piece of pork pie to the value of £1.99 because he had no funds left from that term's grant. A terrible blot on a young life! All for a piece of pork pie that was almost past the sell-by date.

While Patrick was working with the United Nations Centre for Human Settlements in Kenya, we both lived in Nairobi. I heard frequently from the local people who maintained our apartment about the *Harambe* events when villagers gathered to contribute funds to enable a son or daughter of that village to pursue studies at home or somewhere in Europe or America. We also met several people who had to curtail their studies because the funds had been used up and perhaps the crops at home had failed or their land been 'acquired'. On one occasion we were followed through the streets of Dar es Salaam by one such person. Just as I was about to become alarmed by this stalker, he quickly stood in front of us and addressed my husband thus: 'Sir, I detect you to be the Professor Patrick McAuslan. I was a student of law and I have read your book, sir. May I shake your hand, sir. It is a great honour to meet so great a man.' Patrick was visibly humbled and asked the man about his studies only to learn that like most of the people in his village, his parent's crops had failed, he had to abandon his studies and seek employment to help out at home. His hope was to pursue his studies again later when, hopefully, circumstances would improve. This was a scenario repeated time and time again even in the UK.

Events like these made a great impression on Patrick and I believe that much of his work both in and outside the UK was motivated by his desire to reduce inequality and injustice by helping to create opportunities for the less privileged and by creating laws and constitutions which, in a modest way, he hoped would confront the roots causes of poverty and deprivation and enable the *Georges* and *Lennies* to realise their dreams. It is my hope, as I know it would be his, that this book will go some way to encourage the readers to push those boundaries that block the aspirations of many. As a husband and friend, father and grandfather, he has left a lasting impression, not just on his family, but also on others in many parts of the globe.

Finally, and of equal importance, I would like to thank all those colleagues of the late Patrick McAuslan for their role in making the publication of this tribute to his work throughout a long academic career possible. There are a number of individuals to whom particular mention should be made who, despite their heavy workload elsewhere, found the time to liaise with each other, with the contributors and with myself to make an idea a reality. Among them are Valerie Kelley who, although now retired from Birkbeck, continued to work on the project from her home in the North of England; Professor John McEldowney for his unwavering support and advice to me throughout; and Thanos Zartaloudis who undertook the tedious task of co-ordinating and editing the book – a truly great tribute to Patrick by his colleagues.

Note

Dorrette McAuslan was born in Jamaica and grew up in London. She met Patrick McAuslan in London and they got married in 1968 before going to live in Wisconsin in December of that year, where Patrick was a Visiting Professor at the Wisconsin State University. There she became involved in the first psychiatric unit in a general hospital in that state and in the introduction of a new approach to psychiatric treatment and care in the Veteran's Administration Hospital. She qualified as a health visitor before going on to obtain a Master's degree and PhD in public policy and health administration. She held several offices on public bodies in England, among which were, the BBC General Advisory Council; West Midland Regional Health Authority, the Race Relations Board, the Commission for Racial Equality and the National Consumer Council. She was appointed and served 12 years as deputy and later chair of the South Warwickshire National Health Hospitals Trust.

At the same time, she served as a member of the Warwickshire Police Authority, where she steered through the recommendations of the McPherson Report on the death of Stephen Lawrence and became very involved with the in-service training of senior police officers. Dorrette

McAuslan was a member of the Commission of Inquiry into the Education of Children of Ethnic Minorities under the chairmanship of the late Lord Swann, which marked significant changes in the curriculum in state schools and in the methods of training teachers and teaching children. She was, for 28 years, a magistrate in the city of Coventry and a member of the Commonwealth Magistrates and Judges Association.

Introduction

Thanos Zartaloudis, Linda Mulcahy and Abdul Paliwala

With Patrick McAuslan's death what had been a project designed to celebrate his work at a conference organised at Birkbeck Law School on 12–13 January 2012, is sadly also an honorary commemoration of the person and of the work. Yet we shall continue to remember and celebrate him and his seminal as well as multi-faceted contributions to scholarship, education, policy and law making. This volume is only a preliminary part to what is held to be a necessary long-term study of Patrick McAuslan's work and contributions to numerous fields, worldwide, in the time to come.

Patrick McAuslan was a rare person in the academy; a man who attracted widespread respect even among his critics, of whom there are few. Reading the many tributes about him, which appeared in the aftermath of his death in January 2014, we have been struck by the frequency with which certain words are used to describe him. His wisdom, craving for social justice, wry sense of humour, respect for indigenous understandings of rights in the countries where he assisted in land reform, and commitment to public service are frequently cited as his defining characteristics as a person. He has been described as a 'landmark figure', a 'pioneer' and a 'founding father'. He has been honoured as an expert in the fields of law and development; administrative and public law; land law; urban law; law reform; sustainable development; poverty alleviation; law in context and planning law. It may seem like a very English and outdated adjective, but Patrick McAuslan is also widely acknowledged to have been a decent man who provided an exemplary model of what it meant to be a fine scholar, teacher, public servant and person.

McAuslan was undoubtedly an exceptionally able scholar. He graduated from Oxford University having obtained a double first BA and BCL degree in 1961 and went on to work at a succession of prestigious and influential law schools. He was a founder member of the law school at Dar es Salaam between 1961–1966 and enjoyed a brief spell at the London School of Economics in London before joining the University of Warwick in 1968.

Promoted to Professor in 1974, he stayed there until 1986 when he moved back to the LSE and in 1992 joined University College London as Professor of Urban Management. Technically he retired in 1999, though many of us know this to be a myth. He continued to be closely involved in policy circles and held a part-time professorial appointment at Birkbeck College when a new Law Department was established in 1993. He was still enthusiastically teaching there and planning future research projects when he died. The list of the institutions with which he was affiliated is indeed an impressive one, but it is what he did while at each of these universities that gives us insight into the many gifts he left behind.

The scholarship that McAuslan has left us with has long provoked debate and should continue to influence future generations of scholars. He was the author of numerous books, articles and chapters including his landmark monograph, *The Ideologies of Planning Law*, which, like his other work, pioneered the exploration of links between law, society and justice. His long standing interest in contextual approaches to law was heralded in his early book on *Public Law and Political Change in Kenya* in which he challenged traditional accounts of law as a discrete discipline and advocated multi-disciplinary and comparative approaches to law. For Manji (2014) this particular book remains the *locus classicus* on constitutional development under British colonialism and contains an incisive and hard hitting critique of the enduring legacy of repression and authoritarianism. His most recent book, *Land Law Reform in East Africa: Traditional or Transformative?* published in the year before his death, carries a characteristically frank and provocative message about the failure of top-down planning and colonial models of land administration in several East African States. Far from attempting to be an apologist for legally constituted systems of land administration, he argued that those interested in social justice could not fail to recognise that revolution had achieved more than incremental legal reform. This thesis reflects a life-long interest in bottom-up approaches to law reform, which has long endeared him to socio-legal and critical scholars.

McAuslan's work included projects in Africa, Asia, the Middle East, the Pacific and Eastern Europe. He worked in more than 35 countries in the developing world. Most importantly he was acknowledged as one of the foremost scholars and advocates of land reform in Africa where his interventions were later to earn him an MBE for services to African land use and environment in 2001. His promotion of land reform in English-speaking Africa and focus on protecting traditional land tenure, played a significant role in undermining the colonial structures that had been retained at independence. By allowing ordinary people to participate in decisions about land use and enhancing the security of their land rights these reforms contributed to the legal empowerment of millions, and crucially women who might otherwise have been marginalised or excluded.

Equally as significant was the work he undertook as a practitioner, or what Perry-Kessaris (2011) has labelled a 'pracademic'. He regularly acted as an advisor for the UN, the World Bank, the European Union and the Department for International Development (DfID). He worked for several years for the United Nations Environment Programme (UNEP) in Kenya where he authored several policy documents. In the 1990s he took up a senior role in the UN-Habitat Urban Management Programme in Kenya, and was commissioned to convert Tanzania's ambitious national land policy into legislation. The latter resulted in two substantial pieces of legislation on which reforms in Uganda and South Sudan were later modelled. McAuslan possessed the very enviable skill of being able to work effectively at the interface of academic research and policy and to covert an idea into a practice. His ability to do so, to work as both a critic, intellectual and drafter has left him with admirers in academic, political and policy circles.

McAuslan will also be remembered as an enthusiastic teacher who inspired numerous students to enter academic life, the world of land reform or just to be critical and questioning thinkers. As a teacher he provided a model for us all, students as well as colleagues. 'Paddy Mac', as his students were apt to call him, was consistently keen, committed and genuinely interested in hearing what students had to say. While at Birkbeck, students regularly commented on his sincerity, kindness, clarity of thought, humour, ability to get to the heart of the issue and his extensive knowledge of law, practice and politics. McAuslan was never someone who shrank from teaching; indeed, he sometimes taught more than his fair share without complaint and had to be stopped from volunteering to do more. In addition to delivering excellent classes he made an important contribution to ideas about what it was legitimate to teach. His early involvements in educational experiments at Dar es Salaam, where the goal was to develop an indigenous, socially relevant law programme for the newly independent country, is said to have opened his eyes to the limitations of his own legal education at Oxford (Loughlin 2014).

This was, in fact, the beginning for McAuslan of the 'Law in Context' approach whose genesis in Dar es Salaam is described by William Twining (in this volume) who, with McAuslan and A.B. Weston, was one of the three originators of the Dar Law Faculty. The Faculty was subsequently reinforced by luminaries such as Yash Ghai, Sol Picciotto, Aki Sawyerr and briefly even Wolfgang Friedman. As Twining writes in this volume, it was Julius Nyerere's expectation that:

> we should teach East African Law in Context – and context here meant the historic break with colonialism, local circumstances and problems, and the ideology of the first Independence Government. The university should aspire to international standards of excellence, to traditional (Western) academic values, but it must contribute to nation

> building, focus on African problems and conditions, and study law in its local context.
>
> Twining, this volume, Chapter 2

Both McAuslan and Twining were open to this as a result of their own previous African experiences, with McAuslan in Nigeria and Twining in the Sudan. For McAuslan, innovative teaching and research had to go together and the contextual research resulted in perhaps the most significant work on East African law – Ghai and McAuslan's *Public Law and Political Change in Kenya* published in 1970. The book's innovation lay firstly in broadening the traditional understanding of public law to a point at which public law involved a wider set of governance institutions than lawyers were used to at the time; for example, the nature of agrarian administration. Secondly, public law had to be studied in extensive detail involving both colonial history and the transition to independence. Thirdly, the objective of the study was to resolve underlying issues of constitutionalism and legitimacy and in particular whether a system based on charismatic legitimacy founded on the personality of the then president could survive in the absence of real legitimacy of the institutions of governance. The question is as fresh today, over 50 years after independence, as it was then.

McAuslan was to build on this experience when he returned to England where he played a key role in the establishment of the Law in Context approach at Warwick Law School in accordance with the vision of Geoffrey Wilson, the founding head of department. Wilson requested colleagues to develop their own interpretation of a contextual approach to law. Wilson had heard about the impressive new approach to legal education in Dar es Salaam. He had also had discussions about a contextual approach with William Twining who was by then teaching in Belfast. It was therefore not surprising that there would be an 'African' contextual influence in the Faculty with initially McAuslan, Sol Picciotto and Patrick Atiyah (who had been in the Sudan) and subsequently William Twining becoming key players. McAuslan's very contextual underpinning meant that Warwick's different environment required a different contextual approach using policy perspectives inherited from radical English public lawyers (Loughlin, in this volume). He was to take up Geoffrey Wilson's challenge to rethink property law and he developed two innovative courses followed by an innovative book merging the two topics into *Land, Law and Planning (Law in Context)* in 1975. Twining, in this volume, provides an excellent description of the development of the courses and the book. The underlying context within which land law worked was the reality of housing, both public and private and the institutions involved in the provision of housing. Thus the legal transactions involved were broader; for example, council tenancy agreements, studied as processes and within the context of the social reality. This formed the launch pad for an understanding of wider innovative issues of planning law. McAuslan's main innovation, which has subsequently transformed our appreciation of land, property and planning laws, as related by Loughlin, was to transcend the private law and public law divide in the teaching of the subject, but also emphasise the role of law in promoting public policy objectives. No-one thought of the integral connection between private property law and public law, which was the dominant domain of undergraduate legal education and planning law. The book established that private property rights were centrally located within the contextual framework of national planning policy. Equally significantly, the object of study had to be not only the cases and primary legislation but also forms of regulation and, of equal significance, the regulatory process.

McAuslan's second major contribution to Law in Context was to the genesis of Warwick Law School's Law in Development Programme, the longest surviving programme of its kind under the new title of International Development Law and Human Rights. At a meeting in 1980 including McAuslan, Jill Cottrell, Yash Ghai, Francis Snyder and Abdul Paliwala, with McAuslan and Yash being the main movers, the initial idea was for two separate programmes. McAuslan's objective was education of middle level government personnel and for Yash it was the academia. While one emphasised the development of practical skills and the other intellectual skills, it was soon realised that there was no fundamental distance between the two conceptions in the sense that both elements were essential to the projected programme. The *in* as opposed to *and* was a fundamental conceptual marker of the programme. It established both the intellectual and political distance from the embers of Law and Development at Yale and Wisconsin.

That Law and Development movement was already in crisis when the Warwick programme started was vouched for by Trubek and Galanter's essay (1974) on 'Scholars in Self-Estrangement'. They correctly identified Law and Development studies as part of 'development assistance' by the US government and other international and private agencies. The essay fundamentally questioned whether the diffusion of western 'modern' law would lead to development and liberal values. The *in* signified a distancing from the Law and Development movement as well as an openness towards the subject of the relationship between Law and Development in accordance with the Warwick Law in Context approach. It enabled a critical examination of Law and Development, especially questioning simplistic assumptions about the relationship between the two.

As indicated above, the programme's genesis was in capacity building; thus its objective was to enable open inquiry as to the nature of law in developing societies and in particular, the issues which confronted them. The synthesis of McAuslan's initial practical concerns and Yash's wider theoretical objectives led to a programme which has continued to be rich and varied and able to adapt to a changing global environment. It is useful to further relate McAuslan's approach to Wilson's vision of law in context. Wilson's vision was very broad and tolerated a wide range of approaches as described by both himself and Ross Cranston (Wilson and Cranston 1995). Thus Cranston suggests that Warwick Law School encompassed 'pluralism' with the 'approach moving from Patrick Atiyah with his focus at the time on the historical context of contract doctrine, to the theory-laden Marxist approaches at the other end of the spectrum' (Wilson and Cranston 1995, p. 5). However, within this pluralism, Wilson's own preference was to emphasise 'legal scholarship' as an independent discourse.

His approach 'does not begin with law or even legal scholarship and ask what out there is relevant to it. It starts with what is out there and asks about the relevance of legal scholarship to it'. (Wilson and Cranston 1995, p. 239). In particular, Wilson insists that legal scholarship should not be tied to a particular social or human science but be an independent cultural discourse. Wilson also emphasised that the context of law had changed so that it now had to encompass international perspectives. In addition, the context, however broadly conceived, which is the starting point of the examination, has nevertheless to be explored from the legal scholar's perspective.

In many respects McAuslan's approach fitted squarely within this perspective with an emphasis on the study of social issues and locating the role of law within this overall perspective. However, there was an underlying radical ideology in his framework of analysis. For example, in relation to planning law, he saw the balancing between ideologies of private property, public interest and public participation and increasingly promoted participation as a human right. Loughlin and Azuela (in this volume) indicate the tremendous achievements of this approach in relation to McAuslan's work on urban law. However, Loughlin also points to its limitations – the main one being that ultimately it resulted in an instrumentalist perspective for law which could not deal effectively with the fundamental structural changes brought about by neo-liberal dominance in society. In some ways this raises valid questions about the reification of legal discourses and the need to consider legal discourses as complexly interacting with other discourses. McAuslan's strong adherence to the significance of legal regulation also became apparent in the drafting of legislation implementing the Tanzanian National Land Policy when he suggested that legal controls were ultimately preferable to giving peasants a large amount of control:

> Peasants have their share of the good, the bad and the ugly and without pretty close supervision, there would be those who would grab land, oppress their fellows especially women, ignore the law, forget about justice and rights, take and receive bribes.
>
> McAuslan 2013: 116

On the other hand, for Shivji (2006: 180–186) the belief in people was more valuable and the provisions of the Act as enacted would lead to wholesale alienation of village lands under the guise of joint ventures.

These contentious issues go to the very root of arguments about the significance of law in context. Nevertheless, it is no coincidence that both Warwick and Birkbeck Law Schools now enjoy international reputations as leading law schools in the field of law and context and critical legal studies. In this sense, his most important legacy was a passionate commitment to teaching law from the perspective of the deprived and disadvantaged; those who were affected by law rather than those who argued for it or drafted it. The modest but powerful insistence on the combination of technical legal study with inter-disciplinary and critical approaches was perhaps the ever needed reminder, within a generally conventional legal academy, that legal pedagogy and research can change and must change.

For those of us who worked with McAuslan our appreciation of his many talents often focused on the apparently mundane. His regular attendance at academic and social events, his genuine interest in the work of emerging scholars, his skills as an ever modest mentor and most of all his intellectual curiosity and generosity were all evident on a day-to-day basis. As a former head of department at Warwick he was fully aware of the trials of senior management. Behind the scenes, he would frequently offer sage advice, which left one feeling advised and supported rather than criticised or foolish. Though he had the look of someone who was conventional, he was far from it. He had a quick, and at times acerbic wit, and was as ready as the next person to poke fun at life. His life was well lived and he was fully committed to the things he believed in: his family, the promotion of land reform; the need for institutional modernisation in developing and urbanising countries; the improvement of the life of the disadvantaged; the provision of a challenging and socially and critically minded academic education and most crucially the importance of listening and speaking at the right time, with *parrhesia* as well as love.

Summary of the Chapters

In what is the first publication of McAuslan's inaugural lecture in the early 1990s at Birkbeck College, *Scholarly origins of preaching and practice: Lord and Professor in the understanding of modern land law,* McAuslan offers a reflective account of his approaches to legal scholarship with particular regard to English land law, emphasising the need for a new approach to legal scholarship in this field. He offers a lucid and crucial critique of what he explains as the dominant model of writing and researching about land law (focusing on exposition rather than critique of the law), as well as the reasons for it, comparing it to the approach taken, increasingly at variance, by the judiciary and the links to policy making. In doing so, McAuslan reengages with the appreciation and evaluation of the ambition of the Law In Context approach. In particular, he turns further to the role of the Law Commission and the judiciary in the last 30 years to suggest that, interestingly, these have advanced a greater perception of the 'real world of land law', as he calls it, than legal textbooks. Significant markers for the future of teaching and learning in land law are posited with regard to the need to never ignore the pragmatic and political-economic nature of what is at stake in and beside land law and policy, as well as the much needed internationalisation of the approach to the subject.

Twining's contribution *McAuslan in context: early days in Dar and Warwick* narrates and reflects on the histories and contexts of two of McAuslan's educational, as well as substantive, contributions in the foundation and development of two new Law Schools in Warwick and Dar es Salaam. With regard to the early 1960s and the founding of the law school in Dar es Salaam, Twining explains the circumstances and inspirations that led to this initiative, as well as the ideological, pedagogical and strategic decisions and tensions that were confronted. In a tone as personal as reflective, Twining describes and evaluates the impact of this innovative law school in East Africa. Apart from valuable insight offered as to the founding of a new law school, and the lessons one can draw from that in relation to academic reform and pedagogical approaches, it also offers the reader a pragmatic explanation as to how the Law in Context approach was first conceived before it became a more formal 'movement' in the UK and beyond. Next, Twining turns to the founding of the law school at Warwick in the late 1960s, where McAuslan worked for 18 years and where he instituted new pedagogical approaches and research agendas in land law and planning law in particular. The latter contributions have been key aspects of the McAuslan *legacy* and will remain so for the time to come. Twining thus explores their long-lasting significance and influence.

Paliwala's Chapter *Context, political economy and good governance: avatars of Dar legal education* explains and evaluates the so-called multiple 'avatars', of the development of legal education in Dar es Salaam as a legacy of the contextual approach to law developed by McAuslan, Twining, Weston and other founders of the Faculty of Law. The succeeding avatars consisted of a leftist 'political economy of law' perspective which has been superseded since the nineties by an increasing focus on 'good governance' within a neo-liberal context. Paliwala then proceeds to consider legal education in developing countries in the context of wider debates on Law and Development and locates McAuslan's perspectives within these. McAuslan considered legal education to be vital to development and Paliwala suggests that while McAuslan supported the Senian perspective on development as freedom, he remained sceptical about contemporary approaches to law, development and good governance and emphasised the dangers of postcolonial and imperial discourses on Law and Development promoted by International Finance Institutions. Paliwala then explores these contemporary approaches to legal education by considering the changing methodologies of teaching and learning and in particular the development of clinical legal education. He suggests that regional collaborative approaches are essential to the development of emancipatory legal education in the manner envisaged by McAuslan.

Adams, in his contribution *The vagaries of consulting on land policy and land law reform in Africa 1994–2006* offers a wide-ranging account of McAuslan's efforts for the reform of land and planning law in Anglophone Africa in particular, evaluating the battle of ideas and good policy and governance with national interests, administration and the rights of citizens and the poor in particular. Adams's analysis begins with the related perspectives to this battle as they affected Tanzania in the mid-1990s, reflecting on his own involvement and collaboration with McAuslan 'in the field'. This is explicated by paying close attention to the Tanzanian reforms. A counterpoint perspective is then offered with regard to the land law reforms in Uganda in the late-1990s, which are explained in a contextual and evaluative manner. A third example is offered with reference to Lesotho in 2001–2004, where McAuslan proposed a new system for land tenure allocation and protection, assessing, among other things, its aftermath and the continuing frustration in the midst of the long-lasting conflict of ideas between law and politics. The case of Botswana in 2002, where McAuslan and Adams were involved in a thorough review of its land policy, offers the next exemplary case of reflecting on McAuslan's contribution, to then conclude with the example of Rwanda in 2006 where McAuslan and Adams were involved in preparing a country-wide tenure reform programme. In all these exemplary cases Adams brings to the fore a principle that was really at the heart of McAuslan's approach and practice: enablement, marketability and good governance will never suffice unless they are informed by equity and social justice.

Alden Wily's Chapter *Grand larceny in the tropics: Patrick McAuslan's role in limiting legal land theft in Africa* provides another valuable contribution to McAuslan's particular role in detecting, exposing and responding to legal land theft in Africa. This offers a crucial dimension to McAuslan's strategic scholarship and policy proposals that courageously and directly confronted vast issues such as land theft. Wily explains how McAuslan never lost sight of the fact that this is really what was at the heart of proper, critical Law and Development work. The colonial and so-called postcolonial effects on mass deprivation were placed at the core of his motivations and strategy, Wily explains, while considering in its detail and context the programme of land reform in Tanzania.

Loughlin, in his Chapter *The rise and fall of urban law, 1968–1988* interrogates the emergence (during the 1960s) and development (up to the

1990s) of the so-called 'urban law' field of research and teaching. This novel approach, which we owe to McAuslan's vision and research, entails the study of how law, among other things, allocates and dislocates property rights in land, and how it regulates land use. In doing so, Loughlin examines McAuslan's key contributions in the particular period between 1968 and 1985 with regard to curriculum innovation, teaching-led research, and the so-called functional 'style' of scholarship. These landmark innovations formed the ground upon which urban law developed and which Loughlin, furthermore, usefully proceeds to evaluate and critically appraise within the contemporary context.

Stein's contribution *Comparative and international urban land law and policy: a celebration of the work of Professor Patrick McAuslan* sets McAuslan's work within the frame of his central concern with the ideological apparatuses of law. The analysis offers, *inter alia,* a useful revisiting of the ever-relevant discussion among scholars, as well as practitioners, with regard to the instrumentalization of critique and the empiricism of theory. McAuslan's work over decades illustrates the complexity of the matter and the care as well as political lucidity required in confronting it effectively. To locate the unexpressed ideological grounding and interest that inform a law or a policy, becomes then a formative skill that aims not at the mere exposition of the undisclosed ideological elements, between the lines of law or policy, but also a more genuine encounter with them. Such an encounter could be said to aim at enabling legal and, by extension, political possibilities with empirical accuracy as well as principled equity. Within his exploration Stein provides, finally, a consideration of McAuslan's concern and work in relation to climate change as a particular field of problematization, mitigation and adaptation.

Manji, in *Patrick McAuslan, land law and development* provides a reflection on what, she notes, are the most important themes arising from McAuslan's work on land law reform, while focusing on one of them in particular: the purpose of legislative drafting and the different approaches to it. If one of the key characteristics of McAuslan's law reform work was his exceptional ability to conceive and draft complex legal codes while maintaining even-handedness between pragmatism and social justice, Manji's analysis offers us an exemplary glimpse into McAuslan's approach and its operative legal and social cognition. Manji's case in point, in this regard, is the legislative reform on the illegal and irregular allocation of public land in Kenya. She thus analyses first the Ndung'u report of 2004 and then, in this light, turns to reconsider McAuslan's public law approach to the legal framework governing land allocation, which aimed at both doctrinal creativity and analysis, as well as, crucially, critical and inventive scholarship.

McEldowney's *Policy and development: perspectives from public law and political thought – a twenty-first century odyssey* sets out McAuslan's wider contribution to public law scholarship, and perhaps we can say 'strategy', in the historical context of the political and social concerns that inspired and informed McAuslan's approach, over the decades, to teaching, scholarship and practice. McEldowney places McAuslan's innovations in teaching and scholarship within the context of pedagogical concerns as arising from, among other things, the development of the ideology of democratic constitutionalism. Issues such as legitimacy, public participation, public interest, the boundaries of judicial review are matters of direct concern to McAuslan's work, McEldowney emphasises, and help us appreciate, not just the legal but also the political and ethical dimensions of his concern with democratic governance more generally. In the final part, and with reference to exemplary jurisprudence, McEldowney expands on the latter by examining certain areas of constitutional law that 'give rise to concern, exposing the values and justifications for the changes and considering the normative values underpinning political choices and appropriate accountability.'

Azuela in the final Chapter *Public participation and legal standing: Mexican high courts and environmental conflicts* provides an engaging case study of public participation and legal standing in Mexican High Courts which acts, also, as an exemplary consideration of McAuslan's approach to the intermixing of private property, public interest and public participation at both their micro-level and their macro-level impact with regard to the way cities and the environment are transformed. The extension and reconsideration of McAuslan's famous theses in relation to the ideologies of planning law, the public approach to both planning and private property law, and the field of urban law in the empirical context of Mexican urban and environmental conflicts, offers an invaluable tribute to McAuslan's contribution in these fields but also a furthering of his inventiveness and criticality towards twenty-first century jurisprudence, such as the pressing question of how to give content to the right to the environment.

References

Ghai, Yash P. and J. Patrick W.B. McAuslan. 1970. *Public Law and Political Change in Kenya*. Nairobi: Oxford University Press.

McAuslan, Patrick. 1975. *Land, Law and Planning (Law in Context)*. London: Weidenfeld & Nicolson.

McAuslan, Patrick. 1980. *The Ideologies of Planning Law*. Oxford, New York: Pergamon Press.

McAuslan, Patrick. 2013. *Land Law Reform in East Africa: Traditional or Transformative?* London: Routledge.

Manji, Ambreena. 2014. 'The Politics of Land Reform in Kenya 2012'. *African Studies Review* 57, pp. 115–130.

Perry-Kessaris, A. 2012. 'Law and Development: Patrick McAuslan's Odyssey 1961–2011'. Conference at Birkbeck, 11–12 January 2012 (unpublished paper).

Shivji, Issa. 2006. *Let the People Speak: Tanzania Down the Road to Neo-Liberalism.* Dakar: CODESRIA.

Trubek, David M. and Marc Galanter. 1974. 'Scholars in Self-Estrangement: Some reflections on the Crisis in Law and Development Studies in the United States', *Wisconsin Law Review* 1062.

Wilson, Geoffrey P. and Ross Cranston (eds) 1995. *Frontiers of Legal Scholarship: Twenty-five Years of Warwick Law School.* Hoboken, NJ: John Wiley & Sons.

Chapter 1

Scholarly origins of preaching and practice

Lord and Professor in the understanding of modern land law (Inaugural lecture, Birkbeck College School of Law, University of London, 1995)

Patrick McAuslan

Introduction

At the beginning of an inaugural lecture, it is customary for the inaugurant to pay gracious tribute to his or her predecessors in the chair to which he or she is being inaugurated. I have no predecessors for this chair but it is I think not inappropriate to commence this lecture with a public acknowledgement of the vision of the college in establishing the Law Department and the vibrant intellectual atmosphere which in a very short space of time has been created within the department. It is both a privilege and a pleasure to work in such an atmosphere and with colleagues who have created such an atmosphere. Nor indeed should I omit our students from this encomium for the enthusiasm, commitment and variety of intellectual and practical experience they bring to their studies serves constantly to remind us that, despite the best endeavours of the government to create, via a centralising bureaucracy of higher education, a more conformist and circumspect University sector, the profession of university teacher and scholar is still an intellectually challenging and rewarding one.

No-one I believe could accuse the Law Department of being conformist or circumspect in its approach to legal scholarship. Adopting the quadripartite division of English law teachers highlighted by Professor Twining in his masterly Hamlyn Lectures, *Blackstone's Tower*, of expositor, censor, scientist and craftsman, my colleagues exemplify the best traditions of censor, or using more modern terminology, critic.

In keeping with his nascent intellectual tradition of the department, I intend to use this lecture to mount a critique of scholarship on English land law. To stop at that however would, I believe, be rather narrow and introspective; a lecture likely to appeal only to other academic lawyers, a criticism I would have to make of some of the newer approaches to and themes in legal scholarship. I will endeavour to go beyond criticism and discuss the policy relevance of developing a new approach to legal scholarship on English land law. I will then ask and attempt to answer the following questions: what is the dominant approach to writing about land law by academic lawyers and what are its defects; why is this approach so persistent and increasingly at variance with the approach being taken by judges, or some of them, to handling land law disputes in the courts; what are the wider and deleterious effects on policy-making and our understanding of the role of law and law reform in society of this dominant tradition? I will finally offer some suggestions as to how we might escape from the present intellectual straitjacket.

Before I start on this voyage, I should offer a brief explanation of the title to this lecture. It is, as I am sure you are all aware, a shameless plagiarism of the title to Barrington Moore's seminal work *Social Origins of Dictatorship and Democracy: Lord and Peasant in the Making of the Modern World,* a book which had an immense influence on my intellectual development as it had on many other people's. More particularly, the book brought out vividly the connection between the evolution, style, and nature of and conflicts over land ownership and use, and wider social and political evolution and revolution in society including English society. It provided, for those who wanted it, a context within which to understand the evolution of a society's land law and while I cannot hope to emulate the scholarship and intellectual force of that work in this lecture, connecting with it via my title gives some indication of what I will be attempting.

The professors: the dominant intellectual tradition

English legal writing on land law is overwhelmingly that of the exposition of the law, books on what the law is rather than critical texts about the law. But this neat distinction does not sufficiently bring out the narrowness of writing on land law or the apparent inability or unwillingness of generations of authors of books on the subject to provide any form of intellectual vision of what they are trying to do. Nor does it sufficiently highlight the fact that if we can detect any trends in legal writing on land law, it is in a backwards sloping direction. I will give some illustrations on these points.

Take first the three major standard texts on land law; in order of seniority, they are Cheshire's *Modern Real Property,* first published in 1926 and now in its 15th edition; Megarry and Wade, first published in 1957 and now in its 6th edition; and Gray's *Elements of Land Law,* in my view first published in 1981 albeit under the joint authorship of Gray and Symes with the title *Real Property and Real People* and now in its officially 2nd but in reality 3rd edition. In terms of dates of first publication, what might strike an outsider is that a major new book appears about once a generation and one might suppose that these news books would offer a new vision of the subject, taking account perhaps of the changed nature of society and the place and role of land law therein or new approaches to scholarship, both legal and otherwise or, more narrowly, new approaches to the subject evidenced in cases, legislation and reports on law reform.

Nothing could be further from the facts in the case of these books. While the order in which the subject-matter of the books differs from book to book, not merely is the intellectual approach uniform, but the content of the books is uniform, varying only in the amount of space accorded the different topics. The property legislation of 1925, the culmination of a century of land law reform, appears to set the parameters of all the works. A characteristic of them all is their enormous size; the smallest is over 1000 pages, two of the three, over 1150. The size is symptomatic of a deficiency of all the books; the lack of a clearly articulated message in the book which would attempt to explain its overall theme or relate the law to the subject-matter with which it deals, namely land. Note that I am not at this point criticising the books for not being contextual – that is a separate point to which I will return. The criticism here is that the size of the books betokens a failure to prioritise the topics to be dealt with, and that failure in turn stems from the lack of clear overall objectives. It is this I believe which makes land law so daunting for students; they are faced with an enormous mass of words pitched at an aseptic intellectual level, that is free from any contamination caused by the harmful bacteria of reality, which seem to have no connecting theme or underlying message.

Let me illustrate this by reference to the law on mortgages and its treatment in the three books. As we are all aware, the mortgage is the technical legal name given to the mechanism which fuels the housing market, the loan secured on the house bought with the monies provided by the loan. If you don't repay the loan, or more realistically, if you don't keep up with regular payments of interest and repayments of capital on the loan, for those who have repayment mortgages, you are liable to have your house taken possession of and sold by the lender (in legal parlance, the mortgagee). Over the years, a rudimentary legislative framework of protection for borrowers or mortgagors who fall behind with their payments has been created and now operates via benefit offices and courts. The number of people, however, who are in difficulties with their mortgages is very large: over 300,000 homes repossessed in the last five years with 60,000 homes repossessed in 1994; over 200,000 people in long-term mortgage arrears and over one million people with mortgages bigger than the value of their homes, the negative equity phenomenon which can often be a prelude to arrears or actions for possession. Although the figures are significant, the problems of arrears and possession did not spring up overnight; they have been around for some time. The problems have been investigated by several public agencies, NGOs and academic authors; the National Consumer Council in 1985; the London Boroughs Association in 1992; the London Research Centre in 1993 (in a booklet published by HMSO); the Catholic Housing Aid Society in 1992; Valerie Karn and colleagues who looked particularly at the practice and procedures in the courts and Janet Ford both in *The Indebted Society* and later for a Joseph Rowntree study. Now note:

we are concerned here with a legal phenomenon, the mortgage, and with legal procedures in legal institutions connected with that phenomenon when things go wrong, the very issues one might think that academic lawyers would write about and focus on in a textbook dealing with what the law is. Not one of the three books under review make any reference to any of the studies which have examined the operation of the law on mortgage arrears; none of them go below the surface of the few High Court and Court of Appeal cases which have dealt with the subject. Only one mentions the provisions dealing with the payment of mortgage interest as income support. All of them however mention the Payne Commission, the Committee on Judgement Debts, whose report in 1969 led to the present law on providing relief for mortgage arrears. But then Payne was a lawyer, a judge no less, so what his Committee had to say was part of the law and remains relevant to this day. Thus, judging the books on the narrow conception of what they are aiming to do, describing and analysing the law that is, they have consciously circumscribed their own brief. Nor are these authors unique; a survey of articles in the leading academic journal specialising in property law, the *Conveyancer and Property Lawyer*, over the last 25 years, since the passage of the legislation establishing the present legal framework of protection for mortgagors, disclosed only four articles on this part of the law. These four articles, out of some 600 articles, dealt only with the statute and the few reported cases on the statute and not on the operation of the law in practice. Furthermore, no articles have been published on this subject in the last decade. It is rather astonishing, almost one might say frightening, that the problems which hundreds of thousands of people are having in being caught up with this central institution of land law are of no apparent interest to academic lawyers concerned with land law.

The absence of context

It should occasion no surprise when we turn to consider the next issue, the contextualisation of writing about land law, to learn that the position is no better. What do I mean by contextualisation here? I will take as my text the statement of aims of the *Law in Context* series founded almost 30 years ago with the first book published in the series 25 years ago. The editors stated:

> The impetus behind [the series] is a desire to broaden the study of law by proceeding beyond the exposition of legal doctrine to consider critically the law-in-action in its social and economic context. A contextual approach involves treating legal subjects from a broader base than has been normal in the past, using material from other social sciences... that helps explain the operation *in practice* of the subject under discussion ... The series ... will be written primarily for undergraduate students of law.

These were ambitious aims and it is not my intention to consider how far they have been realised. It is I think fair to say that the series has been influential on legal scholarship in general; that is, textbooks outside the series now pay more attention to context than was formerly the case and there has therefore been a general broadening of approach and materials available for legal education. Other factors have been at work but they are not my concern here. Taking the *Law in Context* series itself as my starting point, we find that every basic subject in the standard LLB syllabus, that is, every 'core' subject required to be taught within the LLB if the degree is to gain professional recognition and many of the most popular and professionally-orientated options in the syllabus is featured in the series – bar one; Land Law. This is not for want of trying on the part of the editors of the series; successive would-be authors have for one reason or another not proceeded with their proposals but there have not been that many would-be authors to take on this subject. Clearly a contextual approach does not appeal to land lawyers.

This matter too needs further elaboration. One of the earliest books in the *Law in Context* series was in fact one on a part of land law; *Land Law and Tenant* by Martin Partington, first published in 1975, in many respects a pioneering work which deservedly won high praise. This in itself is revealing; the law of landlord and tenant has had a high political profile for many years. However, it features in standard land law courses and books as the law of leases and for the most part carefully eschews the context of the topic; the provisions of the Law of Property Act 1925 on leases provides the framework for and content of the topic. The closest the standard treatment comes to the real world of landlord and tenant is in connection with the lease/licence distinction. One would have to avoid any discussion of the cases — the basic fare of the standard approach – if one were to pursue the aseptic approach to the topic since the cases themselves bring out time after time that the real issue between the parties is whether their relationship is governed by the protective legislation within which the residential landlord tenant relationship used to be cocooned or whether it had successfully escaped that regime, allowing the landlord greater freedom to get rid of his tenants or lodgers and charge what rent he wants.

So the topic of landlord and tenant, indeed the very title landlord and tenant, was itself making a contextual statement. As might be expected, the content of the book too did reflect context, though only up to a point. The first Chapter is 'Setting the context' and combines legal, historical, statistical and policy-orientated materials very effectively. Thereafter, the content of the materials is overwhelmingly traditional materials; cases and statutes. If we take the Chapter on 'The scope of Rent Act protection', by 1980, the date of the second edition, there was a fair amount of empirical material available on the operation and effectiveness of the Rent Acts, some of it indeed written by lawyers. Yet, apart from a very brief five and a half page historical introduction to the chapter, the remaining 71 pages of materials are extracts of cases and statutes. There are no references to and no extracts of legal and other writings about the real world of the Rent Act. This would seem to confirm the point made earlier: the contextual breakthrough was seen by both the editors of the series and the author as being one of developing this topic for undergraduate legal education rather than as one which pre-eminently could have been the vehicle for a multi-disciplinary approach to the study of landlord and tenant law. To bring the story up to date: in 1992, the book re-emerged, out of the *Law in Context* series, now called *Housing Law: Cases and Materials*, still dealing with the same subject matter but if anything with the contextual element reduced while, in the intervening 12 years since the second edition, the amount of available contextual material has vastly increased.

Clearly, then, something seems to be happening here. Have we stumbled on to the case of the disappearing context? The next example suggests we have. This is Gray's work. Let me start with the credit side. Gray's *Elements of Land Law* is a work of immense scholarship and erudition; it has, I believe, set new standards for the traditional textbook concentrating on a critical and analytical survey of the cases, statutes and official proposals for reform of the law that is. It has I think gone as far as one can down that road. Other textbooks of the traditional genre will in future be judged by reference to this one. It is when one reviews the development of this work that one begins to have concerns. The book started its life, as I mentioned just now as *Real Property and Real People*, a title that promised a new approach to writing about land law. The preface seemed to promise even more:

> The ultimate objective of a university education is not the learning of rules but the critical perception of value. This means not only that the student should be taught to distinguish between a good argument and a bad one. It means also that he should be taught that law does not exist in a moral or social vacuum of the society in which he lives. The task of the teacher is in part to indicate the points at which the legal solutions are not predetermined by some logical system but are instead explicable only in terms of more fundamental value judgements.

If that were not enough to set the intellectual taste buds tingling, the opening chapter promised a veritable cornucopia of intellectual innovation. The reader is informed that: 'in this book we set out to explore the broader connotations of "property" within the strict context of the rules of English property law ... We shall look particularly closely at the underlying ideology of property law and its interaction with key issues of priority and efficiency'. For a law textbook to state explicitly that it was going to discuss the ideology of the law as opposed to just discussing it without making that explicit was almost revolutionary. Worse (or better, depending on your point of view) was to come. The book broke out into foreign languages; it made reference to sociological concepts, to *Gemeinschaft und Gesellschaft*. I recall a good friend of mine, a fellow student at college at Oxford and like me a law teacher reacting rather dismissively to this foray into the thickets of sociology: 'not more Gemeinschaft und Gesellschaft' he said as if every law book at the time made reference to these concepts. The truth was and still is that the overwhelming majority of law students, and dare I say it, law teachers would not know a *Gemeinschaft* from a *Gesellschaft* even if they were translated into English! In the opening chapter of *Real Property and Real People* the authors proceeded to relate these concepts to the development of English land law and, throughout the book, these concepts reappear from time to time. Furthermore, the book made a substantive departure from its potential competitors; it headed the part on leases as 'Residential Security' and included a substantial chapter on housing law, covering the Rents Act, public sector tenants and the homeless. There was still some hesitation about using non-legal sources – only 43 out of 2318 footnotes in a 636-page book were to non-legal references but there was a definite attempt to develop a new contextual approach to the subject.

Twelve years on and into what is effectively the third edition of the work now renamed *Elements of Land Law*, a very definite change has taken place. References to ideology and to *Gemeinschaft* and *Gesellschaft* have disappeared – they actually disappeared in 1987 when the book first metamorphosed into *Elements* – but so too has the very detailed discussion of Housing Law which was one of the best features of the first edition of *Elements*. A chapter on the strict settlement, present in the book of 1981, daringly left out of the first edition of *Elements*, makes an unwelcome reappearance. Perhaps most significant of all changes, is the content and balance of the footnotes. There are now more than 7000 of them in a book of 1168 pages; only 63 are references to non-legal materials and of these 12 occur in the first six pages of the chapter on mortgages. What has vastly increased over the 1981 book are references to US and Commonwealth, especially Australian, cases. Reading *Elements* cover to cover and paying close attention to the footnotes, one would come away knowing a good deal more about what Australian judges think about those parts of Australian land law having similarities with English land law than one would about how English land law was working in practice. It seems then that the author has turned from writing a book on Real Property and Real People and instead has written a book on Real Property Law by a Real Property Lawyer. Real legal scholarship is citing cases from all over the world, not assimilating and discussing even a selection of the vast mass of non-legal scholarship and writing on land, which must surely be the primary context of a book on land law.

For my third example, I want briefly to contrast two recently published cases and materials books, one on land law and the other on contract, prepared by a younger generation of legal scholars. Again, I should make plain that any critical comments that I have of the book on land law are not directed at the industry or acumen of the author; rather I take the book as the latest example of the genre and contrast it with a very different kind of book in order to bring out the point that in a subject other than land law, considerable progress is being made in contextualising materials.

The book on land law is Goo's source book of cases and materials. As is the pattern with books on the subject, it is over 1000 pages. It makes absolutely no concessions whatsoever to context. It is a book of cases, statutory material and some extracts from reports by the Law Commission. The attempt is made to be comprehensive, that is to cover all the topics of the standard land law course. A half apology is made for not including more extracts from reports by the Law Commission which represent the new thinking on land law but it is felt to be essential to provide the students with information on the law as it is at the moment. To revert to the subject of mortgages, that means providing the readers with the usual extracts from the Law of Property Act 1925 and a few other Acts and a selection of decisions from the higher courts but no reference is made either to the role, operations and regulatory framework of the main vehicle for providing mortgages, the building society, or to the day-to-day operation of possession actions in the courts. In sum, one has to say that for all the industry displayed in the production of this book, there has been absolutely no intellectual advance in how to present the subject from the other principal such book *Maudsley and Burn's Land Law Cases and Materials,* which was first published in 1967.

Contrast with this a new cases and materials book on contract by Wheeler and Shaw. The topics covered include chapters on contract theory and contract and state, which in fact includes more discussion of the theory of social contractarianism. The materials in the book embrace economics, philosophy, history, sociology, public law as well as private law, comparative law and work on postmodern legal feminism. These materials and the underlying theoretical positions are worked into all the chapters of the book, so that there is a constant interaction between theory, context and law. The core of the book then is the law of contract, but contract brought alive and placed firmly in its theoretical and social context. The book represents a distinct intellectual advance on the challenge to other approaches to presenting the law of contract, just as its main rival — *Beale, Bishop and Furmston's Cases and Materials on the Law of Contract* with its heavy emphasis on contract as an economic institution – represented an intellectual advance on existing fare when it was first published in the mid-1980s.

There is then a stark, one might say painful, contrast between the intellectual fare offered by the academic community on the law of contract – for the cases and materials book are paralleled by texts and monographs of equal originality and freshness – and that offered on land law which generation after generation follows the standard intellectual approach. There is one exception to this and it deserves to be mentioned. This is the brave, albeit perhaps too short and therefore over simple, cases and materials book on land law by Lim and Green which avowedly set out 'to challenge the conceptual formalism of the orthodox law course and to expand its texts' and so selected texts from history, philosophy, anthropology and literature which the authors hoped would 'serve to unsettle the standard framework of land law, with its fixed questions and "rational order". Let us hope that future editions of this work will expand its own text as well as continuing to expand the texts of land law.

Let me sum up the message so far: it is not possible to understand the operation of land law in and on English society and the relationship between the evolution of that society and the land law by reading the current literature which is overwhelmingly located in a narrow orthodoxy. I intend to try and suggest why land law scholarship is as it is and an essential dimension of this involves turning now to those persons denominated in the other half of the title to this lecture: the Lords. I refer to the judges and the practical men and women of the law. Contrary to what the defenders of the orthodox might say, my contention is that over the years – say for the last 25–30 years – a far greater perception of the real world of land law and its problems, the connection between an evolving land law and movements in society, can be gained by reading the law reports and reports of the Law Commission than by reading the law books.

The central issues of the land law

At this point, it really becomes necessary for me to say what I think the central issues or issues in English land law are since I will be concerned to show how the judges have referred to these issues in their judgements. I would assert that the central issue in English land law is and always has been the tension between, on the one hand, freedom to deal with land in the market and, on the other, protection for the users, and occupiers of land and increasingly nowadays consumers in the market for land. Over the centuries different classes and groups have been accorded either protection from or assistance in dealing in the market with the trend being towards facilitating the operation of the market. But even after the culmination of the century of market-orientated land law reform in the property reform legislation of 1925, the tension has remained and is evidenced by both legislation and judicial decisions.

Examples of each may briefly be given. With legislation, we can point to laws protecting the position of tenants, or regulating the activities of estate agents on the one hand and laws advancing the freedom of landlords or introducing competition into the practice of conveyancing on the other. With judicial decisions, two examples may briefly be given: first, the constant oscillation by the courts on the lease/licence distinction which is the technical legal ground on which the constant battle between landlords' freedoms and tenants' protections has been fought over. Second, the even more technical legal subject area of restrictive covenants where the tension can be described in the modern terminology of inter-generational equity; the text to which one generation of land owners should have freedom by their market transactions to limit what their purchasers and their successors may do on the land in the future.

The Lords: judicial approaches to land law

The problem I have in setting out the evidence for the assertion that the judges and practitioners seem more able and willing to focus on this central tension is where to begin and how to limit the evidence which could be produced. The best way is to approach the matter through an examination of how judges (often it so happens), Law Lords, and the Law Commission have provided social and economic background to and as supplementary explanation for their decisions on issues in land law and its reform. As before, I will confine myself to three examples only and to maintain some consistency of approach, I start off with the law of mortgages.

The central issue in the modern law of mortgages as it operates in practice is how to balance consumer protection and market freedom, the former of which necessitates some kind of regulatory framework over the activities of the principal mortgage loan providers, the latter of which would imply the absence of regulation so as to facilitate and encourage the flow of capital into the mortgage market. This central dilemma in the law of mortgages is perfectly captured in the speech of Lord Browne-Wilkinson in *Barclays Bank plc v. O'Brien*, a case dealing with undue influence and the responsibilities of mortgagees to ensure that one partner in a relationship had independent advice before being persuaded to agree to allowing the family home to be used as security for the other partner's business or financial dealings. The following quotation comes, significantly, from a paragraph in a section of his speech headed 'Policy Considerations', a heading one will look for in vain in the textbooks. After making the points that much private wealth is now tied up in the matrimonial home which is increasingly in joint names of the two spouses and that while the law has rejected the 'outmoded concept' that the wife is subservient to her husband in the management of family finances, it is still the case that in practice many wives are still subjected to and yield to undue influence by their husbands. Such wives can reasonably look to the law for some protection. He goes on:

> It is easy to allow sympathy for the wife who is threatened with the loss of her home at the suit of a rich bank to obscure an important public interest, viz. the need to ensure that the wealth currently tied up in the

> matrimonial home does not become economically sterile. If the rights secured to wives by the law render valuable loans granted on the security of matrimonial homes, institutions will be unwilling to accept such security, thereby reducing the flow of loan capital to business enterprises. It is therefore essential that a law designated to protect the vulnerable does not render the matrimonial home unacceptable as security to financial institutions.
>
> (188)

The Law Commission too has been active in proposing reforms to the law of mortgages designed to make it simpler and more comprehensible both for professionals to use and consumers to understand. That the Law Commission is aware of the underlying social problems behind the technical law comes through clearly from their report on Land Mortgages which features in an early footnote, references to many of those reports and studies on mortgage arrears which I referred to earlier and which do not feature in the scholarly legal literature on mortgages and in one of their central recommendations which is that a special type of mortgage to be known as a protected mortgage be created for mortgages of dwelling-houses.

The second area where judges have perceived and brought out into the open the social problems and the market versus protection tensions behind the operation of what might appear to be a dry-as-dust technical legal institution is that of overriding interests in the registration of title to land. The legal issue is the extent to which pre-existing interests of persons in land should be permitted to take precedence to or override the title of a purchaser of, or lender of funds on the security of, land. The purchaser or lender has in all innocence purchased or lent funds and carried out the normal procedures in accordance with the law to obtain a registered title to the land or registered protection for the loan. They then find someone claiming on the strength of being in occupation of the land, usually a house, that they have a better right to the house and can resist being evicted by the purchaser or lender, in the latter case where the loan is not being repaid and the lender wishes to realise the security.

That puts the matter in as aseptic a way as possible. The reality is that the issue often arises between husbands and wives and mortgagees to whom the husbands have mortgaged the family home, without informing their wives and then are unable to meet the repayments on the second mortgage or the much larger re-mortgage. Here then is another classic example of the tension between protecting the occupier and facilitating the operation of the market. There have been over the years, sharp differences of opinion between the judges on the issue of which side of the line the decisions should fall. While it is perfectly possible to understand the difference between the House of Lords' decision of *City of London Building Society v. Flegg* in 1986 which found for the lender and its earlier 1980 decision of

Williams and Glyn's Bank v. Boland which found for the occupier, on legal grounds connected with the interpretation of various Acts of Parliament, it is not possible to read the various judgements and speeches in those and other similar cases without being very aware that the judges were themselves only too well aware of the financial and social implications of their decisions. One brief quotation from the speech of Lord Wilberforce in the 1980 decision may be given. His whole speech is shot through with a recognition of the changed status and therefore the property rights of wives in respect of the matrimonial home but his final remarks sum up very well the conflict between protection of occupation and facilitation of the market in the light of these changes:

> I ... agree ... that whereas the object of a land registration system is to reduce the risks of purchasers from anything not on the register, to extend (if it be an extension) the area of risk so as to include possible interests of spouses and indeed in theory, of other members of the family or even outside it, may add to the burden of purchasers, and involve them in enquiries which in some cases may be troublesome.
>
> But conceded, as it must be, that the [Land Registration] Act, following established practice, gives protection to occupiers, the extension of the risk area follows necessarily from the extension, beyond the paterfamilias of the rights of ownership, itself following from the diffusion of property and earning capacity. What is involved is a departure from an easy-going practice of dispensing with enquiries as to occupation beyond that of the vendor and accepting the risks of doing so. To substitute for this a practice of more careful enquiry as to the fact of occupation can not, in my view of the matter, be considered as unacceptable except at the price of overlooking the widespread development of shared interests of ownership.
>
> (508–9)

The third example comes from the subject of restrictive covenants, conditions or covenants imposed by the seller of freehold land on the buyer so as to prevent or restrict the buyer from doing certain things on the land bought. Covenants are usually concerned to prevent building on the purchased land or building of a certain kind or particular kinds of user. The land sold with a covenant as part of the sale is called the burdened land; the land retain by the seller is called the benefitted land. The case usually regarded as the start of the law on restrictive covenants, *Tulk v. Moxhay* in 1848, was concerned with the maintenance of Leicester Square as an open space by the prevention of building on it. The issues for the law have always been, first, the extent to which a covenant agreed to by buyer and seller should continue to affect the land bought and sold after the original buyer and seller have died or sold on the land burdened by the covenant or benefitted by the covenant; second, the type of covenants which should be permitted; and third whether the enforcement of positive covenants, that is covenants which require the owner of the burdened land to do something to or spend money on the land, should be allowed. It is obvious that the more liberal the rules on the enforceability of restrictive covenants, the more restricted will be the use of land and this in turn impedes the operation of a free market in land. In the almost 150 years since the decision in *Tulk v. Moxhay*, the law has oscillated between liberality and restriction or it would perhaps be more accurate to say that both strands of judicial opinion have been present in the cases giving judges a choice as to which line to follow: should the wishes of the occupier-seller prevail through the generations or should they be restricted, so facilitating the sale and productive use of the land? While it is not difficult to find judgements of extreme technicality and aridity on this subject over the years, as policy decisions are disguised in legalese, it is also possible to read judgements, particularly over the last 25–30 years where it is perfectly clear that the judges are well aware of the policy implications of what they are doing and are making explicit their decisions to come down on one or the other side of the line. Similarly, when the Law Commission has addressed this subject, it too has discussed the wider policy issues of this species of private planning law.

The reasons why

Why should this be so? Why are the judges, the Lords, more able and willing to tell us about the relationship between the evolution of the legal rules relating to land and the movement of society, more able to advance our understanding of the land law than the Professors? I wish to advance several possible reasons, each of which will I suspect, may, I hope stir up disagreement. The first reason lies in the phrasing of the question; the judges are more willing and able to 'tell us' about the law. Over the last three or so decades, to a considerable extent, I would claim, through the example and influence of Lord Denning, the style and approach of judgements in the courts have undergone a profound change. There is now a much greater collective effort made to write judgements in easy-to-read language, to explain in terms non-lawyers can understand reasons for decisions and to be more explicit about the non-legal factors which have played a background part in decisions. Judges in other words are making more of an effort to explain themselves and their work to the citizenry. Academic land lawyers, on the other hand, are not. The target for the academic lawyer is the law student and the practising profession. Too many land lawyers seem to adopt the position solemnly advanced by a leading academic lawyer only the other day that 'I do not want law to be made interesting to non-lawyers.' So successful have land lawyers been in this regard that, to give just one example, in the 46 year history of the showcase law lectures, the Hamlyn Lectures, which are specifically aimed at acquainting the common people of the United Kingdom with the benefits they derive from the common law in comparison with other European peoples who are not so fortunate – no *Gemeinschaft und Gesellschaft* there – no lectures devoted to land law have been given.

But to say that academic land lawyers do not see their role as being to make land law come alive for the ordinary person, which includes law students, or do see it as being to more than offer a dry conceptual approach to the subject is by no means a complete answer. After all, academic lawyers in other subjects have expanded the scope of their writing and they too have as their main audience students and practitioners. Furthermore, of all the principal private law subjects in the standard law curriculum, land law was the one which was most closely associated with public policy and political and legislative activity in the earlier years of this century, a fact recognised and written about by some of the leading lights in legal academia in those early years. I can mention articles and books making the connection between land law and public affairs and governance by Dicey, Holdsworth and Pollock. What then went wrong?

There is, I think, a vision amongst land lawyers that their subject is to be seen and taught and written about as the most intellectually pure legal topic there is. It is the product not of messy politics or even messy judgements but of pure intellect and reason. Now, most such lawyers know perfectly well that that is not in fact the case but it is the ideal, and it is the ideal that is offered to the world in texts. One of the best and undoubtedly one of the most influential texts which offers this particular vision is Lawson's *Introduction to the Law of Property* first published in 1958 which was, and as the second edition makes explicit, still is aimed at the law student approaching the subject for the first time and the non-lawyer. What is emphasised above all else in this book are the 'clear patterns in the English law of property', the abstractions which have been invented by lawyers, the need for the student to enter:

> the precise, sharp, logical world of the expert conveyance who is constantly using the most refined abstract tools in order to create complex arrangements for the future which cannot, so far as the law in concerned, go wrong and to provide with equal certainty for the happening of untoward events ... The purpose of all this activity is to ensure, as far as the law can ensure it, that the property interests he is dealing with shall ... be managed in the cheapest most efficient way, attracting the lightest possible burden of taxation.

Such an approach has no room for and no intellectual interest in the social and political realities of the legal framework of land management.

A more sophisticated and subtle explanation-cum-defence of this traditional approach to land law is provided by another equally learned introductory work, Murphy and Robert *Understanding Property Law*, written by two lawyers who would, I think, generally be regarded as being in the forefront of the socio-legal and critical legal studies movements. In passing it is worth noting that both these introductory works use the more abstract term 'property' as opposed to the more concrete term 'land' in their title. For these authors, 'the study of land law ... is a gloss or commentary upon these statutory texts [i.e. the 1925 property legislation] and the decisions which have interpreted them'. However, standard textbooks which 'give pride of place to the judges...can obscure the primacy of what lawyers do in their offices, preparing documents which serve as instruments to achieve a client's wishes ... To prepare these documents, lawyers resort to verbal formulae – to forms of words – which have worked in the past, recycling and adapting them to meet the needs of the present'. Then comes the crucial sentence: 'The driving force in the history of land law has been the activity of conveyancers. Their expertise is essentially formulaic and remains so in large measure today.' So, despite the much wider range of disciplines which have been brought to bear in writing this book, the essential message is the same as Lawson's: forget about the economic and social forces that have shaped and continue to shape the law; disregard the role of the judges in this process; concentrate on the verbal formulae that are the heart of the law. Once again, land law is being used to prove that lawyers with a wider vision of law are, *au fond*, real lawyers writing about Real Property.

What is even odder about this stress on the activities of practitioners in their offices is that neither these two books nor the vast array of books on land law actually discuss the activities of practitioners in the land market or therefore notice and discuss what is one of the most striking developments in modern land law, which is the interplay of the forces of deregulation of and competition in services in, versus the push for more consumer-orientated regulation of, the sale of land. That can only be understood by examining what practitioners do and how they are regulated doing it. It is not therefore surprising that recent writing focussing specifically on the regulation of the contract for the sale of land has come from a city solicitor and two trading standards officers, rather than from academic lawyers.

Let me be even more speculative. The role-model held out to the student of land law is the private conveyancer working in his office – I use the word 'his' deliberately – on instruments and documents designed to transfer property and regulate its use and 'preserve it from the depredations of the taxman'. This image of the property lawyer as tax avoider features, remarkably, in both Lawson and Murphy and Roberts. The property lawyer then has, even in the 1980s and 90s, a particular social status. His role is to serve the propertied classes, a point made explicitly in

Lawson, and, like Agag, he should treat delicately as he goes about this task. Not for the property lawyer the concern with the homeless or the tenant faced with an obdurate landlord; that can be dealt with by someone called a housing lawyer. Not even someone faced with de-possession of their home by a mortgagee; that can be dealt with by a social worker or someone from CAB (the Citizens Advice Bureau). The property lawyer deals with socially and economically neutral words and concepts having apparently socially and economically neutral outcomes and only those indoctrinated to believe that are fit to join the priesthood.

Thus, the teacher of land law, either out of conviction or from a feeling of being obliged to do the best for his or her students portrays land law as a set of abstract rules and concepts about property to disguise the fact that it is and always has been about the struggle between the haves and the have-nots and the extent to which market forces should be given free rein so as to facilitate acquisition by the haves or subjected to some regulation in the interests of the have-nots. Nothing could more eloquently demonstrate this than that the two recent and fascinating studies of the evolution of land law and its reform in the nineteenth and early part of the twentieth century, which bring out vividly the political, social and professional struggles which were an essential part of the reform process of the 'land question', are nowhere referred to in the three principal student texts on land law. They are just not a part of the law as presented to the law student.

Where is all this leading to? So far, it has all been a bit introtrospective, deserving perhaps the criticism that it is 'presenting a not particularly appetising picture of lawyers and law teachers talking past each other or to themselves, airing their prejudices and promoting section interests'. There is a view that that is what inaugural lectures are meant to be about but in the third part of this lecture, I want to turn away from introspection and consider the wider import of this failure of legal scholarship to address social and economic issues of the land law and its evolution alongside the technical aspects of the subject.

The internationalism of land law

In June 1996, the United Nations Conference on Human Settlements (Habitat II) will take place. The conference's overall objective as recommended by the General Assembly of the UN in December 1992 is:

> to increase the world awareness of the problems and potentials of human settlements – as important inputs to social and economic growth – and to commit the world's leaders to making our cities, towns and villages healthy, safe, just and sustainable.

The conference comes 20 years after the first such conference held in Vancouver which led to the establishment of the United Nations Centre for Human Settlements (Habitat) where I worked for three years between 1990 and 1993 as the Land Management Adviser in the global Urban Management Programme, working with national and local urban governments in developing countries to improve the management of their urban resources, one of which is land. The Programme, launched in 1986, is a joint venture with the World Bank, the United Nations Development Programme and several OECD, (Organisation for Economic Co-operation and Development) countries. Indeed, it was at a meeting of the OECD's Development Assistance Committee that the idea of such a programme was first aired.

In the early years of Habitat's existence, there was a reluctance to confront issues of land management since these raised sensitive political and social questions. In most cities and large towns in developing countries, large numbers of people, usually the urban poor, live in settlements which are technically illegal; they have appropriated land to which they have no lawful title; they have built houses without seeking or receiving planning permission and they use building materials and techniques which do not comply with the building regulations. They do this not out of some kind of perverse love of lawlessness, but because they have no alternative; they cannot acquire land legally; and the planning and building laws, modelled for the most part on laws from the United Kingdom, France, the USA, and other highly developed and wealthy countries impose standards which are well beyond the economic capability of the majority of the urban population to afford, as well as giving rise to inefficient and rent-seeking bureaucracies which administer the laws and add to the cost of compliance. However, if the urban majority are forced to live a mean life in an 'illegal city', the political and bureaucratic elites benefit from and are happy to maintain this state of affairs since they control the land and the laws and access to both. Thus, any programme aiming to facilitate easier access to urban land, or the regularisation or legalisation of 'illegal' settlements, or more efficient and cost-effective regulations and bureaucratic procedures would likely undermine the political power of those elites. In its early years, Habitat was not about to embarrass those elites so tended to concentrate on less politically contentious matters.

The Urban Management Programme heralded a change of attitude and approach to urban land issues in developing countries. The need for reform; the need to highlight the way power, resources, laws and administrative institutions were abused by elites; the role which secure land tenure, transparent administrative procedures, simpler and cheaper processes for buying, selling and using land and resolving disputes about land; the role in other words which the efficient and equitable functioning of land markets could play in economic and social development, were and still are the agenda of the Programme. This agenda has had a significant impact on the willingness of governments in developing countries to face up to the need to tackle the urban land issue.

At the same time, there has been a concern about urban land issues within developed countries and in the transitional economics of Central and Eastern Europe. The OECD's Urban Programme commissioned, and published in 1992, a study on Urban Land Markets, which stated in its Introduction that:

> The operation of urban land markets is a source of concern to many OECD governments ... the way in which urban land is used is important both to economic performance and the quality of life ... The current phase of fundamental economic restructuring, the introduction of new technologies in cities and the concern for the quality of the environment, both at city level and on a global scale, elevate urban land market issues to a key policy concern of OECD countries in the 1990s.

Similarly, there is a widespread recognition in the transitional countries that getting land markets right is a fundamental precondition for economic growth and social stability and much work is being done on that.

There is little doubt then but that addressing the issues of improving the operation of urban land markets through better urban land management is now firmly on the human settlement agenda and Habitat, the agency, as the Secretariat for Habitat II, the conference, intends to make the issue of secure land tenure as a condition for sustainable shelter and urban development a central one at the conference.

A major problem area in developing more appropriate instruments and institutions for the efficient and equitable operation of urban land markets is the role of the law. As I mentioned earlier, inappropriate laws, implemented in inappropriate ways or more often not implemented are a major factor in the inequitable and inefficient operation of land markets in most cities in developing countries. Similarly, within the transitional countries, considerable attention is being devoted to developing legal frameworks for the operation of land and housing markets. This lecture is not the occasion for a discussion of the general question of the role of law in development or the waxing and waning of practical interest in matters of legal reform in developing countries. Suffice it to say here at the risk of some over-simplification that after a longish period in the 1970s and 80s when little attention was paid by the development community of practitioners and scholars, to law, the 90s are seeing a very rapid reawakening of interest being paid to legal institutions and their role in the creation and operation of a market economy and practices of good governance. Land law reform is then on the agenda of international agencies and of Habitat II.

What is the connection between these matters and English land lawyers? Before attempting to explain, let me enter a caveat about law and the market. Law is a necessary but it is not a sufficient input into the development of both markets in general and land markets in particular. Even with the most perfect set of laws, whether and how a land market will work depends greatly on historical, social, cultural and political factors within a particular nation and there is a great danger that the mistake of the colonial past will be repeated in developing and transitional countries alike as laws modelled on those thought to be successful in providing for market economies in OECD countries are introduced as part of aid packages into developing and transitional countries.

It is here that I believe that a more intellectually expansive approach to a study of and writing about English land law would have a great deal to offer development practitioners and could make a major contribution both to the development of appropriate urban land policies and instruments at Habitat II and to a more sophisticated understanding of the limits and possibilities of law reform as a contribution to the development of a market economy. Furthermore, the failure to develop such an approach has contributed to an incomplete understanding of the relationship between law and the operation of the urban land market in the United Kingdom, which in turn affects policy making here and what our development practitioners offer developing and transitional countries. One has only to read the official government publication, *Urban Land Markets in the United Kingdom,* produced as the UK contribution to the OECD study and the references to 'judicial factors' as a context of urban land policy in the OECD study itself which was written primarily by British economists, to realise that the authors of those important reports had no understanding of the central role the law plays in the creation and operation of land markets, and this is largely because no lawyers in the United Kingdom have written on this subject.

What then are the messages which a broader approach to legal scholarship on English land law could offer the world? In my view, the most important lessons that can be learned from English land law which have wide applicability have very little to do with the technicalities of the law and everything to do with the way the law has developed and the policies behind the law. The evolution of English land law over the last 170-odd years provides a classic case study of the relationship between law reform and the growth of the market economy in a rapidly urbanising society, the characteristic of most developing societies. It draws attention to the extreme difficulties of land law reform; the need to placate those who feel they might lose out alongside the need to take account of new interests, and thus the political dimension to reform; the time-scale of reform, not a one-off exercise taking a year or two but a long-drawn out process proceeding by fits and starts and which never ends; the intimate connection between demands made by landowners, developers and would-be landowners – the urban poor – for land and reform of the law; the end product, not a seamless web of intellectual coherence which is how the reforming legislation of 1925 is presented in the texts but legislation which combines compromises on the details with an attempt to adhere to an overall policy objective; the need to ensure the professions, particularly the legal profession are on board; and last but by no means least, the role of a reasonably efficient judicial system and intellectually capable judiciary which can both settle disputes and play a role in enabling the law to adapt to new situations.

The message for policy-makers in developing and transitional countries would be that land law reform must be seen as an integral part of land reform and not a substitute for it or developed apart from it. The message for the aid community would be that law reform, especially land law reform, designed to facilitate the operation of the market cannot be proceeded with as merely a technical exercise; it touches the most profound nerve-ends of society; if not approached with circumspection and sensitivity, it is likely to destabilise social relations, to alter economic expectations and to set off conflicts between political forces and interest groups. These are not reasons for not proceeding with programmes of reform; they are reasons for proceeding with caution and humility and for taking the long view.

In all this intellectual ferment and practical action on reforming urban land policies and practices in Europe and in the wider world, the voice of the academic English land lawyer is silent. Trapped in his narrow world of verbal formulaic, of abstractness, and of rigorous analysis; he 'spends his time', to adapt Lawson's remark, 'like a spider weaving webs of legal gossamer'. It is an Italian lawyer who has drawn attention to the fascinating debate in Russia in the nineteenth century as to whether land law reform in that country should follow the English or continental approach to land rights and the relevance of that history to today's reforms. It is, for the most part, academic lawyers from the States who have highlighted the policy implications of the English property law reforms and are active in land law reform in the transitional countries. Policy debates and the production of scholarship at the global level both on land reform and law reform proceed without the kind of informed input on the English case of land law reform which only a solid body of legal scholarship could provide. These debates are unquestionably the poorer for the lack of this input.

Conclusions

There is no easy way to begin to correct this imbalance in English legal scholarship on land law. It is clear from past attempts to do so that the 'path dependence' of such scholarship is extremely strong. However, to end this lecture, I will mention two matters which between them, might indicate that the possibilities of change are not completely foreclosed. First, there is the international intellectual climate. Habitat II and its commitment to raise the land issue as a central matter for debate, together with the renewed practical interest in the role of law in development, provides an excellent opportunity, which it is not too late to grasp, for academic land lawyers to turn their attention to the wider issues of English land law which would be of interest and use both to a wider audience of global policy-makers and a narrower audience of law students and laypersons within the United Kingdom.

Second, there is a possible national development on the way. Some of the most interesting academic approaches to writing on land law at present are being developed by women. Likewise, the new contextual approach to Contract Law I referred to earlier is authored by two women and the intellectual boundaries in Criminal Law too are being advanced by women. At the international level, new approaches to land policies and practices are increasingly being driven by the imperative to take account of the gender perspective, and in the States, some of the most interesting writing on property rights is being authored by Carol Rose, an academic lawyer. Is it possible that in our own narrow world of English land law, a wider perspective, a more generous interpretation of intellectual rigour and a greater concern for the social and economic implications of the law may come both from a more gendered approach to the subject and from more input by female authors. If this were to be so, it would be a belated catching up by the Professors with the Lords whose shaping of the modern land law has in part at any rate been driven by the increasing involvement of women in the ownership and management of land.

References

Beale, H.G., W.D. Bishop and M.P. Furmston. 1987. *Cases and Materials on the Law of Contract.* Oxford: Oxford University Press.

Cheshire, G.C. and E.H. Burn. 1994 [1926]. *Modern Real Property*, 15th edn. London: Butterworths.

Ford, Janet. 1988. *The Indebted Society: Credit and Default in the 1980s.* London: Routledge.

Goo, S.H. 1997. *Sourcebook on Land Law*, 2nd edn. London: Routledge/Cavendish.

Gray, Kevin and S.F. Gray. 1993 [1987]. *Elements of Land Law*, 2nd edn. London: Butterworths.

Lawson, F. Henry. 1958. *Introduction to the Law of Property.* Oxford: Clarendon Press.

Megarry, Robert and H.W.R. Wade. 1957 [1984]. *The Law of Real Property*, 5th edn. London: Sweet & Maxwell.

Moore, Barrington. 1966. *Social Origins of Dictatorship and Democracy: Lord and Peasant in the Making of the Modern World.* Boston, MA: Beacon Press.

Murphy, Tim, S. Roberts. 1994. *Understanding Property Law.* London: Harper Collins.
OECD. 1992. *Urban Land Markets: Policies for the 1990s.* Paris.
Partington, Martin. 1980 [1975]. *Landord and Tenant* (*Law in Context*). London: Weidenfeld & Nicolson.
Rose, Carol M. 1994. *Property and Persuasion: Essays on the History, Theory, and Rhetoric of Ownership.* Boulder, CO: Westview Press.
Twining, William. 1994. *Blackstone's Tower: The English Law School.* London: Sweet & Maxwell.

Cases

Barclays Bank plc v. O'Brien [1993] UKHL 6.
City of London Building Society v. Flegg [1988] AC 54.
Tulk v. Moxhay [1848] EWHC Ch J34.
Williams & Glyn's Bank v. Boland [1980] UKHL 4.

Chapter 2

McAuslan in context

Early days in Dar and Warwick[1]

William Twining

Introduction

I first met Patrick McAuslan in June 1961 at the corner of Russell Square nearest to School of Oriental and African Studies (SOAS) and Birkbeck. Along with AB Weston, our dean, we were the first three members not only of the law school, but also of University College Dar es Salaam (hereafter UCD). In the ensuing years we were joined by, among others, Nkambo Mugerwa, Aki Sawyerr, Yash Ghai, Jim Reid, and Sol Picciotto. Patrick McAuslan and I maintained contact until his death, not only as colleagues at Dar, Warwick and London, but also as academics with overlapping interests and, of course, as friends.

This chapter was originally written as a tribute to McAuslan while he was alive. Sadly, it is now a posthumous memoir. The point of the chapter is not only to give an account of McAuslan's experiences and contributions to two law schools that tried to break the mould in English-style legal education, but also to record in print information about their early days and, based on unpublished documents and unreliable memories, to try to evoke some of the spirit of these adventures that cannot be captured by a staid account. So part of this is by necessity personal and anecdotal, but it also tries to analyse the meanings given to 'law in context' and the limits of legal radicalism in two different institutional settings. I am especially pleased that Patrick read and *semble* generally approved of an early draft. Part of his legacy is a rich collection of consultancy reports and materials and a remarkable number of unpublished manuscripts, several of which we hope can be edited for future publication.[2]

1 This chapter was originally drafted as a paper for the celebration of Patrick McAuslan's life and work at Birkbeck in 2012. I was unable to attend, but I sent him a copy and he replied with comments, some of which are quoted in the footnotes. I am also grateful to Abdul Paliwala, Ambreena Manji and the editor for helpful suggestions.

2 At the time of writing work on his professional papers is still ongoing under the direction of Patrick's widow, Dorrette McAuslan.

Dar es Salaam 1961–66

1961–66 were formative years for Patrick and myself. Perhaps the most important aspect of the context was the fact that Tanganyika gained independence in December 1961. University College, Dar es Salaam (hereafter UCD) was started in a rush in the wake of Tanganyika's rapid transition to independence. As late as 1956 the Colonial Office had refused to set any target dates for independence, but casual talk usually suggested 50 years. Even in 1958 Julius Nyerere, by then recognised as the nationalist leader, encouraged Tanganyika African National Union (TANU) to prepare for independence in 20 years. In 1957 in addressing the Trusteeship Council he suggested 10–12 years.[3] In 1960 Tanganyika attained self-government and became independent in 1961. It was, indeed one of the speediest and smoothest transitions in the period of decolonization.

One of Julius Nyerere's first acts as First Minister in 1960 was to announce the need for Tanganyika to have its own university. The University College Dar es Salaam Act (Provisional Council) Ordinance was passed by Legislative Council on 16 February 1961. The first Principal, Cranford Pratt (a Canadian), was appointed in March/April. The first three academic staff, AB Weston, Patrick and myself were appointed in April/May. The first faculty meeting took place in June. The first fourteen students arrived in early October, just two months before independence. By then staff had to be recruited, accommodation arranged, regulations drafted and a curriculum for the first faculty (law) approved. In October, fourteen students from Tanganyika, Uganda, and Kenya had been drafted, some of them diverted from programmes of study abroad. The College had no accommodation of its own until TANU, the ruling political party, agreed to lease its as yet unoccupied headquarters – an act of huge symbolic significance for the College.

There were several reasons why law was chosen as the first faculty. Lord Denning had chaired a Committee on Legal Education for Students from Africa, which reported in December 1960.[4] It was highly critical of the practice of sending African students to the Inns of Court to qualify as barristers and urged that local institutions of legal education should be started as a matter of urgency in several African countries and specifically recommended that a faculty of law in Tanganyika should be set up with all possible speed. One attraction for Nyerere was that law was one of the

3 Oral Hearing of the Trusteeship Council (18 June 1957). Two years earlier at an Oral Hearing before the Trusteeship Council, he had talked of 20 or 25 years (7 March 1955). Nyerere wanted the UK Government to set a target date for Independence, but tended to make rather vague statements about timing without revealing his negotiating position. See Nyerere 1966, pp. 36, 44, 47.

4 *Report of the Committee on Legal Education for Students from Africa* Cmd.1255, 1961 (Denning Report). For details see further Twining 1966; and Manji and Harrington 2003, pp. 376–399.

major subjects not covered at the sister institutions of Makerere and Nairobi, so that UCD could be the first to offer local legal education in East Africa. Legal education had been given a low priority in the colonial period, partly because law was not seen as 'developmentally relevant', partly because law students and lawyers were seen as potential trouble-makers – they had played a major role in independence movements in West Africa. The result was that at independence Tanganyika had only two African lawyers and the numbers were not much higher in Kenya and Uganda. Another factor was that law was and is perceived as a cheap subject, requiring no laboratories or special equipment or accommodation. On this view, all it needs is a room, a blackboard and some chalk. During our second year we taught in the vault of a disused bank. However, a great deal of our early efforts was devoted to building a good law library, the need for which is regularly underestimated by higher education planners.

From the outset UCD aspired to be distinctive. The main inspiration for this came from Julius Nyerere, who was First Minister, then Prime Minister, during self-government and the early years of independence, and the first President of Tanganyika, later Tanzania, when it became a Republic in December 1962. Establishing a university was one of Nyerere's priorities. It was a symbol of nationhood, it was an important part of nation building, and he was determined that the educated elite should share his vision of the ethos of an independent Tanganyika from the outset. Nyerere was a socialist and a committed egalitarian, but he recognised that a well-educated elite was essential to lead, administer and develop the country. He was also a scholar and teacher. He had studied at Edinburgh and admired the Scottish university tradition. So he believed in academic excellence, a fair degree of academic freedom, and above all teaching and research directly relevant to African problems and needs. Nyerere also expounded a philosophy of law that some interpreted as more liberal than socialist. At the opening of the College he said:

> I believe that law is one of those subjects that can only effectively be studied in the environment in which it will be used. … Up to now, the Government has insisted that those called to the Bar in England should have a period of reorientation on their return to Tanganyika before they begin to practice at the Tanganyika Bar. Although many of our graduates have found this an irritating and frustrating regulation, I believe that it has a lot of sound reasons behind it. But these reasons no longer apply when the whole training is done within the territory. … We are just undertaking a Herculean task, the task of building of a united, democratic and free country. An essential part of our national philosophy must be a legal profession of great integrity which not only knows the formalities of law but must also understand the basic

> philosophy which underlies our society. Our lawyers and our Judiciary must, in other words, not only appreciate that law is paramount in our society, they must also understand the philosophy of that law.[5]

The mandate for UCD and the Law Faculty was clear: we should teach East African Law in context – and context here meant the historic break with colonialism, local circumstances and problems, and the ideology of the first Independence Government. The university should aspire to international standards of excellence, to traditional (Western) academic values, but it must contribute to nation building, focus on African problems and conditions, and study law in its local context. These were not empty words and Nyerere was a charismatic leader. Inevitably, over time there were tensions between elitism and egalitarianism; between academic freedom and commitment to national ideology in the context of a 'war on poverty, ignorance and disease'; and between safeguarding security and national sovereignty and liberal ideas of the rule of law. There is also a continuous tension between building on traditions of higher education of the former colonial powers and developing genuinely African institutions. All of these tensions were present from the start, and they surfaced from time to time, but in the early days the founders had a clear and inspiring mandate. Furthermore, Nyerere's reputation and charisma attracted bright and adventurous people who might have been less comfortable in more staid and traditional places, such as Makerere. So, nearly all recruits to the academic staff in Dar were in tune with the goals and ethos of the institution. Nyerere's emphasis on independence, nation building, law in context, rule of law, academic freedom, liberal education, and excellence was music to our ears and being involved at the start of a brand new, innovative institution was immensely exciting.

Our first staff meeting in June 1961 was held on a bench in the corner of Russell Square. The bench has since disappeared. I arrived in good time and noticed a tall, thin, figure shyly loitering and introduced myself; then we waited for our new dean, AB Weston, who was late. When he arrived we quickly learned that all three founder members – AB Weston, Patrick McAuslan and myself – were trying to break free from a narrow and formal style of legal education. AB had started in Australia, spent two years in Oxford, en route to Canada, where he was already known for his unorthodox views. Patrick McAuslan had also been at Oxford,[6] but had spent time in Nigeria during his military service. A year in Chicago and three years in Khartoum had almost cured me of Oxford. So you had three

5 J.K. Nyerere Speech at Opening Ceremony of University College, Dar es Salaam, 25th October 1961, p. 12, excerpted as 'Education and Law' in Nyerere 1966, pp. 130–1.

6 AB Weston and Patrick had been at the same College (Wadham) and were taught by the same demanding tutor, Peter Carter, but at different times.

revolting Oxford graduates, sitting in a park in London, devising the first curriculum for a new institution that none of us had seen: a prototypical neo-colonial scene – except that we were all in the process of rejecting our English legal education.

The agenda was to devise a curriculum for the LLB. For the early years UCD was in a special relationship with the University of London via the University of East Africa, so this was to be a London LLB (Dar es Salaam).[7] The structure was already set, but we were offered some leeway as to the details of the curriculum. The basic principle was that we should as far as possible teach the law of the four East African jurisdictions for which we were to be the sole local institution of legal education: Kenya, Uganda, Tanganyika, and Zanzibar.[8] There had been some prior correspondence, but it is rather surprising that we managed to draw up the world's greatest curriculum in about half an hour – perhaps the shortest ever meeting of the Dar Faculty of Law?

At the end of the meeting, there was a lull in conversation. Being well brought up, I knew how to fill the gap. So I asked my new dean deferentially: 'What are you working on, AB?' He replied: 'I am writing a book on John Austin, the jurist.' This was mildly embarrassing and rather disconcerting, since Austin stood for all that I – and Dar – should be against. Still, better keep on the right side of the dean. 'How far have you got?' I asked. 'I am starting tomorrow morning', said AB. About eighteen months later, AB was on leave, sailing on his yacht in the Mediterranean, when he was involved in a collision with an even bigger yacht. Not much harm was done and the two captains tied up and had a drink. 'What do you do?' asked AB. 'I am a writer', said Leon Uris, the famous novelist. 'What do you write?' asked AB who should have known better. Uris was rather surprised that AB did not recognise his name: 'Oh, pot boilers', said Uris who had made millions from *Exodus* (1958) and other big fat books.

> 'Where have you got to on the present one?' asked AB.
> 'I am only at page 250', replied Uris, 'what do you do?'
> 'I write, too', said AB.
> 'What do you write?'
> 'Oh, I am writing a biography of John Austin, the jurist', said AB.

7 To begin with law students in Dar read for the London LLB, adapted to East African conditions first under the aegis of Makerere, later of the University of East Africa. At the start, this arrangement had some obvious advantages: it virtually guaranteed international recognition at the outset and many arrangements could be replicated rather than invented from scratch. It provided a framework, but allowed a reasonable scope for teaching local law.

8 From the second year we also had some students from Malawi, including Peter Mutharika, who became President of Malawi in 2014.

> Uris laughed, 'There can't be much money in that.
> How far have you got?'
> 'I'm starting tomorrow morning', said AB.
> ... and so on through several episodes.[9]

AB was in the forefront of the context in which Patrick and I found ourselves. This is one of many AB Weston legends. Even if the legends are fanciful, they catch some of his character: he was an adventurer, charming, unconventional, breezy, very clever, charismatic, and a brilliant linguist. Furthermore, he did not take himself too seriously.[10]

As dean, AB took on a few tasks with great energy, but left the rest to us.[11] In that first year Patrick was teaching contract, I was teaching 'introduction to law' and we were co-teaching a course on the legal systems of East Africa (which included the constitutions). Apart from helping to draft regulations, sit on committees, consult with architects, start a library and all the other tasks that are involved in founding a new institution – the first in the country – our initial task was to research local law for the purposes of teaching: there was almost no secondary literature on the law of the four East African jurisdictions; there was quite extensive, but uneven, law reporting, and each country had collections of statutes and legislation that were far from user-friendly. The general literature on so-called 'African Law', largely pioneered by SOAS, was quite helpful, but largely in the black letter tradition, even though Tony Allott and colleagues were enthusiastic proponents of customary law.[12]

The task of gathering local materials would have been hard, especially in relation to customary law, but it was made harder by the fact that this was the period of transition to independence and people talked as if everything

9 This is a reconstruction of a version that AB used to tell. Obviously the exact wording of these exchanges is speculative, but it is pretty close to AB's account of the events. The novel on which Uris was working was probably *Topaz* (1967).

10 He had been a pilot in the Australian Air Force and I remember vividly his trying to take over the controls of a bumpy single-engined plane over the Northern Region as three of us flew up to represent Dar es Salaam at a meeting of the University of East Africa at Makerere. We survived the journey, but arrived like three cowboys in safari clothes late for a meeting at which everyone else was wearing ties and business suits.

11 AB was determined to have 'the best law library in Africa', a task he insisted on dealing with personally and he was pre-occupied with ordering books for the library and touring embassies and High Commissions begging for books and funds. He was also involved early on in a project for an English-Kiswahili Law Dictionary project, see Weston 1965 and Harries 1966, pp. 164–167. One day, as he seemed a bit pressed, I offered to take his lecture for him on the following Tuesday. It was only afterwards that we realised that it was the first class in the history of the institution. We did not think we were making history.

12 For a debate on the value of 'restating' or 'codifying' customary law, see Twining 1964 and a reply by Cotran 1966, p. 72, especially pp. 77–79.

was possible. For example, in 1961–62 in our course on legal systems of East Africa we had to take account of the fact that new constitutions were being introduced or debated for three of the four East African jurisdictions and that all three countries were involved in different exercises to reform their court systems, largely according to different patterns. So the question arose: how could one sensibly teach about law in East Africa in the absence of a secondary literature in a period of momentous change?

In retrospect there were two main options: first, to prepare elementary local textbooks and study aids so that the students could have some solid information to learn; or second to teach about problems of law in East Africa, sacrificing coverage of technical detail and focusing critically on the suitability of the existing state legal systems to the circumstances and needs of the various countries in the run-up to and aftermath of independence. In Nigeria, the local law schools, which were founded in the same period under the leadership of Jim Gower, gave a high priority to producing basic expository works and outlines on aspects of Nigerian law.[13] In Dar, we followed a different strategy.[14]

If we did not produce textbooks, how did our students learn? Essentially, we used English textbooks and casebooks supplemented by local materials. Where the course had distinctive local dimensions, we emphasized the materials. It is sometimes suggested that we followed an American model of cases and materials rather than a British model of textbooks. That is only partly true: like American law teachers, we emphasized primary sources, we were not too concerned with coverage, and we tried to proceed by discussion as much as lectures – which was easy with our first class of fourteen students. But conditions dictated that our approach was distinctive in several ways: first, it had to be comparative because we were dealing with four different jurisdictions from which most of our students came. Secondly, transition from colonial rule and the resulting pressures for change linked with the lack of a developed literature virtually compelled us to adopt an historical approach – which was anyway congenial to both Patrick and me.[15]

Thirdly, since we were dealing in large part with imported legal ideas, institutions and doctrines, their suitability to a new context was continuously put in issue – we *had* to be contextual. In our jointly taught course, McAuslan dealt with the constitutions, and I took on the court systems and a bit about customary law. We frantically combed the local law reports, the statute books, official reports, and newspaper accounts of public debates to supplement the almost non-existent secondary literature. Patrick, I

13 Nwabueze 1963 and 1964, and Park 1963 are admirable examples of this genre of expository textbook. On Gower's views see Gower 1967.

14 On scholarly work emanating from Dar in the early days, see below.

15 See note 22 below (Palley).

remember, was relentless, thorough, and remarkably systematic in this endeavour. Kiswahili is a wonderfully inventive language especially in its use of prefixes and suffixes: *mhuru* means a free man; *kihuru* the language of freedom; *acha* or *weka huru* (to make free, liberate), *uhuru* the concept of freedom (independence). The students tended to give all staff Kiswahili nick names: for example, Jim Reid was known as Bwana Twiga (meaning Mr Giraffe); others were less complimentary; I never learned mine nor Patrick's, but I know that the students constructed a new Swahili word – *KuMcAuslan* (i.e. to do a McAuslan) meaning to lock yourself in your room and do a blitz on your work for 72 hours without a break. If they had extended this to *UMcAuslan* (the essence of M) it would have carried the connotation of relentless, concentrated work over substantial periods of time.

The Law Faculty in Dar has been quite self-conscious. It has celebrated its twenty-fifth, fortieth and fiftieth anniversaries with significant publications, including several house histories that periodise the development of this quite small institution (see Shivji 1986; Kanywanyi 1986, p. 39; Mungi 2002; Mgongo Fimbo 2011). The early days, especially 1961 to 1968 tend to be labelled 'The nationalist phase', followed by the African Socialist or Arusha Declaration phase, then an internally controversial Marxist turn, succeeded by a period of structural adjustment and free market liberalisation. The 'nationalist' label was not inappropriate. In the immediate post-independence period, the buzzwords were 'nation building', freedom and national unity (*uhuru na umoja*). Nyerere himself only fully developed his philosophy of African socialism (*ujamaa*) in the mid-60s.[16] In the early days we were too involved with getting on with the job to articulate a rounded philosophy for legal education.

16 Arusha Declaration 1967; Nyerere 1966. Later, UCD became a centre of Marxist critiques of Nyerere's pragmatic socialism. In one period from 1975 the Faculty was full of tensions and there was a rapid turnover of staff. The famous Arusha Declaration of 5 February 1967, which restated TANU's policy on socialism and self-reliance, introduced a more robust interpretation of socialism. This in turn impacted quite markedly on the Law Faculty, both in terms of curriculum discussion and internal debates about various interpretations of Marxism and socialism. After the retirement of President Nyerere in 1985 Tanzania embarked on a period of liberalisation and structural adjustment, which also impacted on the teaching of law, not least in respect of the fact that Government was no longer (perceived as) the main employer of law graduates. How radical these various shifts in national policy and prevailing ideologies were in practice is open to interpretation. For example, when I revisited the Faculty in 1994, 29 years after I had left, as part of a team reviewing all legal education and training in Tanzania, I asked the Associate Dean about the size of the undergraduate intake and the graduating class. He told me that it was 60 and 65 respectively. I said that this was the same as when I left in 1965. 'Yes', he said in effect, 'You remember the lecture room, it holds 62'. The LLB curriculum was also largely unchanged, but controversy had centred mainly on two or three courses. Financial and Legal Management Upgrading Project (FILMUP) 1994.

The first controversy in UCD was not about neo-colonialism or ideology or the meaning of 'development', or different approaches to teaching law. It was about gowns. And it symbolises rather nicely what Issa Shivji later brilliantly designated as 'The Limits of Legal Radicalism' (Shivji 1986). In a nutshell, the first administrators ordered 50 saffron gowns because we had to have different colours from Makerere and Nairobi; the first academics suggested pragmatically that the climate in Dar was too hot for gowns; an American Professor objected: 'Gowns are just an outmoded British idiosyncrasy like wigs, pinstriped suits and rolled umbrellas. No American student would be seen dead in a gown so why impose this on Africa?' Then a Swedish professor of economics, Eric Svendsen suggested that gowns were politically incorrect, exactly symbolising the kind of neo-colonialism and elitism that we are determined to avoid.[17] A senior Tanzanian administrator, bemused by these squabbling expatriates, pointed out that colourful ceremonies are an important part of African tradition and that a degree ceremony without gowns would be considered very alien. In the end pragmatism trumped climatology, tradition, ideology, and local custom. The administrators said: 'We have already paid for the gowns out of public funds and there will be a scandal if we do not use them.' The Academic Board reached a typically British compromise: gowns should only be retained for 'formal and festive occasions'. Later the students had to be restrained from wearing their gowns when they went shopping or to student dances. This debate, which persisted over two to three years, is almost a paradigm example of the ambivalences and paradoxes of neo-colonialism and post-colonialism for both locals and expatriates.[18]

17 It is worth quoting from Eric Svendsen's eloquent and witty memorandum to the Academic Board of UCD (Minutes of Special Meeting held on 8 July, 1964): 'In this wider framework gowns may be said to be a minor matter. In this I cannot agree, however. To me gowns tend to stress the distance between students and other members of society. They help to create a feeling of belonging, not to society in general and taking part in this society's endeavours to change and develop itself, but rather to a group of higher educated people whose privileges and special conditions are anyway so different from those of other young people that they should not be stressed again. And I fear that gowns may lead to manners and behaviour which like the gowns have not been created or have matured on African soil, but come from somewhere else. ... Finally, I would myself – as a graduate of a Danish University not possessing a gown – rather raise this, than hear it be brought up by somebody else as a semi-argument against my view of gowns. I think that it is a fortunate thing that we originate from different sets of traditions, even if I have to turn the Old Danish fairy tale upside down and let the gownless boy speak to the bewigged emperors.' (K.E Svendsen, Professor of Economics).

18 I am told that the fiftieth anniversary celebrations were marked by a colourful array of gowns, even some from Scandinavia, and that the early Dar teachers there were almost the only academics who did not wear gowns (McAuslan, private communication to the author, 2010).

This is just one of many stories that illustrate how difficult it is to break away from foreign models. With an institution like a university you can make adjustments at the margins, as with gowns, but basic structures, attitudes, habitual practices, and entrenched traditions are much tougher to change, or even to adjust to fit local conditions. This is also true of teaching law. UCD, you will remember, was in a special relationship with the University of London and the first law graduates read for a London LLB. In fact, the authorities in London, while insistent on the 'standards' of the University of London – were surprisingly flexible about content. They positively encouraged us to teach about the legal systems, the constitutions and the laws of East Africa, so far as this was feasible and we tried very hard to do this. In my second year, I had to teach torts – but how could one teach the East African Law of Torts, when there were only a handful of reported cases and no books? Even today, how does one teach about local customary law of wrongs in detail and depth? These are real – and to some extent continuing – problems. We did what we could and in some respects we made a virtue out of necessity.

To start with we had no explicit philosophy about what we were doing: we were working under pressure and we had to get on with the job. But over time, we had to articulate an ethos for the law school and what we were teaching. In 1963–4 McAuslan and Twining were constituted as a small committee to draft an entry for a prospectus for UCD in order to recruit students from East African schools. Patrick did the first draft and I have recently found the original in his distinctive handwriting in my archive. The published version reads as follows:

> In the Faculty of Law at Dar es Salaam, lecturers have been appointed, syllabuses planned and methods of teaching devised, with one single important consideration in mind: the fact that the lawyer in East Africa has to be much more than a competent legal technician. With the coming of independence, the manifold problems that beset developing countries have to be faced, and doing this great changes will have to be made in the framework of society. Lawyers have a vital role to play in these developments for upon them will fall a major share of the work of putting into practice the principles and ideas of their colleagues in the fields of politics, economics and science, and ensuring that the resultant system works fairly and efficiently. Legal education must take account of these facts, and see that students are made aware of and prepared for their future role.
>
> Legal education for East African lawyers must therefore entail more than the accumulation of knowledge about rules of law – to know much law is not necessarily to be a good lawyer, although it is the foundation upon which most legal education must rest. The good lawyer is the one who knows also something of the society in which the

> law operates and the processes by which the law may change and be changed by that society. Thus we teach the law as it exists in East Africa today, but we do not stop there; we use this law as a firm base upon which future developments may be considered. In this way we hope to be able to produce lawyers who will thoroughly have mastered the techniques of the law: how to search out all the relevant authorities on a particular point and marshall them in a coherent form; how to read a case in order to understand it fully; how to analyse and interpret a statute; and how to put across one's point of view in speech and writing. But over and above all this, they will have studied that law against the social and economic background of the East African jurisdictions; and will be in a good position to offer useful contributions to discussions of what the law ought to be.[19]

There are six key terms in that statement that became central themes of our early efforts: technical competence plus local law, local context, development, skills, policy, including practical implementation of policy. Looking back, we may have been naïve, idealistic, too much in a hurry, but I think that we can say that we did our best. We scoured the local law reports for cases, we set up an archives project for local legal records; we gave priority to preparing local teaching materials and developing a local legal literature. We tried to be sensitive to social, political, and economic context: most of the law we taught was imported, but every doctrine, every statute, every case or other transplant had to be subjected to critical scrutiny: does it fit local conditions? In fact, in the early years after independence we could not have ignored context if we had wanted to.

In UCD there was a wonderful 'common course' focused on development: interdisciplinary, university wide, sometimes attended by the President himself.[20] The fact that we had students from Kenya, Uganda, Zanzibar and Malawi, as well as locals, forced us all to be comparative and contextual. Similarly, the situation was one of dynamic change. So the absence of textbooks, the fact that we were dealing with several countries and jurisdictions, the heady political atmosphere and the rapidity of change combined to make it virtually impossible to teach or learn law as a static system of abstract rules. We were forced by circumstance to be contextual, critical, and comparative; and to be concerned with how to *think about* dynamic problems and values; and the students had to study primary sources rather than to rely on textbooks and rote learning of dry facts and bare rules. All of this was immensely exciting. We felt that we were pioneers and truly radical. But looking back, Issa Shivji was right – even the

19 The University College Dar es Salaam, *A Guide for Schools* 1964, pp. 16–17.

20 One of the architects of this course was Sol Picciotto, one of the Dar-Warwick axis.

most committed radicalism has severe limits, especially for law in which tradition is a central characteristic.[21] We had of necessity to rely heavily on English secondary literature – and even 50 years on the new curriculum in Dar es Salaam depends rather a lot on English and American texts.

To sum up the Dar phase: Patrick McAuslan made immense contributions – largely unsung – to the college, to the Law Faculty, and to his students and colleagues. The most visible legacy, apart from former students with many of whom he maintained contact, are his published writings. The two pre-eminent publications emanating from Dar in the early years were Ghai and McAuslan, *Public Law and Political Change in Kenya* (1970) and Iain MacNeil, *Contracts, instruments for social co-operation, East Africa: text, cases, and materials* (1968), two outstanding works of original scholarship, which have stood the test of time and presage later pioneering writings by their authors. McNeil's book foreshadowed his relational theory of contract. Ghai and McAuslan set a highly critical account of the colonial legal legacy in Kenya for both the colonial era and the early years of independence in a clear historical framework. A central theme is the continuities after independence in the development of public law and the institutions of government, including repressive legislation – a theme which is again prominent in McAuslan's recent writings on property and empire.[22] Indeed, many clues to Patrick's later work are to be found in the Dar experience. For instance, he took up land law in Dar by chance, to cover for AB Weston who had been badly injured in a car crash. I have in my archive several memos by Patrick, including a submission to government, co-authored with Yash Ghai, about the idea of a one-party state.[23]

Early days at Warwick

McAuslan returned to UK in 1966 and took up a post at London School of Economics (LSE) in London. I do not think that it is a coincidence that in

21 Shivji 1986. In teaching torts, I still relied on Salmond's textbook and Wright's casebook, supplemented by a few East African cases and some fragments on customary law. Salmond was a New Zealander, Wright was based in Toronto – but that was hardly local. In Jurisprudence we studied almost exclusively Western jurists. At times, as Ghai has argued, concern with context and ideological debates may have edged out concern for basic practical competence. (Ghai 1986, p. 26 ff).

22 McAuslan 2011. The classic example of the advantages of an historical approach to law in times of rapid change is Palley 1966. Ian Smith declared UDI while the book was at the proof stage. The publishers allowed the author to add another chapter to bring the narrative up-to-date. The book became the 'Bible' of the three nationalist leaders, Mugabe, Nkomo and Sithole when they shared a prison cell – the standard joke being: 'Who will sleep with Dr Palley tonight?' This contrasts sharply with expository books on African constitutional law which have anchored in specific texts and soon became outdated, sometimes even before publication.

23 Published as Ghai and McAuslan 1965.

that year he presented a strongly critical paper on legal education in England[24] at a conference on 'the Concept of a Law Degree' organised by Geoffrey Wilson, who was appointed the founding Professor of Law at Warwick in the following year. As significant was a paper on 'Modern Land Law' for the original seminar for the Law in Context series in London in May 1967, which set out his first thoughts on rethinking Land Law. In 1968 McAuslan was appointed to a senior lectureship as a founding member of the Warwick Law School – he stayed there for 18 years and land law and planning became his main focus of attention.[25]

So Patrick became a key founding member of another new law school that was setting out to innovate. Sol Picciotto, another Dar es Salaamite, was also there at the start. He was in due course joined by several ex Dar es Salaamites: Yash Ghai, myself and later, Abdul Paliwala. The Warwick-Dar connection continues. In the UK we soon learned that it was undiplomatic to say 'In Dar-es-Salam we…', although we had in fact pioneered changes such as downgrading of gowns, half-courses, continuous assessment and a legal aid clinic ahead of those in the UK. Of course, the context was very different. Dar had been founded in the heady days of independence; the late 1960s in the UK were not quite as exciting – but they came close in legal education: the Robbins expansion, student unrest, a Labour Lord Chancellor committed to law reform (Lord Gardiner), an outburst of openly critical writings on the legal system by Zander, Abel-Smith and Stevens (1967 and 1968) and others, a wider disillusion with the status quo linked to Harold Wilson's optimism about modernisation were all part of the backdrop.[26]

In the foreground of the context of Patrick's move to Warwick was Geoffrey Wilson, the founding Professor of Law; a very different phenomenon from AB Weston. Time precludes dealing with Geoffrey in

24 McAuslan 1966. Interestingly, Tony Bradley, who had suggested this conference to the Young Members' Group of the SPTL, was unable to attend because he was teaching in Dar es Salaam.

25 At LSE 'I did … planning law on the LLM with Malcolm Grant and Jeffrery Jowell – the dream team!' (McAuslan to the author, 2010) 'It might be relevant to note my first introduction to planning law was when I was a Visiting Professor at Wisconsin Law School Madison in 1969 where I took over at literally a day's notice land use planning law from a professor (whose name I think was Jim MacDonald) who was permitted to join the Environmental Defense Fund in NY for some special project. I used Jake Beuscher's path-breaking materials book on *Land Use Planning Law*. It certainly influenced my thinking on the subject. Jake has recently died with his casebook still in a temporary edition. MacDougal [and Haber's book on land law] also influenced me.' (McAuslan to the author, 2010).

26 A succinct overview of the national context as it bore on academic law in England is Sugarman 2009 and 2011.

detail,[27] but it is important to emphasize that he had a very clear vision of the kind of institution he wished to create. This was to be a *law school* (teaching for law degrees, rather than mixed degrees), the catchphrase was 'broadening the study of law from within'; each individual member of staff had responsibility for rethinking a traditional field or constructing a new one; but how they set about it was up to them. The last point was important. In the early days the curriculum was rather rigid: planning, international law, company law, and labour law were all compulsory in addition to courses that were recognisable as core subjects. So there were few options for students, but individual teachers were given a virtually free hand as to how they approached rethinking their assigned field.

The Warwick Prospectus for 1973–4 contains a statement which contrasts subtly with the equivalent statement for Dar es Salaam:

> The School of Law at Warwick was established in 1967 with the express object of increasing the variety of law schools available to students wishing to read Law in the United Kingdom and this has been done. Instead of concentrating on the study, analysis and memorising of legal rules it has aimed at broadening the scope of legal studies to include the social context in which law and lawyers operate and has chosen for study those aspects of law which are closely related to major social problems such as crime, housing, consumer protection, labour relations, companies, taxation. In addition, it includes studies of international legal problems and, of course, European legal systems. One of the assumptions behind the course has been that law is an interesting subject to study in its own right, both as a discipline and as an important aspect of society, certainly for the three years that cover the normal length of an undergraduate degree. At the same time the School is well aware that the reason why many students choose to read law in the first place is because they or their parents think that they might want to become solicitors or barristers, and many in fact do go into practice. A further aim of the course has therefore been to provide a preparation for practice for those who eventually wish to go on to practice and at the same time provide a course of study for three years which will not seem wasted if students go on to do something else as a career. In the event it has not proved too difficult to combine these aims since in the view of those establishing the law school the kind of preparation that has been traditionally provided for future practitioners needed to be broadened in exactly the same direction that made law studying by students who did not eventually go into practice, namely by putting the law in its context and studying the role of law

27 For Wilson's views see Wilson 1968; 1987; 1994; and 1995. See further Folsom and Roberts 1979.

> and lawyers in society at the same time as studying the way in which they go about their tasks, and giving students the opportunity of reading something other than legal textbooks.[28]

Wilson emphasized history, structures, institutions, processes and social problems in addition to rules and concepts. An implicit theme was that the aim was to understand British society through the prism of law.[29] Wilson also regularly stressed the importance of Europe and international relations. On that view, the Warwick graduate who claimed that his degree had equipped him to understand every page of *The Financial Times* was exemplary. The emphasis on social problems tended to encourage interpretation of 'context' in terms of policy analysis.

What was unusual about the original LLB curriculum was that commercial and consumer law, housing, town and country planning, international law of war and peace, jurisprudence, law of labour relations and employment and the law of companies were all compulsory, in addition to four of the core subjects. If challenged, how could you justify requiring all students to study company law and labour law? The standard answer could be: how can you understand contemporary British society without studying the main institutions of capitalism and industrial relations? A Warwick graduate should not only gain some understanding of law in the context of society, but should come away understanding contemporary society through studying its law. One implication was that students had limited choice of options in two courses in their third year from a quite short list. It was difficult to hold the line on this as the law school grew and in the first major curriculum revision some of the former compulsory subjects became optional – a move that clearly diluted Geoffrey Wilson's vision of a coherent degree course focused on salient social and political institutions and problems.[30]

28 University of Warwick, *Guide to First Degree Courses 1973–74.*

29 John Rex, the founding professor of sociology at Warwick refused to recognise 'Sociology of Law' as a category. This did not prevent the development of a 4-year joint degree in Law and Sociology, but it reflected a significant difference of perspective. I was disappointed that we never managed to establish a joint degree in law and social history – one of Warwick's strengths.

30 The original Warwick curriculum was to some extent 'fact-based'; that is the organising concepts of some courses were social rather than legal categories. There was not a course called 'Torts' or 'Trusts'. In the early days it was easy to harmonise this with the requirements for professional recognition: torts were distributed over several courses: trespass to land and nuisance to Land Law; defamation to civil liberties; economic torts to Commercial Law and Labour Law. To ensure the similar distribution of Equity and Trusts, a special topic was added to Company Law entitled 'duties of trustees and directors compared'. Recognition of the degree for professional exemptions was relatively unproblematic so long as all of these courses were compulsory, but delicate, and quite amusing negotiations were involved when some of them became optional. On 'fact-based classification', see Jolowicz 1970.

At my interview in 1971, I was asked: 'What subject are you going to Warwickise?', meaning what traditional or neglected field of law are you going to rethink in broader terms? I had expected that question and had given some thought to it. I had reduced the possibilities to two: Land Law or Evidence (to be more precise: Evidence, Proof and Fact-finding). But the territory of Land Law was already occupied by McAuslan, so I devoted most of my scholarly efforts for the next 20 years or so to 'Warwickising' fact-finding.[31] The outcome of Patrick's occupation of land was two successful courses, an important book on planning and, in time, his major contributions to land reform and urban planning in nearly 50 countries.[32]

This is how Folsom and Roberts described the actual first year property course at Warwick in which Roberts participated:

> Patrick McAuslan started with the idea of organising a section of the first two years of the [property] curriculum around land and the social problems associated with it. In the first year course this led to the study of housing, law and social problems. The course began with the social reality of housing. Initial investigations were carried out into council housing, the workings of the private market, financial institutions and particular social problems of the day such as squatters and homeless families. Based on an understanding of the social reality of housing, the course then proceeded to both categories of legal rules which exist to deal with realty and transaction skills which are necessary to the creation, disposal and transfer of housing. The focus on legal rules led back to familiar property concepts and the transactions focus led to a study of legal processes (e.g. the mortgage market and the process of conveyancing). Aberrations in the system of rules and transactions could then be viewed from the perspective of the social realities of housing. Finally, one could return to law reform and public policy questions as a result of the basic learning dynamic of the social reality of housing, legal rules and transactions.
>
> Folsom and Roberts 1979, p. 182

31 Both Patrick and I came relatively fresh to our assigned fields. Until then Patrick had been primarily a public lawyer, who had mainly taught Public law, Conflicts of law, and Contract in Dar. I knew nothing of Evidence, other than through the writings of Jeremy Bentham and Jerome Frank, who did not feature in contemporary evidence treatises. Although the inspiration for this was American Realism, Geoffrey Wilson was uneasy about my choice because the category Evidence, Proof and Fact-finding referred neither to a social institution nor to a social problem. So he insisted that the subject I taught in the third year should be called 'Advanced Legal System', leaving the door open for someone else to focus on quite different subject-matters.

32 Patrick's precise count in 2012 was 43 including Somaliland, Somalia and Jersey, but not Zanzibar (as part of Tanzania). (McAuslan to the author, 2012). His influence extended further.

This represented a radical departure from the focus and perspectives of leading textbooks, such as those by Cheshire and Megarry.

McAuslan's second year course, which was eventually entitled 'Land Use Planning and Development' adopted a similar perspective and was equally successful.[33] He had originally planned to do a book on land law for the 'Law in Context' series, but produced *Land, Law and Planning* (1975) instead. This was immediately recognised as being well ahead of the field.[34]

Patrick McAuslan's two courses, along with Patrick Atiyah's *Accidents, Compensation and the Law* (1st edn, 1970) have always been two outstanding models of ways in which one can rethink and change a traditional field. When I was trying to construct a method for rethinking a field for a course or a book based on a contextual approach, I used McAuslan's approach to Land law and Atiyah's approach to compensation for accidents as models of one particular approach within the broad church of law in context. Rather than try to describe how he actually constructed his pioneering courses on land law and land use planning, I tried to *reconstruct* his approach as an ideal type and I called this 'the McAuslan legend'. The approach goes something like this:

Step 1

Choose a suitable organizing category, preferably fact-based,[35] that is directly related to some social phenomenon or socio-political set of problems: for example, land or land use rather than real property, or property, or some abstract legal concept. Similarly, Patrick Atiyah's first move was to substitute compensation for accidents instead of torts or the common law action for negligence.

Step 2

Construct a total picture of the social phenomena involved. In my reconstruction Patrick takes out a map of England and Wales and asks how much land is there and how is it used? Land use can be roughly categorised

33 This later became optional.

34 In 1971 Patrick defined the purpose of the course as follows:

> 'The objective of the course is twofold. At the least, this is a course about planning and so you should, at its end, be able to explain the principles of planning law and the social context in which it operates; to be able to discuss in an informed way, both orally and on paper, the relative merits of different policies and methods of planning. At its best, this is a course about decision-making, taking as its focal point, the area of urban land use, and so you should, at its end, be able to assimilate diverse sorts of information about a problem, come up with a reasoned and realistic solution to the problem, and support it against opposition.'
>
> (course description, 1971–72)

35 On fact-based classification of law, see Jolowicz 1970.

as industrial and commercial, agriculture, housing, transport, amenity (including sport), governance and administration, with regard to each category: what are the main uses to which it is put in practice? Who are the main actors and legal persons affected? What are the main institutions and transactions involved in each type of land use?

Step 3

This construction of a total picture of land and its uses sets a broad context, but it immediately reveals that for the purposes of designing a course or a students' work, quite radical selection is necessary. Patrick decided to focus on two categories, one traditional – housing – and one almost completely undeveloped in legal education in the UK,[36] problems of urban planning. The choice of these two topics from a much wider field could be justified by their social importance, their interest, their practical value for intending practitioners and tradition – conventional real property courses focused very largely on a fictitious mansion called Blackacre, rather like Downton Abbey without the downstairs. Warwick students would be expected to be familiar with the basic concepts, principles, rules and transactions of property law, and housing is a good vehicle for studying these.

Step 4

In this instance there is still room for some more demographic realism, for example: where are the houses and where are the people? The answers to these questions reveal some significant gaps in traditional treatments, in which almost no mention was made of the homeless, squatters, travellers ('gypsies'), let alone council house tenants, who, before Mrs Thatcher, constituted over 50 per cent of occupiers in England and Wales. No wonder that in the late 1960s there was felt to be something 'unreal' about Blackacre. Each of these categories is associated with complex problems and legal responses, involving many fields of law: for example, issues of discrimination in relation to public housing, which had been the tinder for reigniting the Troubles in Northern Ireland.[37] So again, this approach shows up the complexity of problems, the intermingling of different field of law and acute problems of selection. Patrick had the luxury of two full compulsory courses spread over two years and he still had to make some hard choices about focus and educational objectives. Someone adopting exactly the same approach could have come up with a very different design

36 Patrick's starting point was American courses and materials on land use and planning. See note 25 above.

37 i.e. the protests in Caledon (Dungannon) and Derry in 1968; see Boyle and Hadden (1994).

for their course or a contextual book (for further information, see Twining 1997, pp. 53–58).

My only regret is that he substituted his book on planning for the proposed book on land law and then moved on to other things. We still need a book on McAuslan's approach to Land Law. It is my impression that land law/property courses are still highly conceptual, only slightly more linked to social reality (landlord and tenant may be an exception) and it is reportedly still found by many students to be the most mystifying and uncongenial of all the core subjects. Patrick's achievement was to contextualize the study of land law and urban planning in England and Wales, to demystify the problems and transactions, to introduce a public law perspective on what had been traditionally conceived as a private law field, to bring out conflicts in ideology and values, and to demonstrate the importance, vitality and interest of these two cognate fields. In addition to his personal qualities of thoroughness and precision, he also brought a historical perspective – the first chapter of *Land, Law and Planning* is significantly subtitled 'The continuity of problems and laws'. Anyone familiar with Patrick's enormous practical and scholarly contributions to land reform and urban planning in the global South and beyond (see below), will find many clues to his approach in his teaching and scholarship in the formative years at Warwick from 1968–1987.

References

Arusha Declaration. 1967. Tanzania.

Boyle, Kevin and Tom Hadden. 1994. *Northern Ireland: The Choice.* London: Penguin.

Cotran, Eugene. 1966. 'The place and future of customary law in East Africa', *East African Law Today.* British Institute of International and Commonwealth Law, 72–92.

Financial and Legal Management Upgrading Project (FILMUP). 1994. *Legal Education Report.* Dar es Salaam. September.

Folsom, Ralph and Neal Roberts. 1979. The Warwick story: Being led down the contextual path. *Journal of Legal Education* 30: 166.

Ghai, Yash P. 1986. 'Legal radicalism, professionalism and social action: Reflections on teaching law in Dar es Salaam'. In Shivji, Issa G. (ed.) *The Limits of Legal Radicalism.* Dar es Salaam: University of Dar es Salaam.

Ghai, Yash P. and J.P.W.B. McAuslan. 1965. Constitutional proposals for one-party state in Tanzania. *East African Law Journal* 1: 124–47.

Ghai, Yash P. and J.P.W.B. McAuslan. 1970. *Public Law and Political Change in Kenya.* Nairobi: Oxford University Press.

Gower, L.C.B. 1967. *Independent Africa: The Challenge to the Legal Profession.* Cambridge, MA: Harvard University Press.

Harries, Lyndon. 1966. Language and law in Tanzania. *Journal of African Law* 10(3): 164–167.

Jolowicz, John A. (ed.) 1970. *Division and Classification of the Law.* London: Sweet & Maxwell.

Kanywanyi, Joe. 1986. The struggle to decolonise and demystify university education: Dar's 25 years experience focused on the Faculty of Law. *East Africa Law Review* 16(1): 39.

MacNeil, Iain. 1968. *Contracts, Instruments for Social Cooperation, East Africa: Text, Cases, And Materials.* South Hackensack, NJ: F. B. Rothman.

McAuslan, J.P.W.B. 1966. The proper relation between university law teaching and training for the legal profession in England: Some thoughts on our present discontents. Paper read at the Young Members' Conference on *The Concept of a Law Degree.* Cambridge. September.

McAuslan, Patrick. 2011. Fifty years of land law change in Eastern Africa: Transformative or traditional? A preliminary assessment. Unpublished paper, 50th Anniversary Symposium of the Faculty of Law, University of Dar es Salaam.

Manji, Ambreena and John Harrington. 2003. Mind with mind, spirit with spirit: Lord Denning and African legal education. *Journal of Law and Society* 30: 376–399.

Mgongo Fimbo, Gamaliel (ed.) 2011. *Fifty Years of Legal Education in Tanzania.* University of Dar es Salaam.

Mungi, S.E.A. (ed.) 2002. *Forty Years of the Faculty of Law, University of Dar es Salaam.* Dar es Salaam.

Nyerere, Julius K. 1966. *Freedom and Unity: Uhuru Na Umoja.* Selected writings and speeches. Dar es Salaam: Oxford University Press.

Nwabueze, Ben. 1963. *The Machinery of Justice in Nigeria.* London: Butterworth.

Nwabueze, Ben. 1964. *The Constitutional Law of the Nigerian Republic.* London: Butterworth.

Palley, Claire. 1966. *The Constitutional History of Southern Rhodesia 1888–1965: with special reference to imperial control.* Oxford: Clarendon Press.

Park, Andrew. 1963. *The Sources of Nigerian law.* London: Sweet & Maxwell.

Report of the Committee on Legal Education for Students from Africa. Cmd.1255. 1961. (Denning Report).

Shivji, Issa. (ed.) 1986. *The Limits of Legal Radicalism.* Faculty of Law, University of Dar es Salaam. 25th Anniversary.

Sugarman, David. 2009. Beyond ignorance and complacency: Robert Stevens' journey through lawyers and the courts. *International Journal of the Legal Profession* 16: 7.

Sugarman, David. 2011. A special relationship? American influence on American legal education. *International Journal of the Legal Profession* 18: 7.

Twining, William. 1964. *The Place of Customary Law in the National Legal Systems of East Africa.* Chicago, IL: University of Chicago Law School.

Twining, William. 1966. Legal education within East Africa, in *East African Law Today.* London: The British Institute of International and Comparative Law.

Twining, William. 1997. *Law in Context: Enlarging a Discipline.* Oxford: Oxford University Press.

The University College Dar es Salaam. 1964. *A Guide for Schools.*

University of Warwick, *Guide to First Degree Courses 1973–74.*

Weston, A.B. 1965. *Journal of the Institute of Kiswahili Research* 35.

Wilson, Geoffrey P. 1968. The concept of a law degree: Getting on with the job. *Journal of the Society of Public Teachers of Law* (NS) 10: 114.

Wilson, Geoffrey P. 1987. English legal scholarship. *Modern Law Review* 50: 818.
Wilson, Geoffrey P. 1994. Europeanising the English law school *SPTL Reporter*, spring.
Wilson, Geoffrey P. (ed.) 1995. *The Frontiers of Legal Scholarship*. Chichester: Wiley.

Chapter 3

Context, political economy and good governance

Avatars of Dar legal education

Abdul Paliwala[1]

> Support for legal education is not high profile; is not going to produce quick results and might be difficult at first sight to reconcile with a commitment to support legal system reform to benefit the poor. One could however, argue that it's the one Law and Development input that brings together the external and the internal perspectives of Law and Development and the one such input that is highly unlikely to fail: in every society there are some lawyers who are concerned with justice, with freedoms and with advancing the rule of law. If it does nothing else as a community, the Law and Development community should make it its business to argue the case for support for legal education in the South and especially in 'failed states' so as to develop as rapidly as possible that critical mass of national legal skills and knowledge that is the only sure way to build up a national legal culture and so in turn create the undergirding for a legitimate, effective and just national legal system.
>
> McAuslan, 2004

The avatars

The first avatar: the birth of law in context

This chapter is based on a paper presented in 2011 on the occasion of 'Patrick McAuslan's Odyssey: A Celebration of 50th Anniversary of Patrick in Legal Education' at Birkbeck, University of London. That anniversary coincided with the 50th anniversary of the founding of the Law Faculty of the University of East Africa, and also of what ultimately became the University of Dar es Salaam. At the week-long celebrations in Dar es Salaam, I was falsely but delightfully celebrated as one of the founders. The

1 I am grateful for the assistance provided by Masha Baraza, Adithya Chintapanti, Helen Kijo-Bisimba and Pamela Tibihikirra-Kalyegira.

real founders, the first avatars, were McAuslan, William Twining and the late A.B. Weston, subsequently joined by Sol Picciotto, Yash Ghai and others. William Twining has usefully laid down the important contribution of McAuslan to this first avatar. The enormity of the contribution could be seen in the warmth of welcome in Dar to McAuslan by former students, some of the most prominent lawyers, judges and politicians in East Africa. The juxtaposition of highly creative and independent minds in the special environment of an East African law school contributed to the birth and ultimate export to Warwick and beyond of what became known as the 'Law in Context' movement.

That original avatar has left its imprint on Dar legal education in the sense that there is a continuing concern about studying law in its context. Nevertheless, in the period from the 1970s to the 1990s, there was a sharp turn towards a 'political economy of law' approach. Since then, in the third avatar there is, on the one hand, a concern to see in legal education a technicist vehicle for promoting globalisation and on the other, a concern with good governance. The Faculty of Law in Dar es Salaam started life as the sole law school for the three East African countries of Kenya, Tanzania and Uganda and, while the situation is very different now with an expansion of legal education in all of Eastern Africa, the East African Community provides a renewed impetus for considering East African legal education as a whole. Therefore this chapter uses the East Africa-wide context of the first avatar to relate to key issues in legal education today, including in particular the conceptual debates about the nature and role of legal education, the concern with clinical learning and the role of regional collaboration in coherent development.

The second avatar: political economy of law

I did have the privilege of being part of a second 'founding' group. As indicated in my highly personal account in the volume celebrating the 25th anniversary of the law school, 'intellectual leadership in the faculty resided for the first time among young Tanzanians' (Paliwala 1986, p. 48) and as we asserted in the editorial of the *Eastern Africa Law Review*:

> A lawyer intellectual has to analyse the legal forms to reveal the real substance – the exploitative economic and political dominant/dominated relationships that underlie much of law. Failing this critical role, the lawyer is likely to become an 'intellect worker'; a technocrat in the service of the ruling class.
>
> Shivji 1972, p. 1

This critical approach, in different forms continued to be influential in the law faculty well into the Eighties. As late as 1990, the Dar es Salaam

Declaration on Academic Freedom and Social Responsibility of Academics asserted in the context of academic freedom and human emancipation: '3. Education shall prepare a person to strive for and participate fully in the emancipation of the human being and society from oppression, domination and subjugation.'[2]

The substantiation of such an approach could bristle with difficulties. Ghai, who acknowledged that those who met in the intellectual ferment that was Dar in those days became convinced that 'law could no longer be conceived of as a closed autonomous world', nevertheless recognised the potential 'danger of a certain amount of abstractness, and the loss of the specificity of law as a technique and method. Law may dissolve in the wider reality, its specificity dismissed as irrelevant' (Ghai 1986, p. 34). Shivji, the proponent of the 'lawyer intellectual', clearly acknowledged the danger, especially from those who sought theoretical/ideological purity above all else, but asserted that law needed to be taught from the standpoint of the working people.

> This does not and need not mean compromising in any way scientific objectivity and the rigours of academic scholarship. The student had to be taught and learn legal skills thoroughly but he ought to double-up and comprehend their place and role in the existing social environment.
>
> Shivji 1986, p. 17[3]

Both Ghai and Shivji emphasise democracy and legality, but there is a relative difference in emphasis, with Shivji asserting the primacy of the social justice perspective and Ghai asserting that ultimately legality is the best defence against state oppression. While there was a significant difference between the Ghai and Shivji positions, there was a clear difference between Shivji's emphasis on legal skills and an overemphasis on doctrinaire Marxist analysis by a group dominated by Ben Nabudere, who became Chair of Postgraduate Studies.[4]

Subsequent Tanzanian history and Shivji's (1989) own approach to human rights suggests that a thin Thompsonian version of legality as a bulwark against state oppression combined with a right to critique and resist unjust laws provides an appropriate approach to social justice.[5]

2 Available at www.codesria.org/spip.php?article351 (accessed 12 October 2015).

3 Shivji can justify the importance of hard law in his own excellent doctrinal account of the Union Constitution (Shivji 2009).

4 See generally Majamba (2011) for a review of dissertations supervised in Dar es Salaam. However, Majamba does not distinguish between the very doctrinaire Marxism of Nabudere and the more nuanced one of Shivji.

5 E.P. Thompson (1977, p. 269) controversially stated 'And if the actuality of the law's operation in class-divided societies has, again and again, fallen short of its own rhetoric of equity, yet the notion of the rule of law is itself an unqualified good'.

The third avatar: good governance

Fimbo (2011, p. 19) outlines the manner in which the University of Dar es Salaam shifted its perspective in the post-Nyerere period of the rise of economic liberalism. After much deliberation, the law faculty's response was to emphasise 'justice and good governance' in its Five Year Strategic Plan of 1999 (Faculty of Law 1999, Fimbo 2011). This was further reiterated in the Special Committee Report on Teaching and Learning Law of the Dar es Salaam Law Faculty 2005 which was part of Tanzania's Vision 2025:

> To remain a centre of excellence and leading institution in training highly skilled society conscious lawyers and advance frontiers of knowledge through research, and provision of legal services in furtherance of justice and good governance in a challenging world.
>
> Faculty of Law UDSM 2005, s1. 11[6]

As we shall see, while the position remains radical, the language has shifted from 'oppression' to justice and good governance which are the new global terms. The changes in perspectives over the years are chronicled remarkably well in the volume commemorating 50 years of legal education in Tanzania (Fimbo ed. 2011). In particular, Hamudi Majamba develops a fascinating analysis of dissertations by law faculty academics at Dar es Salaam. He outlines the manner in which the law postgraduate programme directed by Professor Nabudere developed a highly ideological doctrinaire version of Marxism-Leninism and dissertations completed tended to reflect this approach. However, the same students when they went to study abroad developed dissertations which tended to reflect approaches of the institution and supervisor concerned. According to Majamba (2011, p. 154), 'the flame of ideological underpinnings that was evident in dissertations written by staff and detonated (sic) during the early days of the establishment of the faculty and evidenced for a number of decades started fading towards the late 1990s'.

The original radical Dar position was a counterpoint to the US-led Law and Development movement which saw the role of law in development as the export of US legal institutions including legal education, only to acknowledge subsequently that this attempted blind export had failed (Daniels and Trebilcock 2004, pp. 127–133; Trebilcock and Daniels 2008, Ch 8; Brand and Rist 2009; Geraghty and Quansah 1987, pp. 87–105; Maisel 2008 p. 465). However, a key consequence of this acknowledgement of failure was that the 'money men' walked away from law and legal education. In the Law and Development movement, law and legal

6 For an interesting analysis of developments in legal education in Uganda, see Tibihikyrra-Palmegyira (2011).

education benefited from the spoils of a market for reform. The rise of what became known as the Washington consensus with structural adjustment programmes had little real place for law, legality or legal education reform. Neither did African governments, partly because of the political threat posed by an emphasis on the rule of law, but equally significantly because of economic problems in the era of structural adjustment. A consequence for Africa and especially Dar was that law schools everywhere were starved of funds and therefore fell into decline (Ghai 1986 p. 26; Ndulo 2002, p. 487).

However, structural adjustment programmes also failed. This led to a new realisation of the centrality of law and the rise of a new Law and Development movement (Nader 2007; Tamanaha 2009). However, there is confusion in this new movement. This arises from a duality of aims and contradictions within the promoting organisations such as the World Bank. Relying, perhaps misleadingly on Douglass North's New Institutional Economics, the World Bank and International Monetary Fund (IMF) became convinced of the need to promote state institutions which supported a market-friendly state with an emphasis on global economic liberalisation (Faundez, 2010, p. 180; Schlemmer-Schulte 2001, p. 697; Maldonado 2010; Faundez, 2014, p. 49).[7] This led to a new market for Law and Development with the spending of enormous sums of money on legal institutional reforms (Schlemmer-Schulte 2001, p. 697).

These market-based second generation reforms were soon accompanied by a new reform agenda which was based on poverty alleviation, with the World Bank promenading its new mission in consonance with Amartya Sen's capability approach to development:

> It is important to give simultaneous recognition to the centrality of individual freedom and to the force of social influences on the extent and reach of individual freedom. To counter the problems that we face, we have to see individual freedom as a social commitment. Expansion of freedom is viewed, in this approach, as both the primary end and as the principal means of development. Various types of unfreedoms leave people with little choice and little opportunity of exercising their reasoned agency. The removal of substantial unfreedoms, it is argued here, is constitutive of development.
>
> Sen 1999, pp. xii–xiii

Thus the secondary aim provided a role for law in social justice for the World Bank:

7 Faundez (2014, p. 49) suggests that Douglass North himself has been highly critical of the simplistic model which does not take into account the prevailing political, cultural and ideological context.

> In the struggle against discrimination, in the protection of the socially weak, and in the distribution of opportunities in society, the law can make a contribution to an equitable and just society and thus to prospects for social development and poverty alleviation.
>
> World Bank 1994, p. 23

However, there is an effective subordination of social development to the market-friendly state. As Faundez and Sarfaty separately maintain, the wider good governance agenda was a child of lawyers at the World Bank; but, the lawyers had to please the economists to get them on side, with the unfortunate result that 'the Bank economists have successfully managed to tame the unruly governance agenda, placing it firmly at the service of the Washington Consensus' (Faundez 2010, p. 182; Sarfaty 2012). Unfortunately, there is a new acknowledgement of the failure of billions of dollars spent on the new Law and Development movement, of lessons not learned (Tamanaha 2009; Carothers 2013, p. 17). The underlying reasons for failure are attributed variously to the writing of laws without sufficient attention to implementation and enforcement and the slowness and difficulties in making appropriate changes through training programmes and consultancies (Carothers 2013, p. 17). Tamanaha attributes the problems to the inability to recognise that any legal changes operate in the social, economic and legal context of the society within which they are located (Tamanaha 2009, p. 4). McAuslan remained similarly sceptical about the new Law and Development. While he strongly supported the Senian perspective on development as freedom, unlike Sen, he was also concerned to emphasise the dangers of colonial or imperial approaches to contemporary Law and Development discourses by global financial institutions:

> Development is about expanding political as well as economic freedoms and should be people-centered. Democracy too should be seen as being about the expansion of freedom and equality and likewise, as a consequence, people-centered. The state and the law should not be a vehicle of domination either in the national or in the international sphere. It should enable and facilitate people-centered development. Such an approach to development and law – international and national – is incompatible with colonialism; or with rule-of-law programmes which seek to focus solely on investor-friendly legal systems; or with 'the restructuring of the legal functions of the state [which] serves to aggravate existing inequalities and social exclusion' and 'reflect the more general features and effects of the neo-liberal state: the privatization of state functions, increased inequalities and a reduced institutional capacity to intervene in society to address those inequalities'; or with the kind of unregulated market-centered land law reforms geared to the individualization of tenure

> which the World Bank continues to urge on countries and from the latest evidence, is again gearing up to impose on countries.
>
> McAuslan 2004, p. 76

McAuslan therefore justified his own contribution to expanding freedom as supportive of:

> (n)ational programmes of Law and Development which involved working with local counterparts, developing legal system reform packages that put access to justice for the poor at the centre of the programme, ensuring that equity was as central to land law reform packages as efficiency, and that constitution-making and the development of local government emphasised participation and rights for the people and accountability and control of governmental powers. These may be old-fashioned examples of legal liberalism but, to adapt Claude Ake's aphorism, there is no part of the world where the principles of legal liberalism are not relevant, if only as an emancipatory project.
>
> McAuslan 2004, p. 77

Legal education

For McAuslan, legal education had a key role to play in this emancipatory project as can be seen from the quote at the head of this chapter. Yet, university-level legal education has not been prominent in donor funding for sub-Saharan rule of law programmes. As Geraghty and Quansah pointed out in 2007 (p. 87):

> Although there was once a recognition in the philanthropic community that support of legal education in Africa was a critical element in the support of humane, efficient, and predictable justice systems, external donors (non-African governments and foundations) have all but abandoned their support of African legal education.

Instead, the focus of rule of law programmes until 2007 was on judicial training, continuing education for legal practitioners and legal infrastructure and law reform (Piron 2006, pp. 275–78 and Ndulo 2002, p. 493).[8] There were some initiatives on legal education reform which increased in significance after 2007, for example the US AID initiative in relation to legal education capacity building in Ethiopia. US AID also provided funding for

8 Within this overall context, some attention was given to legal education at the university level for example in the World Bank funded project on Financial and Legal Management Upgrading (FILMUP) in Tanzania (World Bank 1992).

the development of clinical legal education programmes in Africa which have involved the East African countries. Other initiatives have included those of the European Union in Malawi (e.g., Devex 2008). In addition, there has been establishment of a number of research centres at the University of Dar es Salaam. A most interesting development has been the German-funded East Africa-wide LLM and PhD programme of the Tanzanian-German Centre for East African Legal Studies located at the University of Dar es Salaam (African Excellence Website). However, these initiatives tend to be piecemeal and may also suffer from problems of lack of fit with the local situation. It may also be that, just as was the case at the end of the first Law and Development movement, the end of the second will also lead to a loss of funds for legal education.

The complexity of objectives of Law and Development reform has led to similar complexity in issues for legal education. Nevertheless, should the law student merely be prepared for practice in the global market or should she have an orientation also geared, or more geared, towards democracy, rule of law and access to justice? If the latter, what meaning should be given to the latter approaches? Should these be genuinely people-centred or should they relate mainly to formal legalism? Should the new legal education reforms involve a re-importation of US (or Western) legal culture or do they need to be more culturally sensitive to African issues? To what extent should legal education involve critique of forms of oppression whether local, national or global?

Thus the International Association of Law Schools clearly sees its mission as promoting globalisation:

> (b) To enhance and strengthen the role of law in the development of societies through legal education;
>
> (e) To contribute to the better preparation of lawyers as they increasingly engage in transnational or global legal practice, and when they pursue careers other than private practice, including governmental, non-governmental, academic, and corporate careers.
>
> International Association of Law Schools By-Laws 2.1, 2014

On the other hand, the American Bar Association Rule of Law Initiative (ABA ROLI) *Legal Education Reform And Civic Education* has a slightly different emphasis on citizens' rights against the state. This work promotes legal education reform by assisting law schools in introducing new courses and practical training methods that better meet the needs of tomorrow's legal professionals. A rule of law culture is promoted through civic education campaigns on citizens' rights (ABA ROLI; See also Brand and Rist 2009).

Ndulo, writing in 2002, suggested that the important task was to transform legal education into one which promotes 'a rights culture and a protective and responsive legal system that reflects the realization that good governance is a pre-condition to development'. He considered that contemporary African lawyers fell short of these aims:

> The lawyers produced by the present system of legal education in Africa are trained to become legal technicians. They are encouraged to have little or no interest or comprehension of the policy issues inherent in the law. They are generally reluctant to criticize current law. Even as technicians they have limits, for few are competent to represent national and commercial interests in international transactions, involving complexities of taxation and international finance.
>
> Ndulo 2002, p. 500

These sentiments are further reinforced by Daniels and Trebilcock who call for ideologically or normatively pluralistic legal education which fosters 'critical perspectives on "law in action" or "law in society through clinical legal education and interdisciplinary and empirical teaching and research"' (Daniels and Trebilcock 2004, p. 117; see also Trebilcock and Daniels 2008, p. 117). These are interesting sentiments as to the intellectual dimension of teaching and in some respects reflect the Dar es Salaam Declaration of 1990.

However, there are two problematic aspects in the approach of Ndulo, Daniels and Trebilcock, and other African scholars to legal education (Ndulo 2002; Daniels and Trebilcock 2004; Oduor 2009). While they were highly critical of the ravages of the structural adjustment era, they seem to welcome uncritically the new 'good governance' agenda of the international financial institutions. For example, Brand and Rist almost uncritically accept the virtue of the export of US legal education, in their opinion one of the most important US exports, in promoting democratic values:

> (I)f a lawyer from one legal system studies in a different legal system, he or she takes home something more than a simple transplant understanding of law and legal education. The 'export' in this arrangement is knowledge and understanding of host country systems that can generate further influence on the student's home country legal system and legal education system. Education affects a country's level of democracy, and legal education, in particular, should affect the rule of law component of a democratic society.
>
> Brand and Rist 2009, pp. 3–4

Although they promote a critical approach to national issues in relation to human rights they fail to question the nature of human rights and rule of law discourses and in particular to challenge the global problems which may undermine social justice for the people. Thus Juma rightly urges us to 'take up issues on behalf of the poor, disadvantaged and the marginalised.

Any change in curriculum that fails to re-echo this approach is doomed to fail' (Juma 2004, 9). But to what extent is this an issue which is specifically related to 'poverty' and not the deeper global economic structural concerns with the creation of impoverishment?[9]

Changing methodology of teaching and learning

The issues raised in the discussion of the above avatars raise significant concerns about the methodology of teaching and learning including the curriculum, learning methodology and the structure of legal education. The combination of colonial and post-colonial histories of legal education has resulted in generally remarkably outward looking curricula with emphasis on comparative studies and much greater concern with international issues and even human rights than is common elsewhere.[10] Yet, it was not all external facing. Dar es Salaam Faculty of Law pioneered the contextual approach to the study of law, and developed a remarkable course on Social and Economic Problems of East Africa, which subsequently became the compulsory course on Development Studies (Picciotto 1986). Similarly, legal pluralism and customary law finds a place in much teaching. While there are many differences in approach in African law faculties, there is a general move away from emphasis on 'rote learning' and legal formalism (Manteaw 2008, p. 905; Ndulo 2002; Juma 2004; Daniels and Trebilcock 2004). East African Community countries now provide for a post-university professional qualification course as originally recommended by the Denning Committee on African Legal Education in 1961 and for Tanzania by the World Bank's Financial and Legal Management Upgrading Project (FILMUP) Report in 1992.

Nevertheless, there is a general recognition of a range of problems involving legal education.

> Weaknesses in African legal education include a lack of legal clinics to teach skills and sensitize students to local needs and aspirations, limited course offerings, over-reliance on lectures, scarce legal aid support services, and a lack of perspectives on African juridical and philosophical value systems as they relate to the global legal system. Also, law schools lack adequate learning resources, such as well-stocked libraries, electronic information retrieval databases, information and communications technology, and computers.
>
> Manteaw 2008; Ndulo 2002; Juma 2004

9 Poverty is often regarded as a neutral notion whereas impoverishment is seen as a construction of colonial and post-colonial social structures; see e.g. Baxi (2012).

10 Manteaw (2008, p. 905). Manteaw has a useful appendix of curricula in different African law faculties. For East Africa, see Mchome (2005); for Dar es Salaam, see Juma (2004), Fimbo (2011); Kamanga (2011); for Uganda, see Tibihikyrra-Palmegyira (2011).

> Other factors negatively impact the curricula. Overcrowding and disproportionate student-faculty ratios might impede effective teaching. Inadequate remuneration for faculty might compel moonlighting in second or third jobs and, thereby, affect faculty preparation and delivery. Dysfunctional institutions, lack of a broad-based continental administrative structure (such as the Australasian Association of Law Schools or the European Law Faculties Association) to enhance the legal education process, corruption, poverty, lack of facilities, and scarce resources are all challenges confronting African legal education curricular reform. In addition to these broad challenges, there are a number of specific weaknesses in African legal education.
>
> Manteaw 2008, p. 933; Juma 2004, p. 8–10

> In addition, Ndulo criticizes the heavy 'rule focus' of most law faculties, which rely on 'memorization' instead of providing opportunities for deeper case or policy analysis or critical thinking.
>
> Ndulo 2002, p. 493

I will focus on just two issues relating to legal education here. The first is the clinical method in legal education and the second the need for inter-institutional collaboration throughout Eastern Africa. In the US, dissatisfaction with the Langdellian method and the influence of Deweyan pragmatism resulted in the emergence of the new 'realist' approach to law and legal education in which law had to be learned in its practical application (Twining, 2012, pp. 46–51; Paliwala 2010; Maharg 2007). This pragmatism had two dimensions: the study of law in its social, economic and political context; and emphasis on skills-based learning. In recent years the legal skills movement has become even more significant in Africa with US aid being primarily directed to clinical legal education (Maisel 2008). Yet it would seem that the same issues which affected the export of US legal culture in the first Law and Development era are affecting the current clinical movement. Thus Maisel carefully analyses recent US clinical legal education consultancies in Iraq, China, Russia and sub-Saharan Africa. She suggests that the projects have had mixed success. The most significant reason for failed projects in Iraq, China and Russia was that the projects were too closely associated with US government agencies such as US AID and were attempting to replicate in a new form the 'modernisation' agenda based on individualised litigation and rule of law of the old failed Law and Development movement. Yet, she considers that the projects, which were more independent of US government initiatives such as the Ford Foundation or the Open Society Initiative, had more impact. Even more successful were projects which were a consequence of individual initiatives of volunteers. For Maisel, the most important attribute for success has been that the consultants did not come with a blue print but carefully engaged with local needs both in terms of real local ownership and careful adaptation of the clinic to local needs and circumstances (Maisel 2008).

The successful 'different' approaches all illustrate these tendencies. I will just mention one example here. A law clinic developed in the spirit of experiential learning can provide lessons not only for the learners but also for the teachers. Brook Baker volunteered to go to South Africa and worked with two universities in Durban:

> When I first arrived for a six-month sabbatical in 1997, I was politically and culturally naïve about my prospective students, the two law schools, and the South African legal system, all of which bore the wounds of apartheid and all of which were struggling, despite limited resources, to transform themselves and South African society. Over time, my planned focus of adapting a U.S.-based legal skills and legal writing pedagogy to the South African context transitioned to a focus on culturally competent collaboration with my new colleagues. As I struggled with cross-cultural challenges arising from working in a law school clinic where I supervised students who were advising clients from Indian and Zulu communities, my focus shifted again as I came to learn, slowly, about the HIV/AIDS pandemic that was decimating sub-Saharan Africa. By the end, my stances as a legal educator and a global citizen had shifted from cross-cultural collaboration to international solidarity and I have since become a HIV/AIDS treatment activist.
>
> Baker 2003, p. 145

Thus Baker realised firstly that a successful African clinic was not merely about utilising students' legal knowledge to resolve 'legal' problems, but that apparently legal problems such as marriage, succession and death could be resolved through collective sharing of students' own cultural knowledge of issues such as bride price and inheritance. Secondly, that what appeared as a 'local' legal problem upon the death of a person may in fact be deeply connected to the international intellectual property and trade issues involved in the availability of HIV/Aids medicines; and finally, that the solution to such problems required not merely action by activists in South Africa, but global solidarity action. These dimensions can only be realised where those engaged with clinics see the clinic as a truly critical contextual environment in which issues go beyond narrow legal confines and students are engaged with promoting the development of a legal culture based on social justice.

Therefore the above exploration of the teaching of legal skills suggests a need to define the clinic in terms of the local environment and local needs, while not ignoring the fact that global issues such as globalised intellectual property regimes may be at the root of apparently local problems. In an African context, these local needs may require transcending the notion of individualised advice and a redefinition of clinical engagement which goes beyond learning strictly legal skills and recognises the relationship of law to wider issues of national and global social justice.

A new institutional geography: rethinking collaboration?

The social geography of legal education in East Africa is in the process of a fundamental transformation. The most exciting (and troubling?) development in recent years in East Africa has been the mushrooming of university law faculties and schools: one to 11 in Tanzania and similar numbers in Kenya and Uganda.[11] While there has been some growth in the number of public institutions, the main mode of expansion has been private universities. Many of these are funded by specific religious orders. For example, in Tanzania there are only three public universities offering law degrees. Of the seven private universities offering law degrees or diplomas, five are linked to religious denominations. Only one, Bagamoyo, proclaims a non-sectarian social justice vision.[12]

However, this is not the only transformation. There is a growing emphasis on LLM and PhD programmes. The popularity of these programmes is a result of increasing pressure for an LLM for promotion in public service posts and for PhD for promotion in university posts. While going abroad is still considered prestigious, number and resource pressures mean that local options are the ones most available for a majority of students. My first iteration of this paper reimagined a new model East African Law School. This was based on the original, ideal 1960's concept of a law faculty in Dar es Salaam which provided legal education for all East Africans. I recognised even then that it was a foolish thought to consider a new University of East Africa Law School. Instead the emphasis has to be on forms of collaboration which would improve the quality of education throughout Eastern Africa.

11 There is no accurate account of numbers available currently. However currently there are 11 accredited law schools in Kenya; 11 accredited law schools in Tanzania; 9 accredited and 4 unaccredited ones in Uganda. Information thankfully received from Helen Kijo-Bisimba; Pamela Tibihikirra and Masha Baraza. Some idea can be obtained about the general expansion of African universities from the Wikipedia website e.g. for Kenya http://en.wikipedia.org/wiki/List_of_universities_and_colleges_in_Kenya, accessed 12 February 2015.

12 University of Bagamoyo Website www.uob.ac.tz/index.php/about, accessed 12 February 2015.

The idea of collaboration is not new. It is supported by Ndulo and Manteaw in their careful studies of African, and by Juma and Tibihikirra-Palmeyegira of Ugandan legal education (Ndulo 2002; Manteaw 2008, p. 39; Juma 2004, p. 10; Tibihikyrra-Palmegyira 2011). Moreover, some collaborative forms are already in existence. For example, the East African Community Treaty Article 5 provides for cooperation in education and training and member states agreed to collaborate in order to harmonize curricula, examination, certification and accreditation of educational institutions (East African Community 2009). The community has made proposals for collaboration and discussions are taking place, although progress is reported to be slow (Tibihikirra-Kalyegira, personal communication 2014). The need for collaboration arises because no East African institution has the capacity or resources to develop the needed improvements in the quality of legal education by itself. In particular, there is need to collaborate to develop new methodologies of teaching and learning including the use of technology (Tibihikirra-Kalyegira, personal communication 2014, Oduor 2009). This need is especially heightened when one considers the enormous increase in the number of law teachers throughout the region as a result of the exponential increase in the number of law schools. At present there is no satisfactory provision of instruction in legal education for the legal educators. Equally significantly, while there is considerable academic expertise of international quality throughout Eastern Africa, this expertise is spread thinly throughout the region and students, especially at the postgraduate level, would benefit greatly from a pooling of resources through collaborative approaches and programmes. Furthermore, in the context of the countries involved in the East African Community, the growth of community law and especially the requirements of harmonisation consequent on that growth can best be realised through collaborative work (Tibihikirra-Kalyegira, personal communication 2014). Such harmonisation also suggests the important need for collaboration in the production of legal literature. In some respects this need has been lessened because of the rise of publishing houses such as Law Africa (Law Africa website 2015) which produce East Africa-wide literature and the Pretoria University Law Press (Pretoria University Press Website 2015) which produces Africa-wide literature. Nevertheless, there is need for a concerted effort to develop legal literature with or without the cooperation of the existing publishing platforms. There is also the issue of competition. While the type of growth in franchised institutions which has taken place in other regions (for example, South East Asia) has yet to occur in Africa, this is very likely to take place in the future and will take the form of franchised institutions and online learning. In some respects both forms already exist in the form of the University of London International Programme, but the competition is likely to become greater in the future. Whatever the nature and quality of these external-based programmes the local institutions need to 'up their game' to withstand competition. Of more importance is the fact that only at the local level can there be the relevant incentive and expertise to promote legal education that is attuned to and contextually suitable to local needs. Collaboration can avoid domination by the global institutions and promote specific indigenous theoretical and philosophical approaches both to teaching and learning and to substantive material.[13]

Unfortunately, policies of harmonisation and collaboration which are imposed from above, whether at the national or East African Community-level can seriously undermine pluralism and endanger academic freedom. In Tanzania for example, the Council for Legal Education has not only imposed a standardised curriculum but has also initiated inspections of teaching and learning in law schools (Seka 2012). As Fimbo notes, while the Dar Faculty of Law has adapted itself to changed national, regional and global political economic environment and while national and regional co-operative effort is needed, "Law academics' authority with regard to curriculum development is being undermined, if not threatened by the Government and the University authority" through the imposition of uniformity (Fimbo 2011, p. 42).

There is, therefore, need not for a single perspective in collaboration but a range of perspectives which nevertheless leave open the room for a critical engagement with perspectives which have historically informed East African and African legal education.

Collaboration can take two forms. One is of inter-institutional support mechanisms. The pattern in the United Kingdom involves separate organisations such as a Committee of Heads of Law Schools and more independent general associations such as the Association of Law Teachers and the Society of Legal Scholars which have individual membership. In addition there are subject-based groups such as the Socio-Legal Studies Association and the British and Irish Law, Education and Technology Association. Slightly different patterns exist in Australasia with the Australasian Law Schools Association which combines the functions of a committee of deans and a general academic organisation. The specific pattern is not important; what may be relevant is the existence of forms of organisation suitable to the Eastern African context which involve a collaborative engagement between faculty deans as well as broader engagement between academics. However, while these may provide the framework for engagement and general collaboration, in the United Kingdom we found it necessary to have a national institution with resources and skills to promote a collaborative transformation of teaching and learning approaches, and used models in the US and Australia to develop initially the Law Technology Centre and subsequently the UK Centre for Legal

13 For a general emphasis on Southern epistemologies, see de Sousa Santos (2014).

Education.[14] The approach of the UK Centre for Legal Education was firstly to involve all the law schools in the country; secondly to determine the existing best practices in teaching and learning within law schools and where appropriate in other jurisdictions and other disciplines; and thirdly to promote them through national collaborative projects, seminars, workshops, conferences and publications in hard copy and on the web. In particular, the centre provided an excellent basis for national collaboration on information technology projects, an area which is by nature resource-intensive and thus can benefit greatly from efficiencies of scale. Moreover, it proved an excellent vehicle for raising funds for large scale educational projects. In the process, the centre built a considerable national and international reputation. Sadly it came to an end because of the global financial crisis of 2008. Nevertheless, the existence of a small but well-resourced centre can provide a tremendous impetus for legal education whether on a national or regional basis.

The second form of collaboration is collaborative teaching. Informal forms of collaboration exist already. It is common for Eastern African academics to teach in more than one institution. Furthermore, we have already mentioned the growth of East Africa-wide and Africa-wide legal literature. There are obvious advantages in the development of collaborative models of teaching, especially at the postgraduate level. East African law schools currently possess many staff of international renown in most subjects. However, the expertise in particular subject areas whether it is human rights or international taxation is often spread thinly among institutions. Mounting of effective postgraduate programmes on a regional basis can utilise the strengths of regional academics as supplemented occasionally by academics from other areas. Moreover, collaboration can also be extended to development of teaching materials. Thirdly, student demand for specialist courses can be best satisfied on a regional basis.

There are already significant examples of collaborative teaching and learning within East and Central Africa including the Women in Law in Southern Africa Project (WLSA 2015) based in Harare, the East African School on Refugee and Humanitarian Affairs in Dar es Salaam, and Makerere's Inland Water Resources Management Programme (Makerere University 2015). These are examples of regional short course teaching. The Tanzania-German Centre for East African Legal Studies involves a wider LLM and PhD collaborative programme funded by Germany and involving the University of Bayreuth which is bringing together students from Eastern Africa and also teachers from the region and elsewhere

14 For the role of the centre, see Paliwala (2010, p. 1); For the UK Centre for Legal Education Archived website see http://78.158.56.101/archive/law, accessed 15 February 2015.

(TGCL 2015). The premier law faculties in Eastern Africa also have ambitious LLM programmes intended for region-wide students.[15]

The European Union-sponsored LLM programme in Human Rights and Democratisation at the University of Pretoria, which involves students taking part of the course in Pretoria and part in a number of African partner institutions, is a model for longer term taught course collaboration, although the model in which Pretoria is the core and the partner institutions are satellites may need to be rethought to develop a more balanced collaboration (Centre for Human Rights University of Pretoria 2015). Furthermore, the innovative Pretoria University Law Publishing venture produces a substantial body of Africa-wide legal literature which is distributed free to partner institutions and is also distributed in digital form to students (Pretoria University Law Press 2015). A different type of collaborative venture is the joint Mekelle and Warwick LLM programme which has been run at Mekelle, Ethiopia. Unlike many international franchises in which the metropolitan university retains control, the Mekelle programme was deliberately developed to promote capacity building both in terms of developing LLM-level scholarship and capacity of Mekelle University to take over the programme after five years (Warwick Law School 2015). The programme was modular in the sense that the eight course modules were taught sequentially in four-week sessions over two years. The first two weeks involved students reading and analysing selected texts with the assistance of an Ethiopian academic. This was followed by a more discursive two-week programme run jointly by an Ethiopian and a Warwick scholar. Thus the modular programme escaped some of the problems of travel for law teachers in Ethiopia and abroad. The collaboration between Ethiopian and Warwick teachers enabled capacity building on the part of Ethiopians and a more effective engagement with the Ethiopian context on the part of the Warwick teachers to the ultimate benefit of the students.

There are obvious dangers of institutionalised imposition of values and of motives of financial gain on the part of the metropolitan institutions, whether of the South African, German or United Kingdom variety. Furthermore, it would be inappropriate to suggest which models of collaboration would work best in the Eastern African context. This can best be worked out by Eastern African scholars themselves through concerted discussion of both the intellectual and practical issues. Thus Pamela Tibihikirra-Kalyegira (personal communication 2014; see also, Maina and Oduor 2013 and Oduor 2015) suggests the need for 'Innovative approaches to learning' for example by increasing the availability of e-resources so that not all learning has to take place in the lecture rooms or has to be entirely

15 For example, the University of Nairobi LLM programme lists over 50 taught course modules http://law-school.uonbi.ac.ke/node/1391, accessed 15 February 2015.

dependent on a student getting hold of the required/essential but scarce physical texts and the sharing of resources between law schools including staff exchanges in order to adopt best practices.

Conclusions

It is fitting that this rejuvenation of East African legal education is taking place at a time when debates of 50 years ago about the nature of intellectual tasks involved in law school teaching, learning and research are also being engaged in today by African scholars. This chapter has focused on two dimensions of legal education within Eastern Africa, but using the original Law Faculty of the University of East Africa (now the Law Faculty of the University of Dar es Salaam) as an example. In this third avatar, much has changed since McAuslan and his colleagues founded the law faculty, both in relation to the pedagogical perspectives and the exponential growth of legal education. And yet, there is also continuity. The early emphasis on the need for legal education to fit the socio-economic and political context continues to be the concern of most of those who write about legal education not just in the region, but in Africa generally. There is an ideological difference, however, between the Dar es Salaam Declaration on Academic Freedom and Social Responsibility of Academics of 1990 which suggested that education should 'prepare a person to strive for and participate fully in the emancipation of the human being and society from oppression, domination and subjugation', and the contemporary range of perspectives which vary between the technicist need for lawyers who can deal with economic liberal globalisation (International Association of Law Schools 2014), to a more policy-aware legal education which promotes the culture of good governance and human rights (Ndulo 2002), to a more pluralist but critically aware culture of legal education (Daniels and Trebilcock 2004). There is a clear difference between a purely technicist globalising approach to legal education and approaches which emphasise the emancipatory, critical and rights-conscious role of lawyers. Nevertheless, what is required is not a determination of the 'correct' approach but critical debate among East African legal scholars to inform themselves about the relevance of these approaches in the contemporary situation.

These discussions about the overall approaches would also engage with the debates about the nature of the curriculum and teaching and learning methodology. There seems to be a general consensus in favour of moving away from legal formalism and rote learning to skills-based critical contextual approaches. However, as we saw in the exploration of clinical legal education, there is need for a more critical engagement with the issue of what type of skills and what type of clinic is relevant in the Eastern African context. In particular, Brook Baker's experience suggests that an

African law clinic has to move beyond externally imposed blueprints, and be concerned with wider issues at both the community and global levels to effectively promote social justice awareness and skills (Baker 2003).

Finally, the chapter considered the need for collaboration arising out of a variety of factors including the exponential growth in law schools, the substantive socio-economic changes resulting in changes in law with the consequent need to reconsider curricula and teaching/learning methodologies, the need for enhancing teaching and learning skills and dealing with competitive pressures arising from globalisation of legal education. There are already significant examples of collaborative teaching which have mainly been stimulated by external sources. There is thus great need for collaborative engagement between university schools of law. There is also a need for wider inter-institutional collaboration specifically to promote improvements in legal education generally. This involves consideration of inter-institutional arrangements such as region-wide organisations of law schools and general or specialist subject associations. More significantly, it is suggested that while committees of deans and subject associations can develop general strategies or academic discourses, effective co-ordination of strategies and improvement of teaching and learning skills require a well-resourced institution.

It is clear that none of these issues can be considered in the abstract, but they suggest efforts to support and enhance legal education throughout Eastern Africa. McAuslan asserted this need:

> to develop as rapidly as possible that critical mass of national legal skills and knowledge that is the only sure way to build up a national legal culture and so in turn create the undergirding for a legitimate, effective and just national legal system.

It is therefore necessary to consider ways in which this vision can be brought to life. It was in 1965 at the conference at Cumberland Lodge on East African Legal Education that I met McAuslan for the first time. East Africans have to develop their own vision of legal education and an Eastern African Conference on Legal Education would be an effective way of reinvigorating a legal educational process which would critically engage among other things with debates about the conception of legal education which develops 'lawyers who are concerned with justice, with freedoms and with advancing the rule of law' (McAuslan 2004).

References

African Excellence Website, Tanzanian-German Centre for Eastern African Legal Studies at the University of Dar es Salaam. Available at: www.african-excellence.de/centres/tanzania/eastern-african-legal-studies. Accessed 12 October 2015.

American Bar Association. *Rule of Law Initiative.* Available at: www.americanbar.org/advocacy/rule_of_law/thematic_areas/legal_education.html. Accessed 12 October 2015.

Baker, Brook. 2003. Teaching legal skills in South Africa: A transition from cross-cultural collaboration to international HIV/AIDS solidarity. *Journal of Legal Writing Instruction* 9: 145–183.

Baxi, Upendra. 2012. Global development and impoverishment. In Marc Tushnet and Peter Cane (eds) *Oxford Handbook of Legal Studies Online.* Oxford: Oxford University Press. Available at: www.oxfordhandbooks.com/view/10.1093/oxfordhb/9780199248179.001.0001/oxfordhb-9780199248179-e-022. Accessed 15 February 2015.

Brand, Ronald and D. Wes Rist (eds) 2009. *The Export of Legal Education: Its Promise and Impact in Transition Countries.* Farnham: Ashgate.

Carothers, Thomas. 2013. 'Rule of law temptations'. In James Heckman, Robert Nelson and Lee Cabatingan (eds) *Global Perspectives on the Rule of Law.* London: Routledge.

Centre for Human Rights University of Pretoria. 2015. Available at: www.chr.up.ac.za/index.php/llm-hrda.html. Accessed 15 February 2015.

Council for the Development of Social Science Research in Africa (CODESRIA). Available at: www.codesria.org/spip.php?article351. Accessed 1 February 2015.

Daniels, Ronald and Michael Trebilcock. 2004. The political economy of rule of law reform in developing countries. *Michigan Journal of International Law* 26(99) Fall: 129–133.

The Dar es Salaam Declaration on Academic Freedom and Social Responsibility of Academics of 1990. Available at: www.codesria.org/spip.php?article351. Accessed 1 February 2015.

de Sousa Santos, Boaventura. 2014. *Epistemologies of the South.* Boulder, CO: Paradigm Publishers.

Denning, Lord. (Chairman) 1961. *Report of the Committee on Legal Education for Students from Africa* (Cmnd No 1255). London: HMSO.

Devex. 2008. Construction of an annex to the Faculty of Law at Chancellor College in Malawi. Available at: www.devex.com/projects/tenders/construction-of-an-annex-to-the-faculty-of-law-at-chancellor-college-in-malawi/27266. Accessed on 15 February 2010.

East African Community 2009. *Regional Report: Harmonisation of the East African Education Systems & Training Curricula* (EAC). Available at: www.eac.int/education/index.php?option=com_content&id=73&Itemid=145. Accessed 12 October 2015.

Faculty of Law, University of Dar es Salaam. 2005. Report of the Special Committee on Teaching and Learning Law. *Nyerere Law Journal*: 3, 1.

Faundez, Julio. 2010. 'Rule of law or Washington Consensus: The evolution of the World Bank's approach to legal and judicial reform'. In Amanda Perry-Kessaris, (ed.) *Law in the Pursuit of Development.* London: Routledge, p. 180.

Faundez, Julio. 2014. Douglass North's Theory of Institutions: Lessons for law and development. University of Warwick School of Law: Legal Studies Research Paper No. 2014/13. Available at: http://papers.ssrn.com/sol3/JELJOUR_Results.cfm?form_name=journalbrowse&journal_id=1473996. Accessed 12 October 2015.

Fimbo George M. (ed.) 2011. *50 Years of Legal Education in Tanzania. Development of the LLB Curriculum.* University of Dar es Salaam Press.

Geraghty, Thomas and Emmanuel Quansah. 2007. African legal education: A missed opportunity and suggestions for change: a call for renewed attention to a neglected means of securing human rights and legal predictability. *Loyola University of Chicago International Law Review* 5(1): 87–105. Available at: http://lawecommons.luc.edu/lucilr/vol5/iss1/7. Accessed 12 August 2016.

Ghai, Yash. 1986. 'Legal radicalism, professionalism and social action: Reflections on teaching law in Dar es Salaam'. In Shivji, Issa G. (ed.) *The Limits of Legal Radicalism.* Dar es Salaam: Faculty of Law, University of Dar es Salaam.

International Association of Law Schools By-Laws 2.1. 2014. Available at: www.ialsnet.org/wordpress/wp-content/uploads/2014/12/IALS-Bylaws-Final-12.1.14.pdf. Accessed 10 February 2015.

Juma, Ibrahim. 2004. Control of legal education: Challenges facing the Council of Legal Education of Tanzania. *Nyerere Law Journal* 2, 1.

Kamanga, Khoti. 2011. The UDSM Faculty of Law 1999 Arusha Curriculum Review: A 'Midas Touch', in Fimbo George M. (ed.) *50 Years of Legal Education in Tanzania. Development of the LLB Curriculum.* University of Dar es Salaam Press, 43.

Law Africa website 2015. Available at: www.lawafrica.com. Accessed 15 February 2015.

McAuslan, Patrick. 2004. In the beginning was law … An intellectual odyssey. *Cornell Law Library, Scholarship @ Cornell Law: A Legal Depository.* Available at: http://scholarship.law.cornell.edu/ealccs_pld. Accessed 1 February 2015.

Mchome, S. 2005. Incorporating sufficient East Africa content in the Teaching of Law at East Africa Universities. *Nyerere Law Journal* 3: 86.

Maharg, Paul. 2007. *Transforming Legal Education.* Aldershot: Ashgate Publishing.

Maina, Miano and Maurice Oduor. 2013. Digitizing legal education in Kenya. *Jurist* 13 November 2013. Available at: http://jurist.org/forum/2013/11/maina-odour-digitizing-kenya.php. Accessed 15 February 2015.

Maisel, Peggy. 2008. The Role of US Law Faculty in developing countries: Striving for effective cross-cultural collaboration. *Clinical Law Review* 14: 465.

Majamba, Hamudi. 2011. 'Ideological Inclinations in postgraduate dissertations: Trends in five decades at the Faculty of Law'. In Fimbo George M. (ed.) *50 Years of Legal Education in Tanzania. Development of the LLB Curriculum.* University of Dar es Salaam Press, p. 135.

Makerere University 2015. 2nd Short Regional Training Course on International Water Law, Negotiation and Conflict Resolution. Available at: http://events.mak.ac.ug/events/2nd-short-regional-training-course-international-water-law-negotiation-and-conflict. Accessed 15 February 2015.

Maldonado, Nicole. 2010. The World Bank's evolving concept of good governance and its impact on human rights presented at a workshop on development and international organizations, Stockholm, Sweden, May 2010). Available at: https://view.officeapps.live.com/op/view.aspx?src=http%3A%2F%2Fwww2.warwick.ac.uk%2Ffac%2Fsoc%2Fcsgr%2Fnews%2Fdoctoral_workshop_on%2Ffinal_maldonado_nicole_paper.doc. Accessed 12 October 2012.

Manteaw, Samuel. 2008. Legal education in Africa: What kind of lawyer does Africa need? *McGeorge Law Review* 39: 905.

Nader, Laura. 2007. Promise or plunder? A past and future look at law and development. *Global Jurist* 7(2): 1–24.

Ndulo, Mona. 2002. Legal education in Africa in the era of globalization and structural adjustment. *Pennsylvania State International Law Review* 20: 487.

Oduor, Maurice. 2009. 'A Kenyan experience with LL.M. education'. In Brand, Ronald and D. Wes Rist. (eds) 2009. *The Export of Legal Education: Its Promise and Impact in Transition Countries.* Chapter 3. Farnham: Ashgate.

Paliwala, Abdul. 1986. 'Personal and political influences in legal education in 1971 and 1972'. In Shivji, Issa G. (ed.) *The Limits of Legal Radicalism.* Dar es Salaam: Faculty of Law, University of Dar es Salaam.

Paliwala, Abdul. 2010. Socrates and Confucius: A long history of information technology in legal education. *European Journal of Law and Technology* 1:1. Available at: http://ejlt.org/rt/printerFriendly/12/16. Accessed 15 February 2015.

Piron, Laure-Helene. 2006. 'Time to learn, time to act in Africa'. In Thomas Carothers (ed.) *Promoting the Rule of Law Abroad: In Search of Knowledge.* Carnegie Endowment for International Peace, 275–78.

Pretoria University Law Press website 2015. Available at: www.pulp.up.ac.za. Accessed 15 February 2015.

Sarfaty, Galit A. 2012. *Values in Translation: Human Rights and the Culture of the World Bank.* Stanford, CA: Stanford University Press.

Schlemmer-Schulte, Sabine. 2001. 'The World Bank's role in the promotion of the rule of law in developing countries'. In S. Schlemmer-Schulte and K-Y Tung (eds) *Liber Amicorum Ibrahim F. Shihata: International Law, Finance and Development.* Kluwer Law International.

Seka, John. 2012. Implementing cross-border legal practice within the EAC States: A case of the legal profession in Tanzania. LLM Dissertation, University of Dar es Salaam. Available at: www.academia.edu/7513670/IMPLEMENTING_CROSS_BORDER_LEGAL_PRACTICE_WITHIN_THE_EAC_STATES_-_A_CASE_OF_THE_LEGAL_PROFESSION_IN_TANZANIA. Accessed 12 October 2015.

Sen, Amartya. 1999. *Development as Freedom.* Oxford University Press.

Shivji, Issa G. 1972. Introduction: From the analysis of forms to the exposition of substance – the tasks of a lawyer intellectual. *Eastern Africa Law Review* 5(5): 1.

Shivji, Issa G. 1986. 'Within and beyond legal radicalism'. In Shivji, I.G. (ed.) *The Limits of Legal Radicalism.* Dar es Salaam: Faculty of Law, University of Dar es Salaam.

Shivji, Issa G. 1989. *The Concept of Human Rights in Africa.* Dakar: CODESRIA.

Shivji, Issa G. 2009. *Tanzania: The Legal Foundations of The Union,* 2nd edn. Dar es Salaam: Africa Book Collective.

Tamanaha, Brian. 2009. The primacy of society and the failures of law and development: Decades of stubborn refusal to learn. Faculty Research Paper No 10-03-02. Available at: http://papers.ssrn.com/sol3/papers.cfm?abstract_id=1406999. Accessed 10 February 2015.

TGCL 2015. *Tanzanian-German Centre for Eastern African Legal Studies.* Available at: www.tgcl.uni-bayreuth.de/en/index.html. Accessed 15 February 2015.

Thompson, Edward. 1977. *Whigs and Hunters: The Origin of the Black Acts.* Penguin Books.

Tibihikirra-Kalyegira, Pamela. 2011. Liberalization of legal education in Uganda. Policy Considerations. Dar es Salaam: Law Africa.

Trebilcock, Michael and Ronald Daniels, 2008. *Rule of Law Reform and Development.* Chapter 8. Cheltenham: Edward Elgar.

Twining, William. 2012. *Karl Llewellyn and the Realist Movement*, 2nd edn. Cambridge University Press.

UK Centre for Legal Education Website Archive. Available at: http://78.158.56.101/archive/law. Accessed 15 February 2015.

University of Bagamoyo website. Available at: www.uob.ac.tz/index.php/about. Accessed 12 February 2015.

Warwick Law School 2015. Ethiopia Project at Warwick School of Law website. Available at: www2.warwick.ac.uk/fac/soc/law/ethiopia. Accessed 15 February 2015.

WLSA Website 2015. Women and law in Southern African Research and Education Trust. Zimbabwe website at: www.wlsazim.co.zw. Accessed 15 February 2015.

World Bank. 1992. Financial and Legal Management Upgrading in Tanzania (FILMUP) *Report No 10625-TA June 1992* Available at: www-wds.worldbank.org/external/default/WDSContentServer/WDSP/IB/1992/06/01/000009265_3961002232345/Rendered/PDF/multi_page.pdf. Accessed 12 October 2015.

World Bank. 1994. *Governance: The World Bank's Experience.* The World Bank.

Chapter 4

The vagaries of consulting on land policy and land law reform in Africa 1994–2006

Martin Adams

Introduction

Simply described, a national land policy defines what actions a government intends to take in managing the country's land and related natural resources. In eastern and southern Africa, the period 1990–2006 was one of unprecedented attempts to reform land policy and related laws. In southern Africa international donors and funding agencies sought to support a peaceable transition to multi-racial democracy. In East Africa, land tenure reform and related legal reforms were linked to the peace building effort following civil conflicts. Policy objectives included the harmonisation of received law and customary law, and the transformation of colonial systems of land administration and urban planning, better to serve the majority of the population. Policy and related legislative reform progressed in several countries, particularly where efforts were made to integrate customary and statutory land administration in a national system, and decentralise authority over land administration. In the preface to his final work, McAuslan (2013, p. x) describes his 'lifetime's commitment to grappling with the endlessly challenging and fascinating topic of land law in the region'. He provides us with an authoritive and scholarly review of development and change in the land laws of seven countries in Eastern Africa over the period 1961–2011. The following account describes some of the background to his consultancy assignments in three of these countries – namely Tanzania, Uganda and Rwanda. To these three countries, I have added two more in southern Africa – Lesotho and Botswana. Regrettably, despite promulgating good laws, governments have subsequently amended or implemented them in a way that has undermined their worthy aims. Tension between democratic and traditional forces has frustrated land law reform. There are doubts about the transparency and honesty of the declared land policy aims and whether they are really designed to include the rural poor.

In the 1990s, Professor Patrick McAuslan was one of a few independent international legal advisers called upon to assist governments with the reform of land and planning law in Anglophone Africa. The nature and degree of his involvement differed in each country. In Tanzania 1996–97 he worked on a new legal framework for land administration and management. In Uganda, he helped draft the Land Act 1998 to provide people with secure rights to their land, release their potential for development and provide a lasting basis for the settlement of long-standing disputes inherited from the colonial era. He was invited to become the senior technical adviser to the Land Act implementation project the following year. With the author, he joined a team in Lesotho in 2001, undertaking a national land policy review; similarly in Botswana in 2002 he provided legal support to a national land policy review process. In 2003 he returned to Lesotho to draft a national land code and in Rwanda in 2006 he was asked to set out the scope and content of a new law to provide the detailed legal structure for a new system of land tenure. In other countries, he continued to provide advice on aspects of land policy, also drafting bills relating to aspects of tenure reform and/or physical planning.

Because of the prominence often given by national constitutions to the powers of the state and to the rights of citizens, land law reform was invariably politically sensitive and complex and therefore challenging for those at the heart of the process, especially for an adviser-cum-legal-draftsperson from the former colonial power. When drafting such laws, McAuslan sought to surround himself with a panel of knowledgeable nationals with whom preliminary drafts could be shared and discussed. He would remind critics that his drafts had to be consistent with declared policy, provided they met legal and humanitarian standards and principles. When policy was not clear, he saw it as his responsibility to help public officials clarify their position. If issues were not resolved, the acceptability of his drafts would be undermined. There were several occasions when his work came to a halt in the absence of clear and acceptable policy guidelines on important issues. On such occasions, McAuslan would calmly and steadfastly remind public officers of their responsibilities, signalled by the international agreements to which their governments had signed up; for example the Istanbul Declaration on Human Settlements and the UN-Habitat Agenda (1996) which provide the international policy and legal context for any assessment of a country's land laws and policies. Later he would return to such matters in his writings, modestly reflecting upon the challenges and disappoints he had encountered.

Contrary perspectives in Tanzania 1996–1997

For those working on land rights in Africa in the 1990s, Tanzania provided an example of an outstanding land policy and land tenure reform process. It began when President Mwinyi decided that a national consultative process was required to develop a new land policy. The Presidential

Commission of Inquiry into Land Matters was launched in 1991, and in the following year the Commission travelled to all but two districts, held meetings, heard and read complaints, met officials and travelled internationally. McAuslan was meanwhile with UN-Habitat in Nairobi (1990–93) and was invited to submit evidence to the Commission in neighbouring Tanzania. Professor Issa Shivji of the University of Dar es Salaam was the Chairman of the Commission (1991–92) and a founder and the Executive Director of the Tanzanian Land Rights Research and Resources Institute – HAKIARDI (Shivji 1999).The principal recommendation of the Commission was to vest the radical title of most of the country in village communities and to remove control over tenure administration from the executive to an autonomous Land Commission (Tanzanian Affairs 1995). This was not supported by the government and the report of the Presidential Commission of Enquiry remained unpublished until 1994 (United Republic of Tanzania 1994).

In 1993, the Ministry published a Green Paper on the draft National Land Policy (NLP) which nevertheless drew heavily upon most of the other recommendations of the Shivji Commission. It was presented to Cabinet in December 1994 and was the subject of a public workshop in January 1995. The NLP was approved by Parliament in July 1995 (United Republic of Tanzania 1995). The Tanzanian government approached the British government to make McAuslan available to assist with the drafting of the land laws to implement the NLP. He commenced work in January 1996, assisted by a four-person Tanzanian Support Group (McAuslan 2013, p. 96).

My first sight of the draft of the Tanzanian Land Bill was in September 1997 when I chanced to meet McAuslan in Swaziland. I was briefly in the Kingdom advising on land policy, while he was drafting a Land Resettlement Bill with Lionel Cliffe, covering the statutory resettlement arrangements and compensation of people displaced by public works. I had, in fact, come from Pretoria, where I was assigned as an adviser in the Land Policy branch of the new South African Department of Land Affairs under the Mandela government (1994–99). The Tanzanian Land Bill was therefore of great interest. One of my tasks was to act as secretary of a team guiding the draft of a land tenure reform bill, in the course of which we were wrestling with issues relating to the continuing retention of the state's radical title to land in the former Bantustans.

I had read Professor Issa Shivji's conference paper on 'Contrary perspectives on Rights and Justice in the Context of Land Tenure Reform in Tanzania' (Shivji 1997) and was aware that he had singled out McAuslan for criticism, principally on the grounds that his draft endorsed the 'feudal notion' that the radical title to land in Tanzania should remain vested in the state, with all the bureaucratic controls that this would involve. I was keen to know how McAuslan's work was progressing and his views on the topic. He gave me his draft of the Land Bill to read and I recall being awed by its great detail, breadth and depth, but was tested by its length – 164 pages! As it turned out, the draft was revised and divided into two and brought before the National Assembly in November 1998, finally to be passed in February 1999 as the Land Act and the Village Land Act.

By the beginning of 1998, McAuslan's drafting work in Tanzania on the Land Bill had come to an end and his attention had turned to the need for training Ministry officials and to the design of a public awareness and sensitisation programme.[1] The new legislation would introduce far reaching changes in the administration of land and the operation of a land market in Tanzania. The related administrative work of the Ministry would have to be based on clear and detailed rules of law, designed to introduce transparency, legality and fairness into the allocation and management of public land in the country. The management of village land would be vested in village organisations and the status of village land would be strengthened, making it much harder for it to be appropriated by central government for 'public purposes'. The process of individualisation of title and the granting of 'customary rights of occupancy of indefinite duration' by villages to individuals and families was to commence. A new statutory framework for the exercise of rights in land through market processes – leasing, mortgaging, buying and selling, creation of servitudes such as easements – would come into being. A new system of land courts was to be established to handle all land cases from the village upwards. Specific provisions had been written into the Bill to enhance the opportunities for women to obtain rights in land and challenge practices which discriminated against them.

Taken together, these changes caused some alarm. Officials in the ministry would have to find new ways to do things. More important, these same officials would rightly perceive that opportunities for rent-seeking would be reduced by the new law. A significant reduction in the need to obtain official consent to land transactions, mandated by the NLP, was being queried by middle-level officials. They were concerned about a reduction in open-ended discretions and their displacement by standard forms and feared an increase in outside challenges to their decisions. McAuslan was also concerned about potential opposition to the Bill from the intellectual and academic community. Within some of the more articulate opposition parties, there were lawyers who had been campaigning against the Bill. They argued that the new laws and practices would disadvantage village peasants and favour the urban elite and 'kulak' class.

1 The following three paragraphs are based on correspondence in August 1998 between Patrick McAuslan and DFID (Department for International Development) Kampala, copied to colleagues, in connection with planning a training and sensitization programme in Uganda following passage of Uganda's Land Act 1998.

He was aware of their resentment of his 'foreign input' into land law reform and of being left out of the process.

On the occasions when his drafts were criticised by Issa Shivji and others, McAuslan stoically pointed out that it was not in his powers to alter government policy on such a fundamental issue as the state's radical title. His work could not usurp that of the Attorney General, charged with producing Bills for submission to Cabinet and the National Assembly. He recognised that if tenure reform was to be successful, it had to be accompanied by a major five-year, innovative national training programme on the law and its implementation, for village-level officials to judges. He set out proposals for such a programme, but in the event, the scale and scope of follow-up to the legislation was a disappointment. It was several years before the required manuals explaining the Village Land Act in simple terms became available (Alden Wily 2003).

Some two decades later and in his final published work, albeit in a footnote, McAuslan returns to the issue of the opposition he met in a mild understatement: 'As many people involved in land in Tanzania are aware, there has been something of a difference between Issa Shivji and myself on the genesis and content of the land laws enacted in Tanzania in 1999. This is not the place to reprise these differences' (McAuslan 2013, p. 96).

In this book, he sets out the sequence of events which led to his assignment to Tanzania. He explains the process of his appointment to assist with the drafting of the land laws to implement the NLP which he commenced in late 1995, including a prior meeting at the faculty of law in Dar es Salaam in which he informed Issa Shivji of what he was being asked to do.

Was McAuslan right to adhere to the NLP in drafting the law? Most certainly yes, for such were the terms of his appointment. Whatever he felt personally about this key element of the NLP, there was no alternative but to accept it as 'the bedrock of the land law'. However, he did his best to push the envelope as far as possible and give 'village land, the land used by the majority of people in Tanzania' ...'greater protection than it had had hitherto'... The law 'provides for an elaborate mechanism for the transfer of village land to general public land' (McAuslan 2013, p. 99). Issa Shivji was no doubt entitled to criticise the government's decision to disregard the findings and recommendations of the Land Commission with regard to the radical title. In 2013, the state had yet to establish many of the village-level institutions necessary for the implementation of the law, failing to provide true land tenure security to villages. The Village Land Act's multiple protections for the land rights of communities are secure and good only until the state decides otherwise. This is due to the varying definitions of 'General Land' in the two Acts. The Land Act's definition of General Land as 'all public land which is not reserved land or village land and includes unoccupied or unused village land' (Land Act 1999, Article

2) means that the state has the right to rezone what it feels to be 'unused' Village Land as General Land. Also, under Article 4 section 1–2, the state may compulsorily acquire even clearly used village land for 'investments of national interest' and rezone it as General Land. There are no clear mechanisms in the Village Land Act through which communities can appeal or block such reclassifications of their lands (Knight 2010, Adams and Knight 2013). One must give McAuslan the last word on this very point:

> while drafting I was aware that there were real dangers in creating an administrative system that had the Commissioner of Lands both exercising powers through officials, yet was the person to whom one complained about the behaviour of those officials; in a sense both gamekeeper and potential poacher. I therefore suggested a dedicated land ombudsman as a safeguard for those subject to official power over land. The Tanzanian Support Group was unanimous in rejecting this suggestion: in the words of one member, there were already too many ways for people to complain about government action and it was not desirable to add to them.
>
> McAuslan 2013, p. 115

Counterpoint in Uganda 1998–99

McAuslan's work in Uganda in 1998 was a welcome change from Tanzania. There was broad based support for his participation in revising the draft Land Bill. Initially engaged to address a conference (see below) by the Uganda Land Alliance, a consortium of small NGOs involved in land rights advocacy, he was soon invited to work closely with the responsible Sessional Committee of Parliament and the Ministry of Water, Lands and Environment (MWLE) to help resolve the problems that had been encountered in drafting the law. On the other hand, his assignment to the MWLE as a senior adviser on the Land Act Implementation Project[2] in 1999 was less opportune. He carefully documented both episodes (McAuslan 1998, 2003a, 2003b) which are an invaluable source on Uganda's most important tenure reform and the initial efforts to implement it, a process which has only very recently been revived.

Apart from visits to Uganda to attend workshops in connection with the Land Act 1998, my work with the Department of Land Affairs was keeping me in South Africa. However, I was regularly updated on the bill's progress

2 The project was officially named 'Securing Sustainable Livelihoods through Land Tenure Reform' by DFID.

by McAuslan in connection with the Land Act Implementation Project. In September 2001, I was recruited by the MWLE to work with Michael Aliber on an economic and financial analysis of the Land Sector Strategic Plan for the implementation of the Act. At that stage, difficulties were still being encountered in putting in place the decentralised institutions for implementing the Land Act. It was not until 2013 that Uganda finally published a NLP (Republic of Uganda 2013). McAuslan often reminded us that a detailed understanding of the historical context of a country is essential for judging the appropriateness of a proposed tenure reform. This was particularly the case in Uganda, where internal politics had long been dominated by competition for control over land between the four traditional kingdoms and other major chieftainships and central government. Under the British in 1900, the leaders of the Baganda and their followers acquired the equivalent of registrable freehold rights as individuals, known as 'mailo' tenure in view of the basis of its allocation in multiples of square miles.

At the time of Uganda's independence in 1962, some 13 per cent of the country's land was owned in freehold exclusively by Africans and most of the remainder was administered under indirect rule as crown land. President Milton Obote's desire to strengthen his position soon led to confrontation with the Baganda. Under the 1967 Constitution, all official estates and all land formerly held by the Land Board of a Kingdom or District was vested in the Uganda Land Commission. Then, under General Idi Amin, the Land Reform Decree of 1975 vested all land in the Uganda Land Commission as public land and converted all freeholds, including mailo, into leaseholds. The customary use and occupation of public land was able to continue, but without the protection of the previous tenancy legislation (West 2000). In practice, the Land Reform Decree was never fully implemented in the absence of an effective land administration and without peace and security in the countryside.

In 1986, the National Resistance Movement (NRM) under President Museveni began to restore stability and economic growth. Over the period 1986–1995, several attempts were made to produce a NLP with a view to encouraging land-related investments. Keen to facilitate such a process, the World Bank and USAID funded a major study which reported in 1989, but which did not result in the much-needed policy and legislation. Further consultations took place and a new draft bill was formulated, but was never tabled in Parliament. Finally, the elements of the required reform were included in Chapter 15 of the 1995 Constitution which required Parliament to enact a law before 2 July 1998 (Republic of Uganda, 1995).

The 1995 Constitution vested all land in the citizens of Uganda, provided for customary, freehold, mailo and leasehold tenures and decentralised most of the powers and responsibilities of the Ministry of Lands and the Land Commission to District Land Boards. It provided for persons occupying land under customary tenure to obtain certificates of customary ownership or convert to freehold by registration. It restored mailo tenure and granted secure occupancy to *bona fide* tenants, both pending the enactment of an appropriate law by Parliament. McAuslan's 1998 paper entitled 'As Good as it Gets' was a reference to the 1995 Constitution that gave erstwhile tenants ownership rights, individually on mailo land and/or collectively on Public Land. He was rightly suspicious of the 'Washington Consensus' on property rights and often reminded us of the importance of customary tenure in protecting the rural poor from landlessness. The Constitution provided for the conversion of leasehold to freehold in respect of leases of Public Land, again in accordance with provisions to be agreed by the legislature. In the absence of a detailed NLP, it was up to the legal draftspersons to state how these brave policy pronouncements were to be realised.

By March 1998, efforts to finalise the constitutionally-required Land Bill appeared to have stalled. At the eleventh hour, in late April, McAuslan was invited by the Uganda Land Alliance to participate in the Conference on The Land Bill for Parliamentarians, funded by the Department For International Development (DFID) and organised by the Forum for Women in Democracy (FOWODE), Kampala, April 24–25 1998. The meeting was designed to sensitise MPs and launch a public debate on the Land Bill, which had recently been gazetted (Republic of Uganda 1998). He was asked to consider whether the Bill as drafted was workable and whether it provided for accountability. He replied that he was unable to say as he found the draft unclear and pointed to some examples. Diplomatically, he set out his arguments as follows:

> It is with some trepidation then that I have come to the conclusion that the Land Bill as it stands at present needs more work to be done on it if it is to provide the foundation for a new workable and accountable system of land management in Uganda. Law alone is not a sufficient basis for effective and equitable systems of land management … but it is a necessary basis and an inadequate law, particularly one that leaves so many issues unresolved, gives such wide and unstructured discretionary powers to officials and official bodies and if not meshed in with existing land laws as is the case with the Land Bill, will run a very grave risk of exacerbating the land problems of the country, rather than providing the basis for their solution. It would be a great pity if the philosophy behind the Land Bill – provide the people with secure rights to their land and so release their potential for development, provide a lasting basis for the settlement of long-standing disputes between citizens – failed to be realised because the contents of the bill made it impossible to be realised.
>
> McAuslan1998, p. 13, see also McAuslan 2003a

In the opening paragraph to the paper, he puts his finger on the government's principal motivation for the proposed Land Act, namely its desire to lay the groundwork for the development of a land market, based on individual ownership. He cannily reminded participants of the nub of the vigorous public debate on the recently gazetted draft bill, a debate which 'pitted the local politics of land and dictates of the market for land' (p. 1). As he explains in his paper:

> If I have spent some time in setting the scene in Uganda, it is because as I did so, it seemed to me as if some of the lessons that could have been learned from the colonial past in Uganda not just for Uganda but generally in respect of land tenure reform in Africa have been but imperfectly learned by the protagonists of market-orientated tenure reforms in both national and international aid and lending institutions.
>
> McAuslan 1998, p. 4

Returning to the history of land relations in Uganda, in his paper he referred to a series of 'time bombs' and 'poison pills' embedded in the colonial legacy and the 1962 independence settlement, the consequences of which had not been adequately dealt with in the Land Bill. First, the 'Uganda Agreement' of 1900, between the British government and the Buganda Kingdom, confirmed the Kingdom's ownership of half of the total land area of Buganda. This land was vested in the Kabaka and some 4000 other Baganda notables as freehold (mailo). At the time, much of this land was not vacant but occupied by peasants, not necessarily Baganda. Mailo tenure was abolished by the Land Reform Decree 1975 but was understandably resurrected by the 1995 Constitution as it had been the subject of prior assurances given to mailo tenants by the NRM before coming to power. In 1998, this land was populated by the descendants of the original mailo owners and their tenants, with multiple, overlapping and conflicting interests and rights in land which they regarded as theirs by virtue of customary law.

Secondly, under the same British Uganda Agreement in 1900, a large part of the Bunyoro Kingdom was prejudicially included in the territory of the Buganda in Kibaale District,[3] the so called 'lost counties' of the Bunyoro Kingdom. Prior to independence in 1962, it was agreed between the British and the Ugandan authorities that a referendum would be held in the 'lost counties' to determine whether the land should be returned to the Bunyoro Kingdom or remain as part of Buganda. Not surprisingly, the Banyoro who constituted a majority in the lost counties voted to re-join

3 The former Kibaale District has since been subdivided into the districts of Bulisa, Hoima, Kibaale, Kiriandongo and Masindi, which now have a total population in excess of 1.5 million.

Bunyoro, leaving the legal position of the Baganda landlords and Bunyoro tenants unresolved.

A third 'time bomb' was the division by the colonial authorities of Buganda into two categories: mailo of some 9000 square miles and another 9000 square miles referred to as crown land (West 1972). On mailo, customary rights were not recognised. Nor were they recognised on crown land. Customary occupiers were regarded as tenants-at-will on both mailo and crown land. When freehold or leasehold titles were granted on this land, customary occupiers were expected to move, or remain as tenants-at-will of the new owners.

As a result of McAuslan's comments on the Land Bill at the FOWODE workshop for parliamentarians, he was asked by the Minister to assist in the preparation of the Ministry's amendments to the Bill. He was also asked to support the work of the Parliamentary Sessional Committee which was in the process of examining the bill.[4] He describes how he found himself in the position of an unofficial liaison person between the Ministry and the Sessional Committee and involved not just in drafting technical amendments but in what might be called drafting policy amendments. Thus in the absence of an explicit national land policy and with only the bare bones of the directives and articles in the 1995 Constitution at hand, it was necessary to develop the detail of the proposed law from other laws and statements by the president and ministers on such matters as agricultural development, environmental protection and poverty reduction since the proposed law had been represented at various times as being a positive contribution to all these matters.

The Land Act 1998 inter alia provides for the issue of Certificates of Customary Ownership; for their conversion into freehold titles; for the grant of land in freehold; for the establishment and management of Communal Land Associations; for the registration of interests; and for restrictions on the transfer of land by family members; all to be administered through District Land Boards, Land Tribunals and parish-level Land Committees.

McAuslan had long been a strong advocate of strengthening women's land rights (McAuslan 2010a) and what became of 'the lost amendment' was a source of personal frustration. In 2010, he wrote:

> In Uganda, after the saga of the 'lost amendment' to the Land Act 1998 when an amendment to improve women's rights to land was never formally passed although generally agreed to in the last hectic hours of

4 The Land Bill published in the Government Gazette in March 1998 had already received its first (formal) reading in parliament. After that it passed to the Sessional Committee of Parliament for amendment. At that stage the Committee invited McAuslan to assist in rewriting the bill, which then went back to Parliament for a second reading and passed through with very little debate.

> getting the Bill through the National Assembly by the deadline stipulated in the constitution, I worked with women's groups and the relevant Minister to put together an amendment to the Act to reinstate the lost amendment. The President then announced that any such amendment would threaten the social and economic stability of Uganda – a very unlikely scenario. This did not stop women's groups from continuing to argue for the amendment nor myself from continuing to help them.
>
> McAuslan 2010b

He spent much of the following year in Uganda as an unfulfilled senior technical adviser to the 'Land Act Implementation Project' from April 1999 to March 2000. He was profoundly disappointed and disillusioned by the lack of support from the staff of the Ministry of Lands and DFID. Ministry officials set out to sabotage the project, as its purpose was to implement the Land Act, which in accordance with the Constitution was to decentralise land management to the districts, thus removing power and 'benefits' from officials at the centre. He described the difficulties he faced in a self-deprecating paper for the Lincoln Institute in 2003. He concluded that the creation, passage and implementation of the new land law was a 'major exercise in institutional reform, and such exercises generate a whole host of problems, challenges and opposition that need to be addressed if reform is to have any chance of being successful' (McAuslan 2003b).

Problems relating to the slow progress with land reform also arose from the severe constraints on resources at district level, personnel and funds. The Land Act 1998 decentralised land administration to district land boards and other district and sub-county structures, namely the District Land Office and Land Registry, the District Land Tribunal and the Sub-County Land Committee. The cost of creating the decentralised land administration system in the 69 districts exceeded the resources available, despite the Land (Amendment) Act 2004, which limited the number of the prescribed institutions. Land administration was just one of the functions of cash-strapped district governments. The Land Boards, where they had been established, were not able to cope with the demands placed upon them. Matters which could have been sorted out by the Land Boards went to the District Land Tribunal; there were only 18 circuits to serve 69 districts. One chairperson had to cover up to 4 or 5 districts, thus a large backlog of unheard land cases built up. In desperation, people were taking their land disputes to the magistrates' courts.[5] These problems might have been avoided if there had been a detailed NLP, backed by the necessary budget in 1998.

5 Notes of a meeting between the author and Richard Oput, coordinator, Land Tenure Reform Project (LTRP), MWLE Kampala, 7 June 2006.

I returned to Uganda briefly in early January 2014, a few weeks after McAuslan's death, as part of an effort led by the Ford Foundation Program Officer Dr Margaret Rugadya, to help the Ministry raise World Bank funds for the implementation of the NLP (Republic of Uganda 2013), a consultative policy process in which she had been greatly involved (Rugadya and Scalise 2013). The Land Act 1998 remains central to the NLP and the legal framework for the land tenure reform process in Uganda.

The Land Policy Paper that never was: Lesotho 2001[6]

In former Basutoland, the role of the King and the chiefs was central to land governance. Land was held in trust by the King for his subjects. Except within the confined administrative seat of the colonial government in Maseru, chiefs were delegated certain administrative rights and responsibilities, including that of presiding over customary courts. They were required to provide residential and arable land for all married men, but not for women. The same principle applied to the allocation of grazing for their stock. A Mosotho tribesman was entitled to land without giving anything for it, but he had a duty to use and maintain it. Although the concept of individual absolute ownership was unknown, the rights to residential land tended to be exclusive and heritable.

Following Lesotho's independence in 1966, there had been moves towards more democratic forms of government. These included attempts to replace land administration by the chiefs with a more accountable system under the supervision of central government. The Land Act of 1979 aimed to supplant customary tenure with land administration under Roman-Dutch law by nationalising all rights to land. This caused tension between the state and the traditional authorities who insisted that it was unconstitutional for any authority other than the King to 'make grants of interests or rights in or over such land, to revoke or derogate from any allocation or grant that has been made'. Though, the Constitution also provided that the power vested in the King 'shall be exercised in accordance with this Constitution and any other law'.[7]

By 1996, about 30 per cent of the population of 1.84 million were living in urban areas, with Maseru, the capital, accounting for the largest share, as a result of high rural-to-urban migration and large numbers of mine-workers returning from South Africa as a result of the restructuring of the mining industry. The great majority of Maseru residents inhabited informal settlements on land previously under the administration of local

6 The information sources on Lesotho in 2001 and 2003 are mainly from the author's record of assignments as team leader in both periods.

7 In terms of the Lesotho Constitution 1993, Chapter IX, Section 108 (1) and 108 (2) (Government of Lesotho 1993).

chiefs, without security of tenure, clean water or main drainage. The long-running dispute between the Maseru authorities and the traditional leaders also added to the difficulties of developing sound agricultural land use policies. Insecurity of tenure made farmers reluctant to invest in the land. Piecemeal amendments to the Land Act 1979 had not addressed the fundamental problems of legal dualism (Adams and Turner 2005).

With the new millennium, there was growing recognition that policies were needed for an efficient land market and fair procedures and just compensation for compulsory acquisition of land. Customary land tenure and the Deeds Registry Act, 1967 – an essential adjunct of land held under the Land Act 1979 – discriminated against women's rights to land: to acquire land; to hold land with a secure legal title and to pursue legal remedies with respect to land. Past governments had done nothing to tackle this matter, which offended fundamental human rights. Finally, the Land Act and amendments thereto discriminated against foreigners, discouraging incoming investment. Banks were reported to be reluctant to lend money for land and housing development due to what they considered to be political interference in the land market. Real estate agencies were almost entirely absent due to the impossibility of making a business out of facilitating property transactions.

In 2001, Lesotho was receiving assistance from the World Bank and bilateral donors, including DFID, for the Agricultural Policy and Capacity Building Programme – APCBP (Selebalo and Effler 2002). Government was encouraged by the donors to agree to drawing up a national land policy as a necessary prelude to drafting a new land code. The Land Policy Review Commission (LPRC) headed by a distinguished judge had visited Uganda, Malaysia and Germany and toured Lesotho holding public meetings in every district between March and June 2000, conducting hundreds of interviews and receiving many written submissions. A principal recommendation of the Commission's report was that:

> For the avoidance of doubt the present customary land tenure system must be abolished forthwith as it is not conducive to efficient land management and/or administration, security of tenure, high productivity and economic development. Accordingly all land (including agricultural land) that was held under customary tenure shall henceforth be held on leasehold tenure.
>
> Ramodibedi *et al.* 2000, p. 116

The government's response to the commission's recommendations was awaited. Although not published in full, the principal recommendations were widely known. A task force in the Directorate of Lands, Housing and Urban Development in the Ministry of Local Government (MoLG) had been appointed to prepare government's response to the report in the form of a White Paper on National Land Policy. DFID consented to provide technical assistance, Patrick McAuslan and myself,[8] as well as the necessary running costs for the preparation of a draft White Paper and public consultation. It was agreed that the draft White Paper would be presented to the public, although the form which the consultation would take was to be decided by the Cabinet.

By January 2001, stability had returned to Lesotho following the Southern African Development Community (SADC) military intervention and peace-keeping operation in 1998, although Maseru still bore some of the scars of widespread arson and rioting. The political situation under the Interim Political Authority was uncertain and to some degree fragile. General elections were planned for May 2002, under a yet-to-be tested system of proportional representation. However, senior officials in the executive branch of government could not be sure that a decision on the sensitive issue of public consultation on a new land policy would be supported by their interim Minister or indeed by the National Assembly when it was eventually reconvened. Unfortunately, this fault line between the executive and the legislative branch in matters relating to land policy and land law reform widened rather than closed over the next few years and left many issues unresolved.

McAuslan was sceptical about the feasibility of implementing the recommendation of the Commission to abolish customary tenure 'forthwith'. He circulated an internal note on the subject to the task force.

> The central issue of the Report is the future place of customary law in the land tenure system of Lesotho. The Commission proposes the abolition of customary land tenure and its replacement by leasehold and freehold title. ... The Commission's view is that customary tenure has failed to provide a viable equitable and effective system of land tenure and has contributed to land degradation. It is also clear, reading between the lines that the Commission is of the opinion that the abolition of customary land tenure will deal a death blow to the chiefs' role in land management which they also wish to abolish.
>
> The problem with the proposal is that almost certainly it will not work. Customary law will go 'underground'; it won't disappear. No country in Africa has succeeded in 'abolishing' customary law though many have tried it.
>
> McAuslan 2001, p. 1

8 This was not McAuslan's first assignment to Lesotho. He worked on the town and country planning law and compulsory acquisition law on a DFID consultancy in 1996–97, which sought to adapt planning laws to the developing democratic local government. I had been involved in the preparation of the White Paper on National Land Policy and the preparation of land tenure reform laws in the former 'homelands' of RSA.

He gave examples (e.g. Kenya and Tanzania) where attempts to replace customary tenure with 'modern' statutory law and tribunals with jurisdiction over customary tenure disputes within registered areas had not succeeded. McAuslan's proposals for land tenure law reform were central to the Draft White Paper (MoLG 2001, paragraphs 31–33), which was submitted to Cabinet in June 2001. It proposed to develop a new national law that would reconcile customary and statutory land allocation. This would combine knowledge of Basotho culture and traditions with the experience of land laws and institutions of neighbouring countries, where they had proved successful in grappling with similar problems. It would provide for the confirmation and continuation of existing customary family rights, which were exclusive and heritable and for the large areas of rangeland that would remain communal. It would also provide for common law leases for non-customary land use (residential, commercial and industrial) limited in time and subject to eventual reversion to the community. Such leases would be registrable under the Deeds Registry Act and would be mortgageable and transferable to eligible persons, without the consent of the allocating authority. This was consistent with what was happening elsewhere in southern Africa, given the need to be competitive in attracting foreign investment. The new law should take into account, inter alia, the content of rights (e.g. to occupy and use, to transact, to exclude others and rights of enforcement), new allocations, confirmation and conversion of existing rights, demarcation, recording and registration, dispute resolution, cancellation, expropriation and land rights administration.

With regard to 'the land laws and institutions of neighbouring countries, where they have proved successful in grappling with similar problems', members of the task force from the Directorate of Lands in Lesotho spent a week in Botswana in March 2001, hosted by the Ministry of Lands, Housing and Environment, where land administration had been a co-operative exercise between customary and contemporary land administration over the previous three decades. At the end of February 2001, the Draft Land Policy Paper was expected to be the subject of broad consultations at district level followed by a final consultation workshop. Unfortunately, this was not possible because the Cabinet had yet to approve the draft document. On the morning of Tuesday 19 June 2001, we were invited to wait outside the Cabinet meeting room while it considered a briefing paper summarising the issues in the draft White Paper. After two hours, the government secretary emerged from the cabinet meeting with the instruction that the principal secretary for local government and his advisers should proceed with finalising the draft along the lines which were felt to be acceptable to government. Sadly, no feedback was received from the Cabinet before our work in Lesotho came to an end. The Draft Land Policy Paper was not approved for release before the election in May 2002, by which time government's response to the report of the LPRC was more than a year overdue.

'A reform too far': Lesotho 2003

Back in Lesotho, following the May 2002 elections, a new minister, the Hon. Pontšo Sekatle, assumed the Local Government, Lands and Housing portfolio. At the request of DFID, I flew from Botswana to Lesotho to meet her on 14 October 2002 to respond to her Ministry's request for assistance from DFID with the revision of the land legislation. I was informed that this was an item on the agenda each week in Cabinet and therefore had a high priority. I explained that DFID wanted to know the status of the Draft White Paper on Land Policy to ensure that the legal draftsperson did not waste time revising legislation only to be told that it was not what was wanted. The Minister responded that she wanted the drafting of the land policy and the land legislation to go in parallel and what she required was a white paper which took the form of a 'legislative draft'. She said that the policy paper had to set out the details necessary for the National Land Code. She wanted the Land Code drafted immediately, before the next Cabinet meeting!

The APCBP donors were also keen to ensure that there would be rapid progress with the legislative drafting during the last year of their support project. Accordingly, the Aide Memoire of their December 2002 Supervision Mission stated that work on the land policy, the drafting of the Land Code and implementation planning should be done concurrently, for which technical assistance would be provided by DFID. It also stated that the drafts of the Land Code[9] and the Land Reform Strategic Plan (LSSP) should be completed by the end of June 2003. The decision to run the policy development process concurrently with the legal drafting stemmed as much from the donors as from the Minister. To reduce the risk of the proposed tenure reforms being over ambitious and too costly to implement, as had occurred in Uganda, it was agreed that work on the financial and organisational implications of the reforms should be carried out by Michael Aliber and Lala Steyn in concert with the policy and legal drafting.

McAuslan returned to Lesotho in March 2003 to commence the legal work assisted by two Basotho counterparts. The Draft White Paper on Land Policy that we had helped to write in 2001 had not been published; nor had the September 2000 report of the LPRC, to which the Draft White Paper was meant to be a response. The Ministry's policy guidance for the drafting of the Land Code was limited to a short paper dated November

9 This was to comprise the Land Bill, the Town and Country Planning Bill and the Land Acquisition and Compensation Bill.

2002, which included the Cabinet's response to the LPRC. At the time, Cabinet and the Minister were intent on controlling encroachment of informal settlements on agricultural land by demolishing houses and prosecuting offenders.[10]

The drafting programme, led by McAuslan, was designed to create a new legal framework for the management of land in Lesotho, based on the accepted policies developed in the LPRC and other land policies of government, revising and in many areas replacing the existing statutory land laws of Lesotho. The Land Bill was to provide for the grant of land titles, for the conversion of titles, for better securing of titles, for land administration and for the provision of a new system for the settlement of land disputes. The overarching principles of the Land Bill were threefold.

Principle one

Land occupied by citizens and others would be held as a lease, deriving its legitimacy and legality from the Constitution. Leases would be of three types:

- **Primary leases** would replace the former allocations of land under the Land Act 1979 which had been meant to replace the customary land tenure system. The foundational law that would apply to primary leases would be the 'common law', formerly 'customary law'.[11] The term 'primary' would be given to the lease as it was intended for the time being to be the primary form of landholding in Lesotho.
- **Demarcated leases** would be available to citizens via a process of adjudication of common law interests in land held as a primary lease. Those wishing for greater clarity of their rights would be able to obtain a demarcated lease, registrable in a local register, stating the location and boundaries of the land and the rights and responsibilities of the lease-holder. Such leases would be fully marketable and could be used as security for a loan. It would be for holders of demarcated leases to move from common law to Roman-Dutch law as the foundational law of the lease.
- **Registrable** and **Qualified Leases** would be an existing lease of the Land Act 1979. It was proposed to call it 'registrable' as it would have to be registered in the central Deeds Registry, subject to being surveyed in accordance with the prevailing regulations. The difference to the existing lease under the Land Act 1979 would be the introduction of the

10 In April and May 2004, 201 cases were prosecuted in Maseru. Most of the accused were women (UN-Habitat 2005, p. 41).

11 The reasons for recognizing customary law as the common law are explained below.

qualified lease. This would be a registrable lease, but without the full trappings of final registration.

Principle two

Land management was to be devolved from the centre to elected local authorities. The issuance of primary and demarcated leases was to be managed entirely by local authorities, which would be required to operate in a transparent and fair manner. Registrable leases would also be allocated by local authorities, but, as was the case with leases under the Land Act 1979, the legal process of granting the lease and the registration of the lease would be managed by central government and decisions on dispositions of leases would involve advice from a Land Markets Board, a central agency. While most registrable leases would be for residential purposes and held by citizens, these would also be the principal form of tenure for commercial, industrial and public land holdings and foreign investment.

Principle three

This required the transparent and consistent regulation of the land market. Instead of a rather secretive process of decision-making about what dispositions could be granted and what could be exempted from regulation carried out by the minister (which in practice often meant by officials with no particular expertise in land markets), it was proposed that the regulation of the land market was to be more transparent with criteria for decision-making set out clearly and a Land Markets Board established. A small expert body would provide advice to the Minister, guiding the operation of the land market and the principal actors in order to ensure the growth of an efficient and equitable market.

The financial and institutional planning for the implementation of the legislation was believed to have gone well. McAuslan had conscientiously involved his Basotho colleagues in the legal drafting process and they had presented the penultimate draft of the Land Bill at a two-day workshop on 2–3 June 2003 with members of the Department of Lands, Surveys and Physical Planning (LSPP). This was followed by a meeting with the Minister on 12 June 2003. A number of features of the draft bill proved to be sticking points with the Minister, but none of them was judged at that stage to be unresolvable.[12]

12 Patrick McAuslan's notes of his meeting with Hon. P. Sekatle Minister of Local Government, Lands and Housing, 13 June 2003, to discuss the Draft Land Bill.

First, the use of the term 'common law', a central definition in the draft Bill, to mean customary law, was thought to be confusing. Lawyers in Lesotho colloquially referred to Roman-Dutch law as the common law, a misnomer as it had never been the common law of Lesotho, that is to say the law common to all Basotho and recognised as such. Sebastian Poulter, a noted scholar on Lesotho law, had stated that 'the common law had been introduced specifically to meet the needs of the white population…' (Poulter 1979, p. 14). In the commentary to the Draft Bill, McAuslan explained that the real common law of Lesotho had hitherto been called customary law, but to continue to refer to the basic land law of Lesotho as customary law and the basic land tenure as customary tenure was outmoded. In 2000, the LPRC had recommended that the customary land tenure system be abolished forthwith and that land be held under a new Land Act in future. While this recommendation had been accepted, the government had also recognised that there was a need to define customary tenure clearly which meant that there had to be some set of legal rules which governed and regulated the incidents of the form of tenure under which the vast majority of Basotho occupied and used land. The alternative, to impose Roman-Dutch law on tenure relations throughout Lesotho, would have resulted in widespread disregard of the law and a situation where the vast majority of the population, technically, would be in illegal occupation of their land. McAuslan's solution to this seeming conundrum – abolish customary law but still use it to define rights to land for the majority of the population – was to rename customary law as common law – as the law common to all Basotho - thus deliberately severing it from its traditional roots which, as the LPRC had demonstrated, had given rise to inequity and inefficiency in land relations.[13]

The Minister's exception to the proposal to establish a semi-independent Land Markets Board (LMB) was, in retrospect, predictable. Apart from the additional expense involved, she felt it potentially undermined her authority in matters of land allocation. She rejected the idea that politics should not play a role in deciding on dispositions. She also did not like the provision that the Minister 'may' give policy directives to the LMB. If the Minister 'may' then this meant that someone else could as well. Who were these other people or authorities that could give policy directives to the LMB? Could the LMB, if it had to, not be merely advisory to the Minister or just another Division in LSPP?

After the meeting, McAuslan reflected on what the Minister had said. A superficial reaction was to say that at the end of the day, if the LMB was not

13 The foregoing paragraph is based on Patrick McAuslan's commentary to the Draft Land Bill, June 2003.

wanted, it would not fly. Clearly there was a problem of 'letting go' which he had experienced in both Tanzania and Uganda – particularly the latter where a refusal to 'let go' by central government officials had more or less killed the Land Act 1998. A refusal to let go in Lesotho would more or less kill a land market. What the Bill was proposing was that whereas Ministers had been making virtually all the decisions about dispositions, the new position, via the LMB, would be that they would have virtually no say. This was a step too far. It was unrealistic to expect Ministers to take such a large leap into the dark. Whatever the practice in other countries, where the private sector provided services and managed resources in a market environment, regulated by government agencies, such an approach was not appropriate for land or at any rate land in Lesotho. The Minister's views probably reflected a majority opinion in the Cabinet. In a note on the meeting to team colleagues, immediately following his meeting with the Minister, McAuslan (2003c) concluded that:

> when push comes to shove, the Government will opt for a fudge on land markets; yes in theory; not really in practice since continued Ministerial hands-on decision-making on dispositions would be incompatible with the kind of land market which would persuade investors to invest in land and agriculture. But that will be for Ministers to learn the hard way. Interestingly on the same day as the meeting, *Mopheme, the Survivor,* a local newspaper reported a speech by the Minister of Agriculture urging Basotho to develop commercial agriculture, (calling on) foreign investors to invest in commercial agriculture and 'conceding that the present land tenure system in Lesotho posed serious limitations to accommodate productive commercial agriculture. Could there be a better illustration of the pitfalls of drafting land laws without a land policy in place?

Sadly, uncertainties about the government's policy position on key aspects of the proposed land tenure reforms resulted in the eventual shelving of the Draft Land Bill in 2004, which was considered by aficionados to have provided imaginative and sensible means of resolving Lesotho's endemic land problems. These remained largely unresolved for another six years, until the passing of the Land Act 2010 and the related Land Administration Authority Act 2010. McAuslan's efforts were not entirely unappreciated. In 2010, the Director General and Chief Executive of the Land Administration Authority of Lesotho wrote of the draft legislation:

> The Land Bill, 2004 was innovative in both what it did and produced; regularisation would formalise urban tenures and different types of lease would provide different access points to the formal system

depending on people's needs and means; however, the Bill was a reform too far and it didn't receive the support necessary to progress to law.

Johnson and Matela 2010[14]

Stephen Berrisford, a close associate of McAuslan and familiar with his work in Lesotho in 2003 and the eventual implementation of the Land Act 2010, commented that the two DFID- funded initiatives ultimately transmogrified into the Millennium Challenge sponsored process in 2010.[15]

Some satisfaction: Botswana 2002

In the second half of 2002, McAuslan and I were involved in a review of the national land policy of Botswana, which unlike the other country examples recalled in this chapter was directly funded by the government.[16] Here, Seretse Khama in 1966 had transformed himself into a democratic President of an independent country and in so doing had carried the chiefs with him. Moving quickly with the Tribal Land Act 1968, he had placed the administration of customary land in the hands of Tribal Land Boards, from which chiefs were eventually excluded, but compensated in other ways. Thus land administration in Botswana had been a co-operative exercise between tradition and modernity, while in Lesotho it had been a confrontation.

The context of policy development in which we worked in Botswana was well understood. Up until 2002, the nation's iterative land policy reviews had followed a process extending up to two years and consisting of: (i) a commission of inquiry (or an expert review), calls for written submissions as well as the convening of public meetings with a wide range of stakeholders; (ii) the preparation of a draft report, oral presentations and discussions at a national workshop covered by the media; (iii) a draft paper debated in Parliament; (iv) the publication of a government white paper setting out the policy change adopted, the recommendations which had

14 Johnson (2013) further points out that The Land Act 2010 and the Land Administration Authority Act 2010 were enacted under the auspices of the Land Administration Reform Project and the support of the Millennium Challenge Corporation. Under the Land (Amendment) Act of 2012, the statutory post of the Commissioner of Lands was taken out of the public service and brought under the Land Administration Authority. Similar amendments to the Deeds Registry Act 1967 and the Land Survey Act 1980 took the posts of the Land Registrar and Chief Surveyor out of the public service to consolidate all administration functions under the Land Administration Authority.

15 Stephen Berrisford, personal communication to the author, 31 December 2014.

16 Commenting on an earlier draft, Michael Aliber, the team's economist, reminded me of this important point, which underlines the strong commitment of the then Government to the resolution of its land policy issues.

been accepted, amended, deferred or rejected, with a justification for government having done so; (v) finally, where relevant, the drafting of laws or amendments of existing laws (Adams *et al.* 2003).

Our six months' assignment in Botswana was gratifying. McAuslan excelled both as Legal Adviser and pedagogue. He was one of a team of ten consultants, half of whom were Batswana, charged with conducting a review of the nation's land-related policies and laws. The Permanent Secretary of the Ministry of Lands Botshelo Mathuba was charming, accessible, and very knowledgeable on the subject of the nation's land policy (see Mathuba 1989, 2001). The Legal Adviser's terms of reference were to review the outputs of the national legal specialists and the work undertaken by the team, including the draft reports of the Land Policy Review (Government of Botswana 2003). He made two extended visits to Botswana, during July/August and November 2002 and drafted the final chapter of the Review, namely 'Legal Aspects', covering recommendations on women's land rights, the Tribal Land Act, the Town and Country Planning Act, The State Land Act, land ownership by non-citizens, as well as land registration and survey and the Land Tribunal.

Foresightedly, McAuslan set out proposals for recasting all three land laws – the Tribal Land Act, the State Land Act and the Land Control Act – into one new Land Act divided into chapters dealing with tribal land, state land and land ownership by non-citizens. A further chapter would deal with the Land Tribunal system. Common sets of definitions and of general and miscellaneous powers applicable to all land matters were to be part of the new Act, which would be easier to use and of benefit to officials, professionals and lay users alike. He saw the proposed Act as the first step towards the longer-term goal of a National Land Code for Botswana.

Woefully, in June 2015, Botswana's land policy had yet-to-be updated and the findings of the 2002 Land Policy Review continue to be debated. The land sector had fallen victim to the country's economic success and the consequent rural-to-urban migration. The Tribal Land Act was well overdue for revision and possible incorporation in a unified law (Knight 2010). There were an increasing number of voices raised in the press about tenure insecurity on Tribal Land, particularly for pastoralists (Adams 2013a), and falling standards of governance by the Land Boards. In the peri-urban areas, there was growth in the illicit sale of Tribal Land, self-allocation of land or squatting leading to the proliferation of urban settlements, unlawful land sub-divisions and change of use and land speculation (UN-Habitat 2010).

Full speed ahead in Rwanda 2006

Rwanda has the highest density of population on rain-fed arable land in Africa. In 2001, 60 per cent of rural households held less than a hectare of land. In the period 1960–1990, the population of Rwanda increased from 2.75 to 7.03 million, but in 1994 (the year of the genocide) it fell back to 5.2 million (Musahara 2001, p. 7). André and Platteau (1995) reported the findings of an in-depth case study of a very densely populated area in the northwest of Rwanda, which they conducted during the period 1988–1993. They concluded that the pervasive incidence of land disputes and the threat of landlessness led to rising tensions in social relations and paved the way for more overt expressions of disharmony and violence. They made the connection between these conditions and the civil war that broke out in 1994.

Prior to independence, land in Rwanda was held according to customary law and the received Belgian law. According to custom, usufructuary rights were allocated by traditional leaders and thereafter passed down the male line. After Rwandan independence in 1962, under Article 108 of the new Constitution 1962, Belgian land law continued to be recognised as binding. Article 109 provided for an 'organic land law' which would determine how customary laws would be codified and harmonised with constitutional principles. Land continued to be legally held by customary occupiers, but following the decree law No. 9/76 of 4 March 1976 'all land not held under the written law and (whether) *affected or not by customary law* (italics added) or (by) land occupation belongs to the State'. In 2001, nationwide consultations by the National Unity and Reconciliation Council revealed that land disputes had become 'the greatest factor hindering sustainable peace' (Musahara and Huggins 2005, p. 275). Another two years elapsed before the passage of new land legislation, an indication of the sensitivity of the subject. However, the new constitution was adopted by a national referendum in May 2003, the National Land Policy was finalised and released in 2004 and the 'Organic Law Determining the Use and Management of Land' (OLL) was passed in 2005 (Republic of Rwanda 2003, 2004 and 2005 respectively).

In 2006, McAuslan and I joined a two-year, DFID-funded project, contracted to HTSPE Ltd and led by Clive English, to assist the Ministry of Lands, Environment, Forestry, Water and Mines (MINITERE) to prepare a country-wide tenure reform programme. It aimed 'to secure the land rights of all citizens including the poor and vulnerable, while also supporting national economic development and promoting environmental sustainability' (HTSPE 2006). The project involved the planning of systematic land registration throughout the country, an essential part of which was a programme of 'field consultations' followed by 'trial interventions' in representative districts by a team of young Rwandan graduates led by Elizabeth Daley (Daley *et al.* 2010). McAuslan was asked to consider the legal framework required for the new system of tenure mandated by the Organic Land Law 2005 (henceforth OLL), which abrogated all legal provisions contrary to the law, including customary law. This was his first visit to post-conflict Rwanda, which continued to experience turmoil in land relations with returning waves of refugees (Bruce 2009). He relished the challenge of getting to grips with an unfamiliar legal system and the intricacies of the tri-lingual OLL, drafted in French, translated into Kinyarwanda, the language spoken by most Rwandans, and then into English. The OLL provided the enabling legal framework for land tenure reform. Other legal and administrative instruments were understood to be needed for its implementation.

Until his arrival, there was some uncertainty in the project team as to the meaning of some of the clauses in the OLL.[17] By careful analysis of the French version and by reference to the NLP, which was clearer and more specific on issues of tenure than the OLL, he was able to answer important questions relating to the nature of the land rights created by the law.[18] He confirmed that it was the government's intention to grant title to rural peasants only in the form of an emphyteutic (long term) lease and that any proposal to grant them freehold rights would be unacceptable. In an internal briefing paper[19] he explained that the OLL was a fresh start and that the old law and the problems to which it gave rise were to be left behind. However, he reasoned that before the new law could truly and effectively be brought into operation, a detailed and comprehensive law had to be written covering tenure on individual land; leasing of state and local authority land; title demarcation; adjudication and registration; and dispositions. These were not the only subjects on which new and detailed laws needed to be written, but they were the most important. Without them, people's legal rights and ability to hold land, transact land and develop it would at best be cloudy and at worst non-existent.

In the seven opening pages of his main paper in Rwanda (McAuslan 2006), he set out the basic principles to be taken into account in the design and implementation of the land tenure reforms envisaged in the NLP and the OLL. These were derived from his earlier work for the UNCHS Urban Management Programme (McAuslan 1992) and the Istanbul Declaration on Human Settlements and the Habitat Agenda (1996), to which

17 Uncertainties evidenced by correspondence between the HTSPE UK office and Kigali 07.07.2006.

18 The use of the word 'ownership' in relation to land rights in Rwanda under the OLL had been the source of some confusion. Elaborating on the nature of the land rights created by the OLL, he explained that the meaning of the word 'ownership' in the law had to be understood in terms of Article 30 of the Constitution and Article 3 of the OLL which affirmed that the state had 'supreme power to manage all the national land and guarantees the right to own and use the land'. In other words, the state held the allodial title or dominium over land in Rwanda. Article 5 of the OLL permitted any natural or legal person who 'owns land through various means' to own it on a long-term lease (i.e. an emphyteutic lease) in conformity with the provisions of the OLL.

19 'Basic Rwandan Land Law' unpublished draft, Patrick McAuslan, 20.07.2006.

governments, including Rwanda, had committed themselves. In retrospect, this may seem unduly pedagogic, but in 2006 land administration and management in Rwanda was rudimentary. MINITERE had less than a handful of professionally qualified land administrators and capacity building was a central function of the DFID Project.[20] At that stage, rural and urban land registration was limited to a manual system. The ministry held over 20,000 land applications yet to be processed, which had accumulated over the previous decade. These were mainly for urban land other than in Kigali City, which had its own land administration system (HTSPE 2006).

McAuslan advised that while a strategy of enablement was to be the preferred mechanism for providing access to land and ensuring security of tenure, the role of government should not stop at enabling land markets to operate efficiently and transparently. It should direct its attention to considerations of equity and social justice in the operation of land markets. Government at all levels and institutions of civil society should be involved in working together to remove obstacles to obtaining land and providing security of tenure via the market. Government should desist from actions penalising people, especially the poor and disadvantaged, which lessened their opportunities to obtain and hold on to small parcels of land. He drew attention to a situation in which land consolidation and land sharing should meet the tests of administrative justice and that these should be comprehensively covered by the law. Further, he noted that the OLL contained some important articles on consent to land transactions by family members, but which confined consents to (a) joint owners and (b) with respect to spouses, those who were legally married. He argued that if family members were joint owners, then they should be a party to any legal transaction by virtue of their joint ownership. If consent was to have any usefulness, it needed to apply to family members, particularly spouses who were not joint owners of the land. Another concern was the reference to a spouse legally married. Quoting Rose (2004), he pointed out that there were a huge number of 'illegal' marriages and therefore 'illegal' spouses were left without the protection of the law. He concluded that the emphyteutic lease envisaged by the OLL should be covered by a branch of public law, namely the law governing relations between the state and the citizen. In keeping with the philosophy of the OLL, he recommended that a new statutory code of land tenure and land transactions law should be developed that combined the general principles of customary tenure and existing statutory land laws from the Civil Code.

20 Within a few years, the Ministry built up a cadre of talented and strongly motivated staff, refreshingly free of the rent-seeking behaviour associated with land administrators in neighbouring countries.

The bare essentials of his proposals were contained in the Strategic Road Map (Sagashya and English 2009). However, the comprehensive Land Tenure Decree he envisaged was never drafted. Presidential and ministerial decrees (relating to leases, land registration, land sharing, land consolidation, etc.) appeared during 2007–2011 enabling the OLL to come into effect, but these did not differentiate the OLL significantly from earlier colonial laws and the 1976 law that turned all those holding land under customary tenure into tenants-at-will.[21]

Following a programme of pilot trials in 2008, the systematic land registration programme was implemented by the Ministry during 2009–2013 and covered some 10.4 million land parcels, a process in which the great majority of rights holders are believed to have willingly participated. Thus, in the period 2005–2013, the implementation of Rwanda's NLP was extraordinarily rapid. However, doubts remain about the impact of other compulsory land-related programmes (i.e. Land Consolidation, Crop Intensification and Rural Settlement) on the security of tenure of title holders who are required to participate in these programmes and the impact of land registration on the welfare of women and children, particularly for those in polygamous relationships. Other questions have arisen about the number of intra-family disputes that have surfaced as a result of the adjudication and titling process, even if boundary disputes between neighbours may have decreased. In his final published work, McAuslan (2013, p. 137) revealed his scepticism of the outcome of the process of the systematic land registration programme on the livelihoods of the poor and the motives of the government:

> What appears at first sight to be an excellent example of market-led land reform fully in keeping with modern 'international standard' approaches to land management seems on a deeper and more careful analysis to be a reform *designed* to benefit the urban elites at the expense of the rural poor and to make matters worse, re-exacerbate the long-standing tensions between Tutsis and Hutus.

His view was based upon the writings of four respected, but nonetheless critical studies (Ansoms 2008, Brown 2011, Reyntjens 2011, Smith 2011) conducted several years before the completion of the systematic land registration process. As yet, there is no rigorous quantitative evaluation of the longer-term impact of the programme on the tenure security and rural livelihoods of the poor and vulnerable (Adams 2013b).

21 In June 2013, the OLL was repealed and replaced by the Law Governing Land in Rwanda (No. 43/2013 of 16/06/2013). The extent to which this new law has taken account of Patrick McAuslan's concerns could not be addressed in this chapter.

Conclusion

In the country cases described in this chapter, what Professor Patrick McAuslan achieved and didn't achieve, as well as the reasons thereof, are spelt out. In most cases the environment and issues were uncertain and unpredictable. Throughout he was meticulous, firm and calm, yet passionate about his work. He knew who to involve and to consult and when to insist and when to let go. As an advisor, he could only analyse the issues before him and provide advice taking into account the environment, the history, the politics and the economy. After that, the leadership of the host country had to take over and to decide whether or not to act on his advice. It was unfortunate that in some cases good advice that could have benefited the majority of the people was not embraced because some few decision makers and/or implementers perceived their interests to be at stake.[22] I have described his interaction with public officials, with civil society and with donors and the underlying thinking behind the bills that he drafted, the high hopes that his work inspired and the not infrequent disappointments, sometimes followed by a reassuring note to colleagues explaining why he failed to win over a Minister and why it was to be expected. I understand why McAuslan found this work 'endlessly challenging and fascinating', sometimes disappointing, but not 'deeply depressing'.[23] There have been disappointments, but not depression. Work with colleagues from host countries, who continue to strive to overcome the problems of a dysfunctional land administration, was invariably stimulating. Joint efforts to devise solutions were sometimes rewarded, but whatever the outcome we learnt from the process. As McAuslan reminded us:

> There is always more to be learned; never think you know it all. Wherever you work and whoever you work with, you can always learn from them as they will have had experiences you have not had and they will have an understanding of their own country and its problems that however much reading you do you will never be able to come close to. You may be a consultant but you are still and always a student. (2010b)

In Lesotho in 2003, as in other countries and at other times, McAuslan's contribution may not have been immediately appreciated, but it encouraged and inspired subsequent reforms. I trust that the principles and standards that he set in the region will continue to inspire those that follow.

22 This paragraph is based on comments made by Botshelo Mathuba received on 24.02.2015.

23 See In Memoriam: Professor Patrick McAuslan MBE: by Professor John McEldowney, www2.warwick.ac.uk/insite/news/intnews2/in_memoriam_mcauslan

References

Adams, M. 2013a. Reforming communal rangeland policy in southern Africa: Challenges, dilemmas and opportunities, *African Journal of Range & Forage Science* 30(1–2): 91–97.

Adams, M. 2013b. Assessment of current evidence and data gaps in Rwanda's land sector, report for Department for International Development, Oxford: Mokoro Ltd., September 2013 (unpublished).

Adams, M., F. Kalabamu and R. White. 2003. Land tenure policy and practice in Botswana; Governance lessons for Southern Africa, *JEP* 19(1): 55–74. www.mokoro.co.uk/files/13/file/lria/land_tenure_policy_and_practice_botswana.pdf, accessed 8 February 2015.

Adams, M. and S. Turner. 2005. Legal dualism and land policy in Eastern and Southern Africa, *Land Rights for African Development: From Knowledge to Action,* Nairobi: UNDP, CAPRi and Land Coalition, 31 October–3 November, 2005. https://dlc.dlib.indiana.edu/dlc/bitstream/handle/10535/793/Legal_Dualism.pdf?sequence=1, accessed 8 February 2015.

Adams, M. and R. Knight. 2013. 'Land policy developments and setbacks in the Southern African development community'. In B. Chigara (ed.) *Southern African Development Community Land Issues,* Abingdon: Routledge.

Alden Wily, L. 2003. Community-based land tenure management; questions and answers about Tanzania's new Village Land Act, 1999, Issue Paper 120, *Drylands Programme,* London: IIED http://pubs.iied.org/9295IIED.html?s=DIP, accessed 8 February 2015.

André, C. and J-P. Platteau. 1995. Land relations under unbearable stress: Rwanda caught in the Malthusian trap, Centre de Rechercheen Economie du Développement (CRED), Belgium: University of Namur, September 1995. www.foodnet.cgiar.org/scrip/docs&databases/ifpristudies_ug_nonscrip/pdfs/Southwestern_highlands/Land%20relations%20and%20the%20Malthusian%20trap%20in%20NW%20Rwanda,%20Andre%20a.pdf, accessed 12 March 2015.

Ansoms, A. 2008. A green revolution for Rwanda? The political economy of poverty and agrarian change, Institute of Development Policy and Management, discussion paper, Antwerp: University of Antwerp.

Brown, S. 2001. 'The rule of law and the hidden politics of transitional justice in Rwanda'. In Sririam, C.L., O. Martin-Ortega and J. Herman (eds) *Peace Building and the Rule of Law in Africa: Just Peace?* London: Routledge, 179–196.

Bruce, J.W. 2009. 'International standards, improvisation and the role of international humanitarian organizations in the return of land in post-conflict Rwanda'. In S. Pantuliano (ed.) *Uncharted Territory: Land, Conflict and Humanitarian Action,* Bourton on Dunsmore, Rugby: Practical Action Publishing Ltd.

Daley, E., R. Dore-Weeks and C. Umuhoza. 2010. Ahead of the game: Land tenure reform in Rwanda and the process of securing women's land rights, *Journal of Eastern African Studies* 4(1): 131–152.

Government of Botswana. 2003. Review of Botswana's National Land Policy: Final report, Department of Lands, Ministry of Lands and Housing, 31 January 2003 (unpublished).

Government of Lesotho. 1993. *Constitution of Lesotho* www.google.co.uk/webhp?sourceid=chrome-instant&ion=1&espv=2&ie=UTF-8#q=constitution%20of%20lesotho%201993, accessed 12 March 2015.

HTSPE. 2006. Phase 1 of the Land Reform Process for Rwanda: Developing the Strategic Road Map, Inception report. Hemel Hempstead, HTSPE Ltd., February 2006.

Johnson, S. and M. Matela. 2010. Reforming land administration in Lesotho: Rebuilding the institution, Paper PN-32, Cape Town, *Map Africa Conference* 23–25, November 2010. www.landadmin.co.uk/Documents/PN-32%20Reforming%20 Land%20Administration%20in%20Lesotho.pdf, accessed 12 March 2015.

Johnson, S. 2013. Reforming land administration in Lesotho: A Results Report. FIG Working Week 2013 Environment for Sustainability, Nigeria: Abuja, 6–10 May 2013. www.google.co.uk/webhp?sourceid=chrome-instant&ion=1&espv=2& ie=UTF-8#q=johnson%2c%20s.%20(2013)%20%e2%80%98reforming%20land %20administration%20in%20lesotho%3a%20a%20results%20report%e2% 80%99%20fig, accessed 20 March 2015.

Knight, R. 2010. Statutory recognition of customary land rights: A preliminary investigation into best practices for law-making and implementation (Development Law Service, FAO, Rome 2010). www.fao.org/docrep/013/i1945e/ i1945e01.pdf, accessed 20 March 2015.

McAuslan, P. 1992. Institutional and legal arrangements for the improved administration of land development, Regional Development Dialogue, 13(2) United Nations Centre for Regional Development, Japan: Nagoya, pp. 14–32.

McAuslan, P. 1998. As good as it gets: Politics and markets in the making of Uganda's Land Act (unpublished).

McAuslan, P. 2001. Land Policy Review Commission, Kingdom of Lesotho; Comments, 26 January (4 pages, unpublished).

McAuslan, P. 2003a. 'As good as it gets – politics and markets in the reform of Uganda's land law'. In *Bringing the Law Back in: Essays in Law And Development.* Aldershot: Ashgate.

McAuslan, P. 2003b. A narrative on land law reform in Uganda. Working paper presented at conference on comparative policy perspectives on urban land market reform in Eastern Europe, Southern Africa and Latin America, Cambridge MA: Lincoln Institute of Land Policy. www.lincolninst.edu/pubs/809_A-Narrative-on-Land-Law-Reform-in-Uganda, accessed 20 March 2015.

McAuslan, P. 2003c. Meeting with the Minister. 12 June 2003 (4 pages unpublished).

McAuslan, P. 2006. Implementing the organic land law; The proposed Land Tenure Decree: Issues and Options. Draft, 26 May 2006 (46 pages unpublished).

McAuslan, P. 2010a. Personal reflections on drafting laws to improve women's access to land: Is there a magic wand? *Journal of Eastern African Studies* 4(1): 114–130.

McAuslan, P. 2010b. Emergency Lex – and other improbable tales from the Law Zone, in the Recent News and Reflections, DPU-Associates website at www.dpu-associates.net/node/180, accessed 12 February 2015.

McAuslan, P. 2013. *Land Law Reform in Eastern Africa, Traditional or Transformative? A Critical Review of 50 Years of Land Law Reform in Eastern Africa 1961–2011*, London: Routledge.

Mathuba, B. 1989. Report on the review of the Tribal Land Act, land policies and related issues, Gaborone: Ministry of Local Government and Lands, Government Printer.

Mathuba, B. 2001. Reflecting on customary tenure issues in Botswana. National Land Tenure Conference: Finding Solutions, Securing Rights, Durban: Department of Land Affairs.

MoLG. 2001. Draft White Paper on Land Policy of Lesotho, Directorate of Land, Housing and Urban Development in the Ministry of Local Government, Kingdom of Lesotho (63 pages, unpublished).

Musahara, H. 2001. Land and poverty in Rwanda, Seminar on Land in Rwanda, LandNetRwanda, 22–23 November 2001.

Musahara, H. and C. Huggins. 2005. 'Land reform, land scarcity, and post-conflict reconstruction: A case study of Rwanda'. In C. Huggins and J. Clover (eds) *From The Ground Up: Land Rights, Conflict and Peace in Sub-Saharan Africa*, 269–77, Pretoria and Cape Town: Institute of Security Studies.

Poulter, S. 1979. *Legal Dualism in Lesotho: A Study of the Choice of Law Question in Family Matters*, Morija Sesuto Book Depot.

Ramodibedi, M., N. Hlalele, M. Theko, M. Qoo, L. Thabane, T. Tau, E. Thafene and T.Shaha. 2000. *Report of Land Policy Review Commission*, Lesotho: Maseru.

Republic of Rwanda. 2003. Constitution of the Republic of Rwanda. www.parliament.gov.rw/fileadmin/Images2013/Rwandan_Constitution.pdf, accessed 20 March 2015.

Republic of Rwanda. 2004. *National Land Policy*, Ministry of Lands, Environment, Forests, Water and Mines, February 2004.

Republic of Rwanda. 2005. *Organic Law Determining the Use and Management of Land in Rwanda*, Official Gazette of the Republic of Rwanda, 15 September 2005.

Republic of Uganda. 1995. *Constitution of the Republic of Uganda*, 8th October.

Republic of Uganda. 1998. The Land Bill, *Uganda Gazette* No. 12, March, 1998.

Republic of Uganda. 2013. *The Uganda National Land Policy*, Ministry of Lands, Housing and Urban Development, Kampala, February. http://landportal.info/sites/default/files/the_uganda_national_land_policy-_february_2013.pdf, accessed 8 February 2015.

Reyntjens, F. 2011. Rwanda, Ten Years on: From Genocide to Dictatorship, *African Affairs* 110: 1–34.

Rose, L.L. 2004. Women's land access in post-conflict Rwanda: Bridging the gap between customary land law and pending land legislation, *Texas Journal of Women and Law* 13: 197–250.

Rugadya, M. and E. Scalise. 2013. *Developing A National Land Policy in Uganda: A Learning Process*. Landesa Rural Development Institute. www.landesa.org/wp-content/uploads/National-Land-Policy-in-Uganda_A-Learning-Process_-FINAL.pdf, accessed 12 August 2016.

Sagashya, D. and C. English. 2009. *Designing and Establishing a Land Administration System for Rwanda: Technical and Economic Analysis*, Kigali, MINITERE.

Selebalo, Q. and D. Effler. 2002. The land reform in Lesotho: Will it lead to poverty reduction in rural areas? Fostering Rural Economic Development Through Agriculture-based Enterprises and Services, International Workshop, GTZ-Haus, Berlin, November 2002. www.sarpn.org/documents/d0000268/P236_Lesotho.pdf, accessed 13 February 2015.

Shivji, I.G. 1997. Contrary perspectives on rights and justice in the context of land tenure reform in Tanzania, *Cultural Transformations in Africa*, Centre for African Studies, University of Cape Town.

Shivji, I.G. 1999. The Land Acts 1999: A cause for celebration or the celebration of a cause? Keynote Address to the Workshop on Land, held at Morogoro, 19–20 February.

Smith, S. 2011. Rwanda in Six Scenes, *London Review of Books*, 17 March, 3–8.

Tanzanian Affairs. 1995. The Land Commission's Proposals, www.tzaffairs.org/1995/01/the-land-commissions-proposals, accessed 20 March 2015.

UN-Habitat. 1996. Report of the United Nations Conference on Human Settlements (Habitat II). www.diplomatie.gouv.fr/fr/sites/odyssee-developpement-durable/files/13/Rapport_Habitat_Istanbul_1996_anglais.pdf, accessed 22 March 2015.

UN-Habitat. 2005. Land tenure, housing rights and gender in Lesotho, *Law, Land Tenure and Gender Review Series: Southern Africa*, Nairobi, United Nations Human Settlements Programme. http://unhabitat.org/publications-listing/law-land-tenure-and-gender-review-southern-africa-lesotho, accessed 22 March 2015.

UN-Habitat. 2010. *Land Inventory in Botswana: Processes and Lessons*, Nairobi, United Nations Human Settlements Programme. http://unhabitat.org/wp-content/uploads/2014/07/Land-Inventory-in-Botswana-Processes-and-Lessons.pdf, accessed 25 March 2015.

United Republic of Tanzania. 1994. *Report of the Presidential Commission of Inquiry into Land Matters*, Ministry of Lands, Housing and Urban Development, Dar es Salaam.

United Republic of Tanzania. 1995. *National Land Policy*, Ministry of Lands, Housing and Urban Development, Dar es Salaam.

West, H.W. 1972. *Land Policy in Buganda*, Cambridge: Cambridge University Press.

West, H.W. 2000. *On African Land Holding: A Review of Tenurial Change and Land Policies in Anglophone Africa*, Lampeter and New York: Edwin Mellen Press.

Chapter 5

Grand larceny in the tropics

Patrick McAuslan's role in limiting legal land theft in Africa

Liz Alden Wily

Introduction

Grand larceny – the stealing of other people's moveable property – but what term exists in common law for the stealing of people's land? Given the extent of such theft it is odd there is no ready term for this crime. Perhaps that is the point; much land theft has been engineered by parliaments as perfectly legal. Therefore we must be content with the odd conjunction of 'lawful theft' or more pallid 'dispossession'.

This chapter looks at land theft at scale on the African continent and the contribution of Patrick McAuslan to countering this in his law development work. His contribution is largely unsung by beneficiaries, who rightly see legal curtailment of dispossession as the least they are due. Still, they need identifying: in excess of 50 million landholders in Tanzania and Uganda and tens of millions other Africans who have unknowingly gained through his interventions. His indirect contributions have counted too, such as where his innovative legal norms have slipped across borders (such as visible in the South Sudan Land Act, 2009) or entered the annals of regional guidance for majority land security (McAuslan 2006a).

McAuslan did not move land law in Africa into more just territory on his own, and which, in any event, remains unfinished business (Alden Wily forthcoming). Readiness for change already existed where he went to work and precedents often existed in newly laid policies. Africa does not lack a plethora of scholars and activists and at times politicians and civil servants already on the case of tenure injustice. It was usually they, together with facilitating donors, who sought his assistance in the first instance. Yet, it was the combination of his perspicacity, scholarly excellence, non-combative manner, and the authority he carried in a continent where chief justices, attorney generals, ministers, and scholars had been among his students that so frequently triggered tipping points.

The fundamental issue that was (and remains) at stake is straightforward: are the indigenous unregistered land interests of some 680 million rural Africans (to be more than one billion in 2050)[1] worthy of protection as property rights? Up until the 1990s most land laws in Africa said not (Ghana was a main exception). Lack of formal entitlement descending from received (and imposed) tenure norms was only one impediment. More excuse was found in customary rights, that were neither fungible as a detachable commodity nor easily identifiable as belonging to an individual natural or legal person, the preferred locus of property in European norms. The holding of rights to land collectively was particularly scorned. However, this was not least because such communality expressed dangerous levels of amorphous solidarity and physically embraces the very millions of hectares of resources which colonial and then post-colonial polities wished to retain a firm grasp upon; that 1.8 billion hectares on the continent covering valuable forests, mineral-rich rangelands, marshlands and waters that still fall within the oft-unrecognized customary sector (Alden Wily 2011a). Legal acknowledgement of these lands as already owned would constrain the freedom of administrations to control, benefit from and dispose of these assets at will. Accordingly, such lands were defined as unowned wastelands, *herrenlos*, *terres sans maîtres*, or *el baldío* and thereby by default, state property.

This was, of course, not a new story but rather one embedded in common and civil law, adopted with alacrity into laws for colonies, and with no less alacrity sustained by post-colonial governments as independence got underway from the late 1950s (Alden Wily, 2011b). McAuslan drew attention to early common law case law engineered to establish the mechanisms for lawful mass dispossession (McAuslan 2007). A notable case met the need for the King of England's Bench in 1604 to find that the lands of Ireland were unowned in order to legitimise their transfer to 100,000 Scottish and English settlers in following years and whose tenancy to the English Crown would, inter alia, generate massive 'profit and prerogative' for the King (Dorsett 2002, pp. 9–13). Awkwardly, the Irish appeared to operate an ancient, written, and vibrantly practised customary property law so the counsel for King James, Sir John Davies, was forced to prove that regime was flawed and should be discounted. For this he seized upon the Irish custom of tanistry by which families and clans approved heirs through election. This, Davies successfully established, was 'backward and unreason - able', unlike the 'superior' English custom of primogeniture. Election deprived the oldest son ('naturally the most worthy man of blood and

1 Refer to www.prb.org/pdf14/2014-world-population-data-sheet_eng.pdf for growth of the total population of Africa from 1.136 billion people in mid-2014 to a projected 2.428 billion people in 2050 (last accessed 4 July 2015). Refer to https://esa.un.org/unpd/wup/Publications/Files/WUP2014-Highlights.pdf (accessed 4 July 2016) for UN projection that while the proportion of rural dwellers will decline from 60% in 2014 to 44% of the total population of Africa, they will number 1.068 billion people by 2050.

surname') of 'certain ownership of land', demoralising his expectations ('even debauchery could result') (ibid.). This in turn did not serve public good. Ergo, Ireland was merely occupied not owned in accordance with English common law and with such vacancy and the King of England could legitimately claim to own Irish lands.

A second case that McAuslan refers to is the better-known *Johnson and Graham's Lessee v. William M'Intosh* heard by the American Supreme Court in 1823 (US 1823). This was similarly designed to establish that indigenous populations did not own the lands they occupied and was used to facilitate state-supported land takings. For this, Chief Justice Marshall brought assumed rights of discovery to new depths; this purported to grant discoverers not only political sovereignty over conquered territories (*imperium*), but also original ownership of all lands within them (*dominium*). Sales by native Indians were therefore invalid; they held 'a mere right of usufruct and habitation, without power of alienation' (ibid., p. 569).

In any event, Marshall argued, Indians could not have been real owners as they were not cultivators and therefore could not have acquired 'proprietary interest in the vast tracts of territory which they wandered over... they had no individual rights to land' (ibid., p. 570). This had philosophical support; although John Stuart Mills was yet to develop his defining thesis on property (1859). John Locke (1689) and Adam Smith (1776) had already established that real property only comes into being by man's labour. To boot, Marshall added, Indians are 'heathens and savages and the force used to acquire title by conquest therefore finds some excuse in the character and habits of the people' (ibid. p. 589).

As we know, few English escaped dispossessory land law themselves. Around the same time as Marshall's ruling, millions of rural poor were finally being ejected from their lands to make way for the roads, railways, factories, housing estates, commercial sheep farms, and mechanised cultivation feeding the Industrial Revolution or, more exactly, to make way for the financial killings which landlords could make from selling these lands (Hobsbawm 2011 (1962)). Customary rights had already been dramatically impaired some centuries earlier following Norman transfer of lands to particular lords but had settled in practice into majority rights of possession and use, including the meadows, moors, fens, and forests maintained within and beyond manorial domains (Linebaugh 2010). However, by the industrialising eighteenth century, Parliament, made up of wealthy (land) lords was only too willing to endorse some 200 acts of enclosure and eviction between 1760 and 1830, cumulating in an all-encompassing law of 1945 that established dispossession of customary occupants as in the public interest. This was, the social historian, Thompson, observed '...a plain enough case of class robbery ... played according to the... rules of property and law laid down by a parliament of property-owners and lawyers' (1991 (1963) p. 237). In short, by the time Britain expanded its empire into

Africa, the norms of capitalism as unavoidably dispossessing the majority rural poor in the interests of growth and expansion were already entrenched in common law.

The great dispossession in Africa

European civil laws were no less dilatory in establishing how their governments could legally steal lands at scale, implicit in no less august tomes than the French Declaration of the Rights of Man (1789) (much of which borrowed from the American Constitution) and subsequent Napoleonic Civil Code (1804). When it came to land rights, protection was afforded only to the individual, and the better-off (male) individual at that. By the time the powers met in Berlin in 1884–85 to divide Africa into preferential trading zones, all were well equipped to ignore the fact that Africa was already owned (and the reservations of the American observer set aside: Huberich 1947, pp. 1207–1221. Accordingly, the General Act of the Berlin Conference on West Africa, 26 February 1885, only required the powers to inform each other when they expanded their coastal enclaves (Article 34) and to establish sufficient authority 'to protect existing rights', meaning their own rights, not those of Africans (Article 35). Africans were not entirely forgotten; a watching brief over their moral wellbeing was established and Africans were to be beneficiaries of the blessings of (European) civilisation (Article 6).

In practice, commercial competition among the powers was so great that economic protectionism rapidly segued into political protectionism in the form of colonies and protectorates to better secure trading and resource-capture privileges. Proof that Africa was unowned became a more anxious task in this project. Without this, the greater expanse of the African hinterland could not so easily be taken at will or for free. Solution was delivered in tens of sovereignty-cum-land laws enacted around the continent between 1896 and 1914 (Alden Wily 2011b). These established European Heads of State as the ultimate owners of land and resources within rapidly expanding colonies and from whose hands alone real property could derive. While Britain and Germany favoured the issue of absolute (or long lease) entitlements to entrepreneurs or to regularise earlier coastal land purchases from chiefs by trading companies and missionaries, France and Belgium found it easier to allocate millions of hinterland hectares to home companies, and to require them on the side to collect taxes, establish ferries and other tasks for the colonising state. By 1900 over seventy per cent of present-day Gabon and Republic of Congo were under title to forty-two French consortia (Gray 2002, p. 142). Elite natives, such as those in Liberia who wore top hats and had glass in the windows of their huts or who, like sophisticated Arabs along the Nile in the Sudan who had sharia documentation, could also acquire titles (Alden Wily 2007; Salih 1982).

Initially, to keep the peace and food supply going, native farm occupancy was not unduly disturbed. But the nub of strategy was in respect of the two billion hectares of uncultivated lands up and down the continent. To double-lock these against local claims, laws declared these lands to be wastelands or *terres sans maîtres.*

The road to land robbery was not smooth. Land takings and relocations multiplied as colonies were told to pay for themselves (a fact that was accelerated by the demands of two world wars), with launch of large-scale schemes for rubber development by Firestone in Liberia to million-acre schemes variously launched by the British and French. However, protests, boycotts of European goods (introduced by the ton in the cotton and kettle line), refusals to sell food to European traders, and armed rebellions put down with brutal force, did little to change dispossessory law, other than slowly open up entitlement opportunities for emerging African elites with contacts and means (Alden Wily 2012a). Some tribes did better than others. Early on, worldly-wise kings in the Gold Coast and Lagos Island played the British at their own game by bringing their demands to Westminster (Amanor 2008). Much later, the Meru tribe of Tanganyika would demand restitution at the Trusteeship Council of the UN (Larsson 2001).

By 1960, what had begun in the 1880s as a device to capture exclusive markets for millions of unsold goods from depressed Europe, and then capture of lucrative raw materials at no cost (Hobsbawm, op cit.), had become more genuine conviction that African land rights did not have attributes of property, and that it was not in the natives' own interests to consider this to be so. By then class formation was playing a main role, turning local elites into abetters of the *res nullius* thesis to make it easier for themselves to acquire the lands of their neighbours at minimal cost (Alden Wily 2012a).

Exceptions were few. These included American-settled Liberia (where issue of Aborigine Titles to communities was possible until 1956); Ghana, where swathes of especially forested lands were exempted from state dominium due to the powerful chiefly interventions noted above, along with the Protectorates of Bechuanaland and Lesotho and the Swazi Kingdom within colonised South Africa, where tribal tenure remained more or less intact. Elsewhere, millions of Africans found independence did not remove their subordination as permissive tenants of state on their own customary lands, until such time as those lands were needed for higher purposes, or until titling programmes such as launched in the 1960s began to systematically transform customary occupation into received law freehold entitlements, extinguishing all semblance of 'backward' customary tenure (Okoth-Ogendo 2002).

As frustration mounted in the late 1980s as to the slowness and paucity of these schemes, and as structural adjustment conditions for IBRD

(International Bank for Reconstruction of Development) loans demanding a free market in land for foreign investment began to bite, African governments ventured into what were referred to as land administration reforms. Inevitably, and usually with reluctance, this brought policy makers face-to-face with the legal underpinnings of mass dispossession, the formalisation of customary lands as marketable commodities notwithstanding (Alden Wily 2006). The contemporary wave of transformation from single-party to multi-party democracy, along with the endgame liberation of southern Africa from racist regimes, added fuel to the fire of slow-burning tenure change, with slowly gathering persuasion that customary possession deserves respect in the modern age as amounting to ownership, too long denied. Legal scholars began to frame the transformation needed; as McAuslan in due course wrote:

> Customary tenure is – and always has been – one of the foundational elements of the land laws of all states in Africa. It is not an add-on to received law; indeed, received or imposed law is the add-on. Received law thus needs to be adapted and adjusted to indigenous law, not vice versa, and proponents of received law should be advancing the case for legal pluralism.
>
> McAuslan 2006b, p. 9

This had, in practice, been an implicit if unarticulated objective in McAuslan's law development work in the reformism that was beginning to take hold in anglophone Africa from the early 1990s. We may now turn to his role in this trend. For lack of space I will focus upon his seminal contribution as lead drafter of the new land law in Mainland Tanzania in 1996. By the time that law came into force in 2001, McAuslan had followed this work up with critical inputs into the final draft of Uganda's new land law (1998) and with which he took the time to involve himself in early application as a land programme adviser (McAuslan 2003). Further, as Martin Adams elaborates in this volume, McAuslan would bring his East African experiences to bear in his many contributions to new land policies and laws in other African states such as South Africa, Lesotho, Botswana, Somaliland and Liberia.

The Tanzania case

The background to McAuslan's involvement in drafting Tanzania's land legislation is important, as a massive amount of spadework had already been undertaken and his founding achievement was to nurture and build law firmly upon the pro-poor and pro-majority norms that had come uncertainly the fore. By the mid-1990s a continent-wide tug of war was crystallising between market-led and rights-based imperatives in the resurgent push for financial and capital market liberalization in developing countries spearheaded by the IMF and IBRD in these years (Stiglitz 2001). In respect of resulting land and property rights review, the pre-eminent contribution in Tanzania was by Professor Issa Shivji, appointed to chair a Presidential Commission of Inquiry into Land Matters. This sat throughout 1991 with broad instruction to find out what was driving land grievance and to propose institutional, policy and legal remedy with implied expectation that this would settle upon rapid and final conversion of customary rights into state-granted rights under received common law (Government of Tanzania 1994). The commission travelled the country holding 277 public meetings, setting the tone thereafter for land commissions across the continent to be public and consultative. Its report covered multiple topics but with a firm focus on the status of the indigenous tenure of more than 20 million rural Tanzanians (now around 32 million people).

The commissioners concluded their report with recommended principles of national land policy. Inter alia, these aimed to devolve land rights governance to village level, taking advantage of Tanzania's existing regime of 8,367 elected village governments (village councils, now approximately 14,000) whose customary lands, exclusive of forest and wildlife parks and reserves, covered 70 per cent of the country. The commission recommended that title be vested in village assemblies, the adult constituencies of each village. Customary rights to these lands were to have equivalent force with rights obtained through tenure forms introduced by British colonizers in the Land Tenure Ordinance, 1923. This provided surety for natives to use and enjoy public lands, not to own them, amended in 1928 to imply equity with non-native granted rights of occupancy, albeit with contradictory rights of the colonial state to alienate native lands at will also confirmed (Wily 1988). In the 1992 recommendations of the Shivji Commission, non-village lands were to be known as national lands, owned by the national community, and administered by an autonomous National Land Commission. At one stroke these provisions would have deprived the President of his radical entitlement to all Mainland Tanzania and closed off millions of hectares for land takings without compensation.

Not surprisingly, Shivji's recommendations did not meet with favour by the post-socialist administration of President Mwinyi. Alongside his known interests as a businessman keen to see an entirely open market in land encouraging and enabling sales of fertile farm lands by rural Tanzanians, Mwinyi came from the deeply embedded centralism of the Ruling Party, long used to taking over customary lands at will much as the predecessor British colonial administrations had done. A useful instrument for this had been put in place by the Rural Lands (Planning and Utilization) Act, 1973. This permitted Government to issue Orders extinguishing customary rights in specified areas to free lands up for allocation to the growing ranks of private investors, parastatals, and public-private partnerships for large-scale wheat, seed bean, and other schemes. Orders targeted the expansive pastoral lands of northern Tanzania, complemented by policies instructing pastoralists to settle down as ranchers (Wily op. cit.). Evictions triggered by nine such Orders had prompted challenges in the courts (Maina 2007). Frustrated at its hands being tied, the state enacted the Regulation of Land Tenure (Established Villages) Act, 1992. This was presented as an enactment designed to resolve mounting dispute over the ownership of farms left behind by families when coerced to settle in aggregated settlements under the villagization programmes of the 1970s. The law claimed to solve the problem by simply extinguishing all such rights.

Coincidentally, or more likely otherwise, this law was enacted just as Shivji's Commission presented very different recommendations to the President. These neatly encapsulated what was at stake: protection of majority rights to their lands or protection of the right of the state to co-opt local lands for ill-concealed private purposes. The answer came within a year. The Regulation of Land Tenure Law, 1992 was struck down by the High Court as unconstitutional in failing to protect customary rights (October, 1993). The Attorney General appealed but the High Court ruling was upheld in 1994. The issue settled upon whether customary rights had incidents of real property, which, as described above, most colonial and post-colonial laws and courts had decided was not the case. Now Judge Nyalali of the Court of Appeal decided otherwise, ironically by reinterpreting the ambivalent intentions of old colonial land law of 1923, still in force at the time. He said:

> We have considered this momentous issue with the judicial care it deserves. We realize that if the Deputy Attorney-General is correct, then most of the inhabitants of Tanzania mainland are no better than squatters in their own country. It is a serious proposition.
>
> Judgement, 1994, *Attorney-General v. Lohay Akonaay and Another*, reported in [1995] 2 LRC 399

The judge's timing was right. The Shivji's Commission report was being circulated in civil society circles and international advocacy for rights-based reform was stimulated. The Government could not avoid calling together representatives to debate a new national land policy, which was finalised in June 1995 (Government of Tanzania 1995). Cabinet had already decided it would not surrender ultimate title in the President (December 1994) and made this its bottom-line. Nevertheless, neighbouring Uganda would be inspired to take up that baton. Its 1995 Constitution did away with the inherited common law distinction between radical title and estates in land by vesting title directly in customary or other lawful landholders such as those holding more formal rights of freehold, leasehold or *mailo* – a regime unique to Uganda – (Article 237, National Constitution of Uganda).

In other respects, the new Tanzania National Land Policy trod an uneasy line between Government determination to bring as much customary property into the marketplace and the protection of those rights without formalisation, such as it was now interpreted that colonial land law had allowed, colonial and post-colonial interpretation and practice aside. Majority customary land rights were clarified once and for all as equal in law with statutorily granted rights, to be known respectively as Customary and Granted Rights of Occupancy. The Rights of Occupancy terminology retained colonial naming of rights throughout anglophone Africa, and served to remind the populace that ownership of the entire country remained vested in the president.

The policy of 1995 set aside dictates of agricultural policy in 1987 that had launched grants of 99-year leaseholds to village governments (councils) with directive to sub-let house parcels to individual farmers. The policy relocated councils as non-landholding land managers, mandated to facilitate identification, formalisation and allocation of rights. This countered centralist tendencies that had seen members of President Mwinyi's Administration (1985–1995) deride village councils as a mistake of Nyererian socialism. Mwinyi's 1987 policy made titling compulsory to aid land market development and collateralisation, along with the implication that each village area need only include farm and house parcels along with a little extra commonage for expansion (Government of Tanzania 2011). Nomadism was outlawed, intended to restrict land claims by Barabaig (much of whose lands had been taken for Canadian-funded wheat schemes) and Masai pastoralists who occupied much of northern Tanzania. After global adoption of the Convention of Biodiversity at Rio in 1992, restriction upon pastoralist land claims and use included the intended declaration of numerous new wildlife and forest reserves, alongside a political determination to expand commercial farming (Alden Wily 1997). Cumulatively, these pressures upon customary rights threatened to remove the greater proportion of the 61 million hectares making up the customary land sector. At worst, village lands could be confined to the variously calculated six to eleven per cent of the country area under active cultivation.

The process of entrenching the new land policy in law opened opportunities for adjustments. An implicit choice facing the drafters of new land law was whether to swing the balance of the law into a programme of conversionary customary to statutory entitlements (such as was still being applied in neighbouring Kenya) or to reassert pride of place for majority customary interests and norms, and to also curtail opportunities for losses, such as in the name of conservation. Well-known to the University of Dar es Salaam where he had taught between 1961 and 1966, McAuslan was invited to assist in the drafting of the new land law and did so during 1996. Under his guiding hand, the drafting team focused upon closing the gaps against land theft, limiting administrative malfeasance through heavily prescriptive procedure, and yet not so entirely disabling state determination to retain controlling privileges that the new land law would be rejected. At the same time, it was bound to respect the dictates of the new National Land Policy.

The Draft Land Bill appeared in November 1996. With more than one thousand sections and sub-sections it was long and also in legalese difficult for the lay community to read. Little of substance was altered in the three years it took to be enacted (1999),[2] and then the five years it took to come into force (May 2001). This followed issue of Regulations, also drafted by McAuslan. The bill itself had been transposed into two laws, a Land Act, 1999 and a Village Land Act, 1999, mainly to reduce bulk, and perhaps partly in line with McAuslan's recommendation that 'there is a strong case for created as complete a statutory code for village land as possible…' (McAuslan, 1996: 39).

Inconsistencies arose in the process of turning one law into two. One of the more important was the status of 55 million or so hectares of communal forests and rangelands within the village land sector, purposely neither occupied nor farmed by villagers, but retained for water catchment and limitation of soil erosion, for multiple wood and non-wood products, pasturing and fishing and as land reserves into which later generations might expand farming. Although demonstrable as used if not for farming, such lands have a long history of being officially regarded in effect as unowned wastelands. Without demonstration of active use, such areas risked being excluded from village lands in the adjusted definition of general land made to the original bill, general land being distinctive as directly controlled and allocated by the Commissioner of Lands, not by villages.

In practice, general land comprises urban and rural lands under private title (Granted Rights of Occupancy or leaseholds) and presently covers only two per cent of the total mainland country area (Deininger, Selod and Burns, 2012: 83). The meaning of general land ascribed to it by the Land Act maintained McAuslan's meaning as 'land which is not reserved or village land' to which final drafters added 'and includes unoccupied or unused village land' (s. 2). No such addition was made to the definition of general land in the Village Land Act, a contradiction that has not been remedied until the present.

The addition reflected the growing determination of the Tanzanian state as the 1990s progressed to make as much land available as possible to foreign and local investors. McAuslan himself ensured that compulsory acquisitions for public interest 'shall include investments of national interest' (Land Act 1999 s. 4 (2)), extending provision of the Land Acquisition Act 1967 that already stipulated that lands could be taken 'for use by any person or group of persons who, in the opinion of the President should

2 A main change was reduction in provisions relating to dispute settlement, entered into a more elaborated Land Disputes Courts Act, 2002.

be granted such land for agricultural development' (Land Acquisition Act 1967 s. 4 (1) (g)).

In his commentary on the draft bill submitted in November 1996, McAuslan queried National Policy stipulation that a foreign company could not directly obtain rights to land in villages (McAuslan 1996, pp. 40–41). He provided a circuitous and somewhat ambiguous route for this in providing for a village council to issue leases, sub-leases or other derivative rights that appear to not be descendant from customary rights or Certificates of Customary Rights of Occupancy (Village Land Act 1999 s. 32–34). Nor are any of the provisions bound by explicit sanction against foreigners or foreigner companies applying for such non-customary rights in village land (Village Land Act 1999 s. 32–34). Nevertheless, it remains the norm that should a foreigner or foreign company seek to use village land, this may only be acquired through the sought area being transferred from village land to general land for onward allocation to the applicant. Amendment to the Land Act in 2004 makes it possible for such lands to be granted directly to the investor by the Commissioner for Lands as a Granted Right of Occupancy, or to be acquired as a derivative right or as an interest within a joint venture with a citizen(s) (Land Amendment (Amendment) Act 2004, section 3 amending section 19 of the Land Act). Meanwhile, citizen investors and groups may easily acquire access to village land through numerous provisions for applications by non-resident citizens and non-village organizations in the Village Land Act.

How far the concerned land is voluntarily or compulsorily transferred from village to general land is also complex. First, McAuslan and his drafting team laid down that a village land shall be divided into communal village land, land which is being occupied or used by an individual, or family or group of persons under customary law, and land which may be made available for communal or individual occupation and use through allocation by the village council (Village Land Act 1999 s. 1 (1)). The last category bears uncomfortable resemblance to the notion of unused, unowned, wasteland as touched upon above, and could explain the attempt of legislators to secure 'unoccupied and unused land' as general land. The reality is that with a few possible exceptions in the far south of the country (or anywhere in Africa), there has rarely been a single hectare within the African customary sector that does not have a community owner. That is, a substantial class of unwanted and unused lands such as the term wastelands expresses simply did not – and does not – exist. Second, and curiously, the law only provides for communities to refuse transfer of areas that are less than 250 hectares, the decision concerning larger areas being left to the Minister (Village Land Act 1999 s. 4 (6)). This was evidently not a mistake on the part of the drafting team; 'The procedures allow for proper consideration to be given to the interests of villagers but at the end of the day for the government to obtain land it needs' (McAuslan 1996, p. 13).

In practice, central Government found it difficult to persuade villages to surrender any part of their village territories to Government for onward lease to investors. Early circulars after enactment of the land laws requesting village councils to surrender unused lands to Government for allocation to investors became more forceful. By 2009, President Kikwete and fellow businessmen were so agitated by the failure of the village land sector to (so to speak) put itself up for sale, that he announced that the obstructive Village Land Act would be amended (Kilimo Kwanza Resolution ('Farming First') 2009). Popular resistance to the passage of such a bill has grown in an increasingly wary peasant sector that sees its land assets sought on all sides (Redfern 2011; Kitabu 2011; Makoye 2013). Salutary experiences publicised in the local and international press have help alert ordinary rural citizens to the risks. These include cases where, having been persuaded by local officials and politicians to give up lands in return for promises of jobs, wells, and services, not only have these not materialised but bankrupted investors have then sold off the land to recoup losses – and often to those same politicians with whom villagers have no benefit-sharing agreements (The Oakland Institute 2012, Massay and Kassile 2014).

Outside the agricultural sector, the law has also not been able to halt attempts to evict communities to create new Game Controlled Areas or to expand National Parks, for private rather than public purpose (Legal and Human Rights Centre, 2010, Orozco-Quintero 2014). Nor has the pledged introduction in 2012 to limit allocations to investors to 10,000 hectares been formalised or expected to apply in the proposed SAGCOT (Southern Agricultural Growth Corridor of Tanzania) initiative; this, with much backing from the US and other governments, has earmarked nearly a third of the country for commercial farming developments, leaving some millions of villagers wondering how far their local private and communal lands will be swallowed up (Kiishweko 2012; Hatcher 2013; Provost and Kabendera 2014, Massay and Kassile op. cit.).

For all this, there is a great deal in the Tanzanian environment that protects rural land rights in ways still not commonly mirrored around much of the continent, and which confronts revival in dispossessory trends identified as a new 'global land grab' (White, Hall and Wolford 2012). Part of this protection is driven by customary landholders themselves, increasingly educated, digitally and internationally connected, organised, and more demanding each year that their elected leaders at all levels are accountable to their electorates (Hall *et al.* 2015). However, even in these more politicised respects, immense strength is drawn from the new legal paradigms and protective procedures that McAuslan and his team laboured over, albeit with flaws such as illustrated above.

Positive aspects of these may be collated here. First, the land law is explicit at every turn, such as where urban domains encroach into village lands, or where customary rights exist in lands that have been made Protected Areas, that customary interests cannot be wilfully discounted or treated with less respect than rights secured through state-issued entitlements. Furthermore, the law makes it clear that these rights already exist and cannot be impaired on the grounds of not being formalised. Any hint that titling means extinction of customary rights was cast out with clarity, in that titling is no more than certification of what exists, and not replacement of customary rights with statutory rights as had so solidly been entrenched as the norm around the continent. Appropriately, McAuslan's team chose to ignore a policy directive that registration be compulsory. That this was nevertheless desirable was made clear by bountiful procedures for rights to be adjudicated and registered by the village itself, through essentially no cost procedures.

Just as critical was the fact that the new laws established that customary rights could be owned not only by individuals, but also by couples, families, groups, or whole communities as determined appropriate by the community. This meant that collectively owned local forests, pastures and marshlands were at once acknowledged as owned. These common properties could be double-locked through issue of collective titles if desired. More powerfully, the Village Land Act 1999 pre-empts exclusion of these lands from the customary domain by requiring that each community identify and describe its common properties in the village land register prior to adjudication and issue of deeds to individuals or families in respect of 'private' house and farm plots (Village Land Act 1999 s. 13).

This is complemented by the flexibility offered in the law as to how the perimeter boundaries of each village land area are established, including through inter-village agreement rather than through external survey and mapping and/or the directives by local district councils or land officials (Village Land Act 1999 s. 7). As may be expected, such inter-village consultation sees villages include all their lands, leaving no unowned areas between their respective areas. Such agreement has since been made compulsory in the Land Use Planning Act 2007. It is this, more than any other provision that has frustrated Government expectation and intention that unsettled lands outside settlements would fall to the state as general land. Statistically, Government might have anticipated that only 25 or 30 per cent of the national area (or even the 11 per cent actually settled and cultivated), not 69–70 per cent as is the case today, would be defined as village land (Jayne, Chamberlain and Headey 2014).

The equivalency of customary rights with statutory granted rights protects village land in other ways. Compensation is equally due at public acquisition for either, and this includes lands owned in common as much as lands owned for farming or residential purposes. In addition, the procedures for public acquisition are sufficiently multiple and requiring of public information and proven consultation at every stage, and are so expensive to deliver given the multiple heads under which payment must be made, that this route for land takings has somewhat diminished in utility since enactment. Further, as remarked earlier, the law is insistent that no land may be transferred out of the class of village land until the type, amount, method and timing of the payment of compensation has been agreed with the village council. For example, cost constraints forced the central forestry department in 2002 to abandon plans to establish new state reserves and to look to communities themselves to create protected forests out of their lands, a task in which it has been unusually successful (Alden Wily 2012b; Government of Tanzania 2012).

Additionally, both by terminology and provisions, the laws have taken much of the sting out of the power of the President and his Commissioner of Lands to help themselves to untitled lands. In the first instance, while transfers of land from village to general or reserved land are permitted, the procedures for this also demand local consultation and consent, including in respect of the type, amount, method and timing of payment of compensation. The powers of the President were truncated with precise clarification as powers of trusteeship only (Land Act 1999 s. 4 (1)). This policy objective is reflected in so many procedures that its meaning cannot be glossed over as titular. In addition, the meaning of public land shifted with the new land laws. Although the entire country continued to be referred to as Public land as it had since 1923, with customary rights now given the same protection as titled rights, past inference of public land as unowned lands was done away with. That is, all land in Tanzania since the land laws came into force in 2001 has an owner, customary or otherwise, titled or untitled.

The equivalency of granted and customary rights was furthered in powerful ways. For the first time, it became advantageous in Tanzania to hold a customary rather than statutory state-granted right; the term of customary rights is unlimited (while Granted Rights of Occupancy are limited to 99 years), the identity of owners more flexible, conditions of tenure determinable by communities themselves, and revenue deriving from issue of deeds retained by the community.

The land laws also took seriously National Land Policy's instruction that the elected village councils have administrative authority over land matters. Through this, Tanzania achieved devolutionary land administration, strengthened the village as a viable entity and married customary rights more deeply to community rights. Customary rights have always been definable as community derived rights, and upheld only for so long as the community desired, a fact often forgotten in presumption of such rights as stemming solely from the past and struggling to survive in the modern world. By failing to centralise the administration of these rights into district council or more remote central government hands, and instead legally embedding determination of these rights in a modern, community-based governance context, the Village Land Act assures the survival of community-based tenure into the future as a vibrant regime in the hands of the living community. This may be further illustrated by the absence of any attempt in the law to require ascertainment of codification of customary land law. Each community may, within the boundaries of equity and justice, define its individual, family and collective rights to land and resources within its village area domain, and around which it may, in addition, establish village government-based regulation (Village Land Act 1999 s. 8). This entrenched definition of customary rights as the prerogative of the community and also took the steam out of conflicting customary rights acquired in the past and those acquired under the villagization programme and since. It did this by defining customary rights in their true colours, as rights deriving from and sustained by community consensus, and not necessarily ancient in their origins. That is, the law threw back decisions as to what land rights must be upheld within the community land area upon the living community.

The empowerment elements of these arrangements should also not be missed. By locating decision making and protection of right upon the community, and additionally, installing the land register at village level at the village level, the land laws restructure the powers of both District Council and the Land Commissioner as more oversight than administrative, and in the process, further the survival of community governance (village councils). This is not to say that battles of power between district and village councils and attempts by the Land Commissioner to exercise his powers have disappeared, but that a more equitable playing field has already evolved, reinforcing the managerial powers of the Land Commissioner to general land, but that a more equitable playing field is in place. This has encouraged other laws and most notably in the natural resource sector to take subsidiarity more seriously in their own legal paradigms. It is not incidental that McAuslan was requested to return to Tanzania to lead the drafting of the most progressive of these laws, the Forest Act 2002.

A critical feature of that law deserves mention. Questions arose during the drafting of the land law as to how lands already taken into the custody of governments as 'forest and wildlife protected areas' should be handled. As well as it not being clear that customary rights had been duly extinguished at gazettement of such reserves, it was evident that rights of access and use had only been considered and no compensation paid for their loss, let alone for the loss of lands that were often the most precious forest and rangeland resources of communities (Alden Wily and Dewees 2001). McAuslan and his team took the opportunity to locate the category of reserved land in the land law as less a tenure class than indication that the concerned private, community or national land was subject to preservation in accordance with conservation laws. Wherever customary land rights could be demonstrated within a Local Government of National Reserve, these rights were to be protected or to be fully compensated for if extinguished. The way was also opened up for communities as much as Government to be deemed the owner of a particular forest. The Forest Act is accordingly quiet in relation to who owns forest reserves and deals rather with management responsibilities. Community ownership of a forest of national importance is not precluded, and in accordance with the Land Act, there is provision for transfer of such assets from general to village land (Land Act 1999 s. 5 (3)).

It would be inaccurate to describe the Tanzanian land laws as perfect. Many criticisms take issue with the highly procedural and thus administrative nature of the laws. However, with hindsight it is precisely the entrenchment of detailed procedure that helps curtail wilful misinterpretation of principles or abuse of process, including those by the state. The jury is still out on a number of other issues, such as whether provision for village land registers has been successful, whether the multiple forms that are provided systematise allocations, help or hinder villagers.

As a whole however, the laws have come to be seen as a gold standard on the continent, including the handling of matters beyond the central issue of collective land interests discussed above, such as in the treatment of women's land rights, the interests of the urban poor, and (in contradiction of the Policy) to not only refrain from outlawing nomadism but also to provide pastoralists with mechanisms to share lands over any amount of area as most appropriate to their land-use regimes. It is therefore not surprising that as new land laws gather on the African continent that the terminology and constructions of Tanzania's land laws appear, and in particular with regard to the handling of majority customary property rights.

In this, the contribution of McAuslan and his team may be ranked among the peerless. Grand larceny affecting African tenure has far from ended and, yet, Tanzania's laws lay down instructive ways by which the brakes may be applied and upon a foundation that comes very close to making customary land law, not common or civil law, the basis from which this should proceed. In the process the notion of Africa as *res nullius* is irrevocably damaged.

References

Alden Wily, Liz. 2006. 'Formalizing the informal: Is there a way to secure human potential through land entitlement? A review of changing administration in Africa'. Chapter 15 in B. Guha-khasnobis, R. Kunbur and E. Ostrom (eds) *Linking the Formal And Informal Economy Concepts and Policies.* Oxford: Oxford University Press.

Alden Wily, Liz. 2007. *So who owns the forest? An investigation into forest ownership and customary land tenure in Liberia.* Sustainable Development Institute and FERN, Monrovia and Brussels.

Alden Wily, Liz. 2011a. 'The tragedy of public lands: Understanding the fate of the commons under global commercial pressure international land coalition'. Rome. Available at www.landcoalition.org/publications/tragedy-public-lands-fate-commons-under-global-commercial-pressure. Accessed 12 April 2015.

Alden Wily, Liz. 2011b. 'The law is to blame. Taking a hard look at the vulnerable status of customary land rights in Africa'. *Development and Change* 42(3) May 2011.

Alden Wily, Liz. 2012a. 'Looking back to see forward: The legal niceties of land theft in land rushes'. *The Journal of Peasant Studies* 39(3).

Alden Wily, Liz. 2012b. 'From state to people's law: Assessing learning-by-doing as a basis of new land law'. In Jan Michiel Otto and André Hoekema (eds) *Fair Land Governance: How to Legalise Land Rights for Rural Development*, p. 85–110. Leiden: Leiden University Press.

Alden Wily, Liz. Forthcoming. 'Res Communis: Unfinished Business in Africa'. In Patricia Kameri-Obote and Collins Odote (eds) *Essays in Honour of Professor HWO Okoth-Ogendo: Thoughts on Land Law in Theory and Practice.*

Alden Wily, Liz. and Peter A. Dewees. 2001. 'From users to custodians: Changing relations between people and the state in forest management in Tanzania'. World Bank Policy Research Paper 2569.

Amanor, Kojo Sebastian. 2008. 'Sustainable development, corporate accumulation and community expropriation: Local and natural resources in West Africa'. Chapter 5 in Kojo Sebastian Amanor and Sam Moyo (eds) *Land and Sustainable Development in Africa.* London and New York: ZED Books, pp. 127–157.

Deininger, Klaus, Harris Selod and Anthony Burns. 2012. *The Land Governance Assessment Framework Identifying and Monitoring Good Practice in the Land Sector.* Washington, DC: The World Bank.

Deininger, Klaus and Derek Byerlee. 2011. *Rising Global Interest in Farmland: Can it Yield Sustainable and Equitable Benefits?* Washington, DC: The World Bank.

Dorsett, Shaunnagh. 2002. 'Since Time Immemorial: A story of common law jurisdiction, native title and the case of tanistry'. *Melbourne University Law Review* 3: 1–26.

Government of Tanzania. 1994. 'Report of the Presidential Commission of Inquiry into land matters'. *Volume I. Land Policy and Land Tenure Structure.* The Ministry of Lands, Housing and Urban Development, Government of the United Republic of Tanzania in cooperation with The Scandinavian Institute of African Studies, Uppsala, Sweden.

Government of Tanzania. 1995. *National Land Policy.* Dar es Salaam: Ministry of Lands, Housing and Urban Development.

Government of Tanzania. 2012. *Participatory Forest Management in Tanzania. Facts and Figures.* Dar es Salaam: Ministry of Natural Resources and Tourism.

Gray, Christopher. 2002. *Colonial Rule and Crisis in Equatorial Africa. Southern Gabon ca. 1850–1950.* New York: University of Rochester Press.

Hatcher, Jessica. 2013. 'Tanzania's agricultural revolution: Land grabs or a welcome business boom? Global Development, *The Guardian*, 20 June 2013. www.theguardian.com/global-development/2013/jun/20/tanzania-agriculture-land-grabs-business. Accessed 2 December 2014.

Hall, Ruth, Max Edelman, Saturino Borras, Ian Scoones, Ben White and Wendy Wolford. 2015. 'Resistance, acquiescence or incorporation? An introduction to land grabbing and political reactions "from below"'. *The Journal of Peasant Studies* 42(3–4): 467–488.

Hobsbawm, Eric. 2011 [1962]. *The Age of Revolution 1789–1848.* First published by Weidenfeld & Nicolson Ltd. Abacus 2011.

Huberich C.H. 1947. *The Political and Legislative History of Liberia. Volume II Constitution and the Laws of the Republic 1847–1944.* New York: Central Book Company Inc.

Jayne, T.S., J. Chamberlain and D. Headey. 2014. 'Boserup and beyond: Mounting land pressures and development strategies in Africa'. *Food Policy* 48: 1–17.

Kiisheweko, Orton. 2012. 'Tanzania takes major step towards curbing land "grabs"'. Global Development, *The Guardian*, 21 December 2012. www.theguardian.com/global-development/2012/dec/21/tanzania-major-step-curbing-land-grabs. Accessed 2 December 2014.

Kitabu, Gerald. 2011. 'Experts question land laws in agricultural investments'. *Guardian on Sunday Newspaper.* 16 October 2011. Dar es Salaam. www.ippmedia.com/frontend/functions/print_article.php?l=34440. Accessed 20 August 2013.

Larsson, Rolf. 2001. 'Between crisis and opportunity. Livelihood, diversification, and inequality among the Meru of Tanzania'. Lund Dissertation on Sociology 41, Lund University, Denmark.

Legal and Human Rights Centre. 2010. *Tanzania Human Rights Report 2010.* Dar es Salaam.

Linebaugh, Peter. 2010. 'Enclosures from the bottom up'. *Radical History Review* 105: 11–27.

Maina, Chris P. 2007. 'Rights to communal land ownership'. Chapter 8. Chris P. Maina and Helen Kijo-Bisimba (eds) *Law and justice in Tanzania: Quarter of a century of the Court of Appeal.* Dar es Salaam: Legal and Human Rights Centre and Mkukina Nyota Publishers.

Makoye, Kitzito. 2013. 'Tanzania farmers accuse biofuel investors of land grab'. *Thomson Reuters,* 18 July 2013. www.trust.org/item/20130718134927-q50zx?view=print. Accessed 2 December 2014.

Massay Godrey Elseus and Telemu Kassile. 2014. 'Land-based investments in Tanzania: Legal framework and realities on the ground. The Land Deal Politics Initiative'. The Land Deal Politics Initiative, International Institute of Social Studies, The Hague.

McAuslan, Patrick. 1996. 'Clause by Clause Commentary. A Draft Bill for The Land Act prepared for The Ministry of Lands, Housing and Urban Development', United Republic of Tanzania (on file with the author).

McAuslan, Patrick. 2003. *Bringing the Law Back In: Essays in Land, Law and Development,* Aldershot: Ashgate.

McAuslan, Patrick. 2006a. 'Improving tenure security for the poor in Africa'. Framework paper for the Legal Empowerment Workshop – sub-Saharan Africa. LEP Working Paper No. 1. Food and Agriculture Organization of the United Nations, Rome.

McAuslan, Patrick. 2006b. 'Legal pluralism as a policy option: Is it desirable? Is it doable?' *From knowledge to action.* Esther Mwangi (ed.) Washington, DC: CaPri.

McAuslan, Patrick. 2007. 'Land law and the making of the British Empire'. Elizabeth Cooke (ed.) *Modern Studies in Property Law* 4: 239–262.

McAuslan, Patrick. 2013. *Land Law Reform in Eastern Africa: Traditional or Transformative?: A Critical Review of 50 Years of Land Law Reform in Eastern Africa, 1961–2011.* Aldershot: Ashgate.

Okoth-Ogendo, H.W.O. 2002. 'The tragic African commons: A century of expro - priation, suppression and subversion'. *Land Reform and Agrarian Change in Southern Africa Series,* No. 24, School of Government, University of the Western Cape, Cape Town.

Orozco-Quintero, Alejandra. 2014. 'Case Study Report: Uvinje Village & the Saadani National Park Tanzania'. Ottawa: IDRC/CRDI.

Polanyi, Karl 2001 [1947]. *The Great Transformation: The Political and Economic Origins of Our Time,* 2nd edn. Boston, MA: Beacon Press.

Provost, Claire and Erick Kabendera, 2014. 'Tanzania: Large-scale farming turns small farmers into mere labourers'. Global Development, *The Guardian,* 18 February 2014. www.theguardian.com/global-development/2014/feb/18/tanzania-large-scale-farming-small-farmers-labourers. Accessed 2 December 2014.

Redfern, P. 2011. 'Report exposes dangers of biofuel deals in Tanzania as UK firms go bust'. *The East African Newspaper,* Outlook section, November 7–13, 2011: 33. Nairobi.

Salih, K.O. 1982. 'British policy and the accentuation of inter-ethnic divisions: The case of the Nuba Mountains region of Sudan 1920–1940', *African Affairs* 89(356): 417–436.

Stiglitz, Joseph Eugene. 2001. Foreword to K. Polanyi. 2001 (1947). *The Great Transformation: The Political and Economic Origins of Our Time,* 2nd edn. Foreword by Joseph E. Stiglitz; introduction by Fred Block. Boston, MA: Beacon Press.

The Oakland Institute. 2012. 'Understanding Land Investment Deals in Africa. Tanzanian villagers Pay for Sun Biofuels Investment Disaster'.

Thompson, Edward P. 1991 (1963). *The Making of the English Working Class.* Penguin Books.

White, Ben, Ruth Hall and Wendy Wolford (eds) 2012. 'The new enclosures: Critical perspectives on corporate land deals'. *Journal of Peasant Studies* 39: 3–4.

Wily, Elizabeth. 1988. 'The political economy of African land tenure: A case study from Tanzania' *Development, Issue 2,* School of Development Studies, University of East Anglia.

Cases

US, 1823. *Johnson and Graham's Lessee v. William M'Intosh,* 21 U.S. 543, 1823.

LRC 1995. *Lohay Akonaay and Another v. The Hon. Attorney-General,* High Court of Tanzania at Arusha, Miscellaneous Civil Cause No. 1 of 1993 (Unreported) and Court of Appeal of Tanzania, Civil Appeal No. 31 of 1994, reported in [1995] 2 LRC 399.

Chapter 6

The rise and fall of urban law, 1968–1988

Martin Loughlin

Introduction

This chapter examines the emergence and flourishing of an innovative approach to studies of the way in which law allocates property rights in land and regulates changes in land use and the physical environment. This approach, it will be argued, evolved in a small number of English law schools during the late-1960s and extended its influence through to the 1980s, when it began to fall from favour. The innovation arose essentially from the adoption of a sociologically determined object of inquiry. Rather than taking the relevant legislation as the frame for legal analysis, this approach took the phenomenon of urbanisation to be the critical object of investigation. Such an approach required a fundamental reorientation in the nature and purpose of legal study: if by urbanisation is meant the spatial consequences of the processes of social and economic change, then once this is taken as the object of legal inquiry, the range of questions about the role that law plays in those processes radically alters. The term I use for this reorientation of legal inquiry is 'urban law'. I propose to focus my investigation in this paper on the work of Patrick McAuslan, the undisputed pioneer of this novel approach.

In 1968 McAuslan joined the newly established law school at the University of Warwick as one of its founding members. The founders were agreed that the law school should break with the traditional methods of law teaching that had evolved in England over the previous century and they set about designing a new curriculum. Their objective was to displace the inherited tradition, that of immersion of the student in the common law method by way of intricate case analysis, in favour of the teaching of law as a branch of the social sciences. Their immediate challenge was to devise a curriculum suitable for instructing students in the technicalities of law while, at the same time, exposing them to the role of law in society. This was an ambitious objective, both intellectually and pedagogically. Some subjects – criminal law, constitutional law and even common law subjects such as torts – lend themselves more readily than others to this mode of instruction.[1] None appears, however, to present a greater challenge than the law relating to property and land. This is 'lawyer's law', parts of which are about as arcane as law can get. To McAuslan fell the responsibility of designing the curriculum with respect to property and land.

In this chapter, I will examine and evaluate McAuslan's achievements over the period from 1968 until 1985, the period from the founding of Warwick Law School to the moment 18 years later when he left to take up the chair of public law at the LSE. The contribution he made to legal education through the development of methods of teaching property and land law is an important part of this account. That contribution is, on any count, considerable; he may not have been alone in bringing about a significant adjustment in the orientation of teaching and writing in this field, but it is evident that no British scholar could claim to have played as influential a role in bringing the social and economic aspects of property law to the forefront of the curriculum.

That, however, forms only one of the two main strands of this chapter. The other concerns the contribution McAuslan has made to legal scholarship with respect to this field. In the course of developing innovative approaches to the teaching of property and land law, he was able to establish what became in effect a new sub-field of legal scholarship, that of 'urban law'. This rich and complex field was devoted to a systematic examination of law's impact on the shaping of the processes of urbanisation. Through this exercise in reconceptualization, the traditional categories of law were opened up for examination. The study of urban law entails consideration of the intersected character of, for example, land law, housing and environmental law, common law and statute law, private law and public law, and also an evaluation of the suitability of legal concepts and procedures to realise public objectives with respect to the spatial consequences of social and economic change.

I will argue that with respect to this ambitious scholarly agenda McAuslan achieved only partial success. This objective could be met only by bringing about a fundamental reorientation of the subject and this could be achieved only by developing a robust set of legal methodologies and, ultimately, by propounding a sociologically-orientated theory of law. McAuslan made considerable advances towards realising that goal but was hampered by the deployment of a functionalist legal method linked to certain political assumptions about the nature of social progress. Once the

1 For a selection of early work of Warwick scholars in these fields see: Farrier 1980; Wilson 1966; Atiyah 1971. Farrier's book appeared in a new series starting in the 1970s and edited by McAuslan; and Atiyah's book was published in a new series also established in the 1970s and co-edited by William Twining, Professor of Law at Warwick from 1972–82. Wilson, the editor of the constitutional law casebook, was the founding head of Warwick Law School.

economic and political developments of the 1980s had eroded the basis of these assumptions, his radical agenda for urban law could not be realised.

Curriculum innovation

Students at Warwick Law School were introduced to the law of property and land through two foundational courses: 'Introduction to the Law of Property and Land' in the first-year and a second-year compulsory course, 'Law, Planning and the Use of Land'. Each was designed to provoke questions about the social function of law. Rather than organising the course through the conventional statutory frameworks (respectively, the Law of Property Act 1925 and the Town and Country Planning Acts 1968, 1971) these courses were structured in a way that highlighted contemporary issues of socio-economic importance.

The primary objective of the first-year course was to introduce students to the basic concepts of property law by organising the subject around the workings of housing markets. The period under consideration was one of considerable social change in the field of housing, the main factors of which were: an incremental growth in the rate of owner-occupation financed mainly by building societies that were subject to strict regulation (and often their own strict policies); a growth and then decline in the proportion of council housing (which peaked in the 1970s with municipal ownership exceeding 30 per cent of the UK housing stock and then rapidly declined after the Housing Act 1980); a shift in government policy after 1968 from the clearance of sub-standard housing to that of rehabilitation and improvement of the existing stock through grants and area action policies; a growth in numbers – and social and political prominence – of homelessness; and a major growth in the phenomenon – and certainly social salience – of squatting, not only in response to homelessness as such but also as a movement that sought to highlight inefficiencies and inequities with respect to changes that were taking place in housing markets.

A course organised around such factors obviously remains well-suited to the task of introducing students to such basic concepts of land law as land tenures, including fee simple, tenancies, licences and bare occupancy, as well as such attendant rights as overriding interests (with respect to the family home), covenants and mortgages. By structuring the course in this manner, however, students were also required to reflect on a range of socio-legal issues that traditionally had been felt to lie beyond the remit of the law curriculum. What are the social and political implications of promoting a property-owning democracy? (see e.g. Macpherson 1973). What type of legal entity are building societies, how are they established and regulated, and what impact do their own policies (e.g. of red-lining certain housing areas as being high risk and therefore unsuited for lending) exert over the structure of the housing market? (see e.g. Boddy 1980). To what extent are landlords able to exploit their economic power and use legal techniques for avoiding the security protections provided by the Rent Acts? (see e.g. Partington 1975). What have been the implications of granting local authorities immunity from legal enforcement of their tenancy agreements?[2] How were the legal protections accorded to the fact of possession exploited by squatters' movements, and what have been the responses? (see e.g. Prichard 1981; Bailey 1973). What were the main techniques by which local authorities were able to minimise obligations imposed on them by the homeless persons legislation of 1977? (see e.g. Hoath 1983). By requiring students to engage with questions of this nature, and by giving them access to the relevant socio-economic literature,[3] the aim was to take students beyond the conceptual technicalities of property law and to encourage them to think about the various roles performed by law and lawyers in the construction and regulation of housing markets.

The general approach established in the first-year course was consolidated in the second year by a course on law, planning and the use of land. In certain respects, this second-year course was even more radical in its conception. Previously, a subject like land use planning law had been regarded as a special sub-field of administrative law, and it had been taught in universities mainly as a professionally-orientated foundational subject for non-law students seeking qualification as town planners. At Warwick, by contrast, it formed a core component of the degree programme. This is explained by reference to the method of teaching 'law in society'. One of the characteristic features of modernity has been that of urbanisation. Although only 12 per cent of land in the UK is allocated to urban uses, these urban centres form the hub of economic, commercial, social, cultural and political existence. In that sense, we live in an urban society. The key issue that the Warwick course sought to investigate was the role of law in shaping and regulating the processes of urbanisation.

Again, the period under consideration was one of considerable significance with respect to urban phenomena. During the post-war period the urban landscape of Britain altered dramatically as a result of the promotion of major town centre redevelopment schemes, the carrying out of slum clearance and housing renewal projects, the construction of motorways and other trunk road schemes to deal with the rising levels of car ownership, the facilitation of major infrastructure projects (oil refineries, gas reception terminals, electricity-generating plants) to meet growing energy demand, and later the adoption of a variety of initiatives to address the

2 See e.g. Hoath 1978; and note the tenants' charter reforms introduced by the Housing Act 1980, Pt II.

3 A distinctive feature of the Warwick approach involved the extensive use of photocopied packs of cases and materials containing a wide range of socio-economic as well as legal literature.

phenomenon of de-industrialisation and the so-called 'inner city problem'. Its significance is indicated by a tremendous growth in the volume and range of social scientific inquiry devoted to assessment of the social, economic and political impact of urban change.

The ambition of Warwick's sociological orientation to the teaching of the law of property and land is revealed by the fact that, to an extent greater than any other sector of social change, urbanisation raises questions that cannot adequately be addressed as a matter of social inquiry without having regard to legal concepts, procedures and techniques. Patterns of urbanisation are greatly influenced by the nature, incidence and status of property rights in land. Who owns land? How extensive are the beneficial rights of ownership? To what extent is it felt necessary to regulate these beneficial rights in pursuit of the public good? Who defines – and through what processes – this 'public good'? In what ways might property rights be re-conceptualised in an attempt to internalise the extensive externality effects of certain urban land uses? Given the highly regulated nature of land markets within an urban society, how are the shifts in land values attributable either to public action or public regulation to be equitably addressed? Such are the types of question that are immediately raised once the professionally prescribed framework of the subject is removed and the role of law in these processes of urban change directly addressed.

Even in a purely technical sense, the field is vast. The way in which the various statutory codes of public health, housing, land-use planning and environmental protection have evolved in an intersected fashion since the nineteenth century must first be explained. This in itself is intricate, because each builds on the other, extending its remit from small and discrete parcels of land (insanitary public health conditions in designated housing units), to larger spatial areas (slum clearance through housing powers), to an overall efficient arrangement of land uses (planning schemes across the entire area of a local authority) and finally to an even broader awareness of impact of other environmental media on land use (environmental pollution controls).[4] This type of inquiry also demands an appreciation of the ways in which the private law of land use intersects with public law, involving, for example, some consideration of the way that the common law of nuisance or the drafting of covenants and leases have been used as instruments of land use control.

The regulatory land-use framework must also be supplemented by consideration of the range of positive powers of public authorities available

4 There is also a temporal aspect of the evolution of these codes with the formative period of the public health code being 1848–1875, the housing code 1868–1925, the town planning code 1909–1947, and the environmental pollution code beginning with the Alkali Acts of 1863 but not becoming consolidated until the 1990s.

to promote public infrastructure projects and also to facilitate the realisation of private redevelopment schemes. This not only involves the study of compulsory purchase powers and procedures and of the related compensation schemes, but also an examination of the way in which local authorities use their corporate status to form joint enterprise development companies with private developers or enter into other types of partnership arrangements. And it requires students to look beyond public general legislation to appreciate the way in which the technicalities of private Bill procedures can be used to circumvent the otherwise prohibitive transactional costs of major development schemes.

Over and above all that, this approach to property and land-use law requires students to extend the range of their studies beyond the positive law laid down in statutes and cases to consider the techniques by which flesh is put on these formal legal frameworks by use of secondary legislation, circular advice and policy guidance notes and to appreciate the manner in which the complex mechanisms for the allocation of grant finance from central to local government has a major impact on policy formulation at the local level. This, in short, was the radical agenda McAuslan sketched out when drawing up the Warwick curriculum for teaching the law of property and land.

Teaching-led research

In developing his teaching materials, McAuslan received considerable assistance from the rapidly growing social science literature on the nature of urban change, the factors behind it, and analyses of the winners and losers in the process of urban change. A rich vein of social inquiry was opened up, ranging from empirical investigations of the deployment of these powers in particular schemes for slum clearance, town renewal, conservation, and the establishment of new towns (see e.g. Davies 1972 on Newcastle-on-Tyne; Dennis 1970 on Sunderland; Saunders 1979 on Croydon; Blowers 1980 on Bedfordshire; Schaffer 1970), through more generalised analyses of the worldview of key decision-makers (see e.g. Pahl 1970; Simmie 1974), to studies of the attempt to use statutory mechanisms, such as inquiries, to open up broader policy questions.[5] Helpful though they might be, these social analyses of urban questions merely threw into relief the lack of any critical legal inquiry into the role of law on the operation of these processes. There existed a great void, and Warwick's

5 See e.g. Tyme 1978; Starkie 1982; Wynne 1982; O'Riordan, Kemp, Purdue 1988. It might be noted that the first public local inquiry relating to the siting of a nuclear power station (Bradwell, Essex in 1956) concluded its business within two and a half hours. The Sizewell Inquiry, by contrast, formally opened on 26 July 1982, commenced its hearings on 11 January 1983 and closed on 7 March 1985, after 340 days of hearings taking over two years.

reorganisation of its law curriculum meant it could no longer be ignored. This is the void that McAuslan set out to fill.

He was, of course, not alone. His Warwick colleagues contributed a number of innovative studies on law-in-action, notably Martin Partington's book on *Landlord and Tenant*, Ann Stewart's *Housing Action in an Industrial Suburb*, and Neal Roberts' *The Reform of Planning Law* (Partington, 1975; Stewart 1981; Roberts 1976a). I too made a contribution through a series of studies of aspects of development control (see e.g. Loughlin 1980a, pp. 1–22; 1980b, pp. 171 –192; 1981, pp. 61–97; 1985, pp. 229–248). Academic colleagues from other institutions also began to research previously neglected aspects of legal issues relating to urban questions.[6] And important primary material on law-in-action was generated through the work of such initiatives as the Community Development Projects and law centres that had recently been established and were operating in some of the more deprived parts of urban areas.[7] But McAuslan was undoubtedly in the vanguard. His leading role was exhibited not only through his teaching and writing, but also in his organisation of a series of urban law conferences in the 1970s and 80s bringing together colleagues working on these subjects, his work for the ESRC and Nuffield Foundation setting an agenda for socio-legal investigation of urban issues,[8] his editorship of the newly established book series, *Modern Legal Studies*,[9] and his establishment in the 1970s of a new journal, *Urban Law & Policy*, which provided a showcase for this new type of legal scholarship.[10]

The fruits of this pioneering work were most clearly exhibited in his teaching text, *Land, Law & Planning*, published in the 'Law in Context' series (McAuslan 1975). In this book, constructed from the materials for his Warwick course, McAuslan included excerpts not only from statutes and cases, but also from government policy documents, from plans, inquiry reports, academic commentary, and even newspaper reports. It was given an overall thematic structure by means of interlinking text designed to guide the reader through the issues the materials were raising. As stated in the preface, the objective was to use 'the medium of law to provide materials for an analysis, discussion and criticism of the decision-making

6 See e.g. the work cited above n. 2. Also Prichard 1981; Bailey 1973; Hoath 1983; and Alder 1979.

7 See e.g. Loney 1983; Arden 1977; Arden and Partington 1994. Note also the work of the Legal Action Group, produced through their LAG Bulletins.

8 In 1977 McAuslan produced a report for the (then) Social Science Research Council on the state of socio-legal research on urban planning and in 1983 he served as a member of the Nuffield Foundation's Inquiry into the state of the UK Planning System (chair: Lord Flowers).

9 In addition to Hoath's two books in the series (1978 and 1983), Prichard's (1981), Alder's (1979), there was my own: Loughlin 1986.

10 The journal, which started in 1978, was co-edited by McAuslan together with Otto Hetzel of Wayne State University; it ceased publication in 1988.

process and some of the policies that lie behind and are implemented by that process in land-use planning in England' (McAuslan 1975, Preface, xxvi).

Land, Law & Planning marked a radical break with previous teaching materials on planning law. The standard legal texts on the subject – Heap, *An Outline of Planning Law* and Telling, *Planning Law & Procedure* – were basic black-letter textbooks. They amounted to little more than commentaries on the main legislation and contained no critical analysis or even detailed analysis of the legal ambiguities and complexities of the subject.[11] This is perhaps not surprising, since they were in effect cribs used for the purpose of passing professional examinations.[12]

McAuslan's book rejected the organisational scheme of the statute in favour of a more explicitly sociological approach: how does law shape land use? From this starting point, the range of legal concepts to be taken into account expands considerably. Private law instruments – restrictive covenants, nuisance law, long leasehold schemes – have had a significant, though neglected, influence over the shaping of land use. Beyond the main statutory planning framework, there are many more specialised area designations – national parks, areas of outstanding natural beauty, sites of special scientific interest, conservation areas, clearance areas, general improvement areas, housing action areas etc. – that need to be taken into consideration. So too must other positive powers of public authorities, such as their powers of compulsory acquisition of land for a broad range of purposes and their ability to promote private Acts of Parliament. Once this comprehensive approach is taken to considering the influence of law on land use, it inevitably follows that the types of question that are thrown up for consideration alter. Consequently, rather than taking for granted the benefits of legal processes, students were introduced to decision-making theory, raising a broad range of issues concerning appropriate procedures for plan-making, project approval, inquiries and legal challenge. As McAuslan explained: the 'lawyer who intends to play a part in the planning process is likely to be able to make a useful contribution ... if he or she has had the opportunity, during their education, to think about and discuss what the aims of planning are, how far the process is apt to implement the aims, and what are the ways that the law helps or hinders that process by

11 Heap 1987; Telling 1973. Davies 1978 was similar in style but it did contain more detailed analysis of the case law than the planning law texts.

12 It might be noted that during the early 1980s Malcolm Grant produced a new legal textbook that established new standards of rigor and analysis in the field: Grant 1982. McAuslan characteristically gave it a most positive review in 1984, p. 237: 'There is no question but that this is a quite magnificent book; scholarly, accurate, perceptive, comprehensive and readable. Planning law has come of age as an intellectual discipline and we are all indebted to Malcolm Grant for so surely putting it on the map.'

interposing its own values, assumptions and practices' (McAuslan 1975, Preface, xxvi).

In welcoming the work in review, Neal Roberts pointedly noted the irony of having to compare it with American case books on this subject in order to undertake a proper evaluation of this 'unique' contribution to English planning law scholarship. It is ironic, he explained, because all the key scholars who promoted its post-war development in the USA had invariably turned to the English legislation and procedure for guidance. Roberts also noted the stark contrast between the English and American teaching arrangements. By the 1970s, he commented, 'the number of American law professors interested in, and teaching land use had grown to some 250 and virtually every law school had planning courses and advanced seminars'. Such courses, he added, 'have a marked emphasis on social science (some 25 per cent of coverage) and deal extensively with not only case law but also administrative law and theory' (Roberts 1976b, pp. 608–610). The fact that McAuslan had managed, in such unpropitious circumstances, to publish a volume that stands comparison with the best of these American books, Roberts concluded, stands as testament to the scale of the achievement.

Scholarship in the functionalist style

McAuslan's scholarly agenda should by now be obvious. There is a great deal of talk nowadays about the benefits of 'research-led teaching'. But Warwick's distinctive achievement had been to promote 'teaching-led research'. The reorganisation of these courses around social questions raised challenging issues for students. They also set out an ambitious agenda for research and writing, especially for the teachers.

McAuslan's agenda should first be set in context. Although he broke the mould in reconceptualising the field as the study of urban law, the nature of that achievement can be properly assessed only by placing it within broader twentieth century developments in public law thought. The early decades of the century had been dominated by the controversy over whether the category of administrative law exists within the British system and, if so, how it might be conceptualised. The orthodox position, expounded by Dicey and his disciples, was that the concept was entirely offensive to the common law tradition and that, to the extent that administrative power was growing, it presented a basic threat to the British constitution and ought to be strictly curtailed (see Loughlin 1992, esp. ch. 7). During the interwar period, that orthodox view was directly and systematically confronted by two LSE-based lawyers, William A. Robson and W. Ivor Jennings. Situating themselves within the Fabian socialist orientation of the Webbs, Robson and Jennings developed a distinctive functionalist approach to public law (see Loughlin, 1992; Loughlin 2005, pp. 361–403).

The significance of McAuslan's scholarly agenda for urban law can best be grasped only once situated within the Robson-Jennings approach.

The functionalist approach regards law essentially as a tool of social integration. Distrusting abstract conceptualism, law is treated as a bundle of techniques and procedures to be deployed in the service of the public good. This public good is most obviously determined by the 'sovereign will'; consequently, statute law is recognised as the highest form of law-making. But it is also recognised that, given the complexities of modern society, statute law is able to express this will only in general terms. Statute law is therefore obliged to delegate to administrative officials the powers they need to put flesh on the bare skeleton of the primary legislation; this equips them with the instruments they need efficiently and effectively to realise those public objectives. The growth in the number and type of legal powers assigned to officials for these purposes leads to the emergence of a large body of administrative law.[13] For administrative lawyers like Robson and Jennings, the growth of administrative law was evidently a good thing. This is because in their worldview administrative law is a phenomenon associated with a general theory of modernisation. Its existence reflects a progressive evolution of society from bourgeois capitalism towards the planned society of a socialist commonwealth (Webb and Webb 1975).

Right from the outset, then, the intense political conflict between classical liberalism and evolutionary socialism that shaped British party politics for much of the twentieth century managed to insinuate itself into an ostensibly technical debate over the nature of administrative law. In the mentality of the common law judiciary, rights (especially rights of property) require strict protection, whereas for administrative officials acting under legislative authority they are to be qualified in the public good. The perceived threat to (negative) liberty presented by the growth of administrative power is contrasted with the promotion of (positive) liberty through the exercise of this administrative power. Administrative law was born in circumstances of political controversy, and this legacy has shaped professional understandings ever since (Loughlin 2009, pp. 151–177).

During the interwar period, Robson and Jennings did a great deal to lay the groundwork of the scholarly study of administrative law with their many treatises on such subjects as public health law, housing law, town and country planning law, and local government law. Much of this writing was relatively technical; this is not surprising since they recognised the importance of writing treatises that could explain the legal framework of these new fields in ways that would assist lawyers and officials charged with operational tasks (see e.g. Chapman and Robson 1933; Jennings 1934;

13 Robson 1951, p. 32: 'no modern student of law or political science has today the slightest doubt that there exists in England a vast body of administrative law ... The problem is not to discover it but rather to master its widespread ramifications and reduce it to some kind of order and coherence.'

Jennings 1936). But their political orientation was never far from the surface (see e.g. Robson 1951; Jennings 1933). The election of a Labour government in 1945 did a great deal to establish a consensus over the significance of the welfare state, to quieten the political controversy surrounding the very existence of administrative law, and thereby to permit administrative law slowly to develop alongside the traditional categories of law (Griffith and Street 1952; de Smith 1959).

If recognition had been accorded by the 1960s, this was mainly because the subject had been converted into a technical category that could be taught by the formal methods of statutory interpretation and case analysis. And this was the traditional method of law teaching that the Warwick approach in general was seeking to displace. The way forward was to break with this by now conventional approach to administrative law in favour of a socially-orientated course construction. In place of a course on administrative law that divided according to the formal categorisation of the executive's legislative, adjudicative or discretionary powers and of techniques of judicial supervision, such a course would need to be devised around a social question. In accordance with what policies, and through what powers and procedures, does the state control the migration of persons across its borders? Through what legal forms does the state realise its commitments to provide a platform of benefits and entitlements to citizens according to need? Such newly established courses as Immigration Law or Social Security Law became the means by which administrative law-in-action could be studied. And this was the orientation that explains the emergence of the phenomenon of urban law. How, it was asked, does law work to shape the spatial impact of social, economic and political change?

Urban law scholarship

In both a practical and intellectual sense, Robson and Jennings had during the interwar period laid the foundations of the subject that was to become urban law. The task taken up by McAuslan was to build on that platform. He did so not only by systematising their work of integrating law and policy but also by drawing on recent critical social research to develop a sociologically-informed analysis of urban law. But there is continuity, not least in the general ideological orientation of the line of analysis. In the post-war years, Jennings had moved away from the field to focus primarily on comparative constitutional law and he acted as an adviser on constitution-making across the Commonwealth (Bradley 2004, pp. 716–33, esp. 727–33). Yet Robson's career is of more immediate relevance. In part arising from his wartime experience in government (see e.g. Robson 1941; Robson 1943), Robson had by the 1940s become much more interested in the administrative process and in policy-making and when in 1948 he was elected to a chair at the LSE, it was to the Chair of Public Administration. Robson retained his research interests in the social and political aspects of urbanism, but law was no longer a central feature of those investigations (see e.g. Robson 1972). The challenge for McAuslan was to incorporate Robson's policy insights but retain legal analysis as a central aspect of urban analysis.

The parallels between Robson and McAuslan are striking. In his inaugural lecture in 1948, Robson had adapted Maine's generalisation: while Maine in the nineteenth century had claimed that the movement of progressive societies has been from status to contract, Robson argued that in 'the twentieth century we are moving from contract to public administration' (Robson 1948, p. 3). In 1971, we find precisely the same sentiment being expressed by McAuslan. Noting that planning had emerged in the twentieth century as a function of social complexity, since 'more regulation, control and guidance was needed to maintain social equilibrium', he claimed that: 'Just as equity was needed to outflank the fossilisation of law from the fourteenth century onwards, and statute law was used for the same purpose in respect of equity and common law from the early nineteenth century onwards... so planning is needed to outflank the fossilisation of law, legal attitudes and values in the twentieth century to enable governments to respond to new challenges' (McAuslan 1971, pp. 247–74, at 274). Planning, both scholars were suggesting, is becoming the master science.

But whereas Robson had more or less given up on the legal profession, McAuslan saw the essential task as that of restoring law's status within the modern state. This could be realised only by jurisprudential renewal. Law and planning, he claimed, are engaged in a common task: that of the regulation of society. The challenge was that of promoting the renewal of legal concepts, values and theories so that law and lawyers would become better equipped to perform a central role in the managed/planned state. For McAuslan, this meant reform not only of the legal profession to shift them from their emphasis on private property rights but also a reform of the planning profession to shift them away from the assumption that planning is a technical science which equips them to understand better than ordinary people what constitutes the good in the context of urban change. Only through these twin reforms, he suggested, would lawyers and planners be able to work together to enable government to promote the public good.

During the 1970s, McAuslan wrote eloquent and strident critiques of the deficiencies in the orientation of both professions. In his 1974 article, 'Planning law's contribution to the problems of an urban society', he elaborated on the failures of lawyers to rise to this challenge. Noting that the growth in the volume of planning law in the twentieth century is matched only by the growth in complexity of the social problem with which it is intended to deal, he asks whether the structure and values of planning law has now become 'a positive hindrance' to the objective of realising 'a better urban environment' (McAuslan 1974, pp. 134–152, at 134). The complexity and formality of law are identified as contributing factors but the private property orientation is the key problem.

The planning profession is not exempt from his criticisms. Planning is becoming a much more sophisticated undertaking, extending beyond spatial planning to embrace all fields of policy and administration. Yet every extension in the scope of planning 'gives more support to those planners who have a messianic, almost a megalomaniacal vision of what their role is in society'. Inside too many planners, he complains, 'there is an Albert Speer struggling to get out' (McAuslan 1974, p. 139). McAuslan suggested that by the 1970s, this was leading to a 'crisis of legitimacy' in the planning profession. It had been generated within the profession 'both because of its perceived results and because of the powerlessness that most people feel in the face of the system which ... is still a closed one' (McAuslan 1977, pp. 238–240, at 240). Interventions of this nature invariably end with a clarion call. What is needed, he concludes, 'are lawyers educated to realise that the law has long standing connections with human rights and civil liberties, and that a system of planning founded on those principles might make a better contribution to the solution of urban problems than one founded, as now, on property'.[14]

The final version of the line of argument he had been developing is produced in 1980 in his major work, *The Ideologies of Planning Law*. The book draws on an incredibly broad range of issues, materials and literature to throw up fascinating insights into, and analyses of, the practices of urban planning law. But its thesis can be succinctly stated: planning law 'lacks objectivity and neutrality so that ... the law, its administration and official interpretation ... is itself a major contributory factor to the continuing disarray of planning'. This is the case because, far from being a neutral medium, law is 'based upon and available to implement three distinct and competing philosophies or ideologies which dominate or conflict at different points of the system'. The three are first

> that the law exists and should be used to protect private property and its institutions; ...[s]econdly, the law exists and should be used to advance the public interest; ... [t]hirdly, the law exists and should be used to advance the cause of public participation against both the orthodox public administration approach to the public interest and the common law approach of the overriding importance of private property.
>
> McAuslan, 1980, p. 2

14 McAuslan, 1971, p. 152. See also ibid, p. 240: 'The trumpet then has blown an uncertain sound; it remains to be seen whether the soldiers will now know where to go.'

Having tracked the influence of these ideologies through a wide range of studies, McAuslan concludes that the first two are the dominant ideologies and that, although there are from time to time clashes between them, there is none the less a fundamental community of interest between their proponents. He argues that this 'community of interest is basically a shared understanding that the existing governmental and social structures, the existing balance of property relations... must be maintained and preserved against too swift or radical an attempt to alter it' (McAuslan, 1980, p. 213). The by now familiar critique is again offered: what is needed is a commitment to work, via the creation of new legislation, new institutions, new procedures, towards new decision-making processes which will have as their aim more open government, more searching debates on major policy issues, decisions bringing about positive discrimination in the allocation of resources in favour of deprived persons and groups in the community, and an institutional framework which allows those groups power, subject to appropriate safeguards, to determine their own future (McAuslan, 1980, p. 272).

It is evident that this is primarily a political critique. It expresses a failure of political will, a failure to challenge the existing structure of property relations and entrenched administrative power. In a detailed chapter devoted to the Community Land Act 1975 – the latest (and last) attempt to introduce a collectivist framework of land value recapture – McAuslan explains how 'a reasonably clear principle designed to effect a fundamental change in the planning system has been converted into an immensely complex and confusing piece of legislation' because of the need to co-opt private developers (McAuslan, 1980, p. 119). The 'rise and fall of the principle behind the Community Land Act', he argues, 'is only the latest ... of this ... use of the law to deradicalise, in the name of practicality, a political principle'.[15] Whereas Robson and Jennings had expressed faith that the development of a modern administrative apparatus could be used to overcome the existing structure of property relations and be used to promote the public good, McAuslan expresses a more sceptical conviction. It is not just the lawyers with their entrenched private property interests who need to be overcome; it is also the administration itself that acts as a force to preserve the established order.

Written in the last phases of the Labour government and published within the first year of the newly-elected Conservative regime, the book does not end on an optimistic note: 'For lawyers and others openly to espouse such a democracy in the likely future climate of society and government will take courage and faith', he concludes, and this places 'a heavy burden of responsibility on those lawyers who opt for the challenging

15 McAuslan 1980, p. 142. It might be noted that the entire scheme was repealed by the Conservative government in 1980.

task of making a reality of participatory democracy'. (McAuslan 1980, p. 274).

McAuslan could not have foreseen the scale and nature of the changes to government that would follow from four successive terms of Conservative administration and which resulted in the scale and ambition of the post-war planning system being comprehensively rolled back. But this political reality drastically undermined any chance of his clarion call being answered.

Urban law: The limits of functionalism

By the 1980s it was evident that the ambitious challenges McAuslan had been presenting to lawyers and planners throughout the 1970s had been effectively undercut by political change. This was a development well beyond scholarly control, but the question I want to raise is the extent to which that scholarly ambition was circumscribed by virtue of the functionalist method McAuslan had adopted. Had not the scholarly ambition of developing a sociologically-informed analysis of urban law been undercut by virtue of this being harnessed to a political programme in which law was conceived not as a medium through which the changes in power relations might be charted but as an instrument for realising certain political objectives?

The functionalist method that McAuslan inherited from Robson and Jennings treated law merely as a tool of political will. As it emerged in British public law thought, this functionalist style was linked to a belief in evolutionary progress: the degree of progress was to be measured by a steady and continuous growth in the public sector. The public law challenge was essentially that of establishing the appropriate guidance, control and evaluation mechanisms that would enable public bodies effectively and equitably to realise the public good. McAuslan's 1970s critique seemed to boil down to the claim that lawyers and planners had not adequately responded to this challenge. But his critique contained little that might question the idea that law was primarily a tool of political will. When the Thatcher regime began to deploy legal instruments for the purpose of rolling back the public sector and prioritising market mechanisms, the limitations of functionalism in public law were exposed.

Initially, it seemed that McAuslan would use this critical political moment to deepen the theoretical basis of urban law. In his Chorley Lecture of 1982, there are elements of the familiar critique. He thus argues that as a result of their focus on institutional forms, administrative lawyers have paid insufficient attention to the general structures and processes of the welfare state and this has left them 'ill-equipped to deal with, or make sense of, the major clashes of policy and ideology taking place within our system of administrative law' (McAuslan 1983, pp. 1–20, at 2). But this critique is followed by an ambitious attempt to reconstruct the field on the basis of a sociological category. McAuslan argues that the development of administrative law can best be understood from the perspective of social science by reference to the concept of 'collective consumption'. This concept, which had been developed mainly by the neo-Marxist sociologist Manuel Castells, refers to those services and facilities which, given the nature and scale of their tasks, have to be organised, planned and delivered on a public (ie collective) basis (see e.g. Castells 1977; Saunders 1981; Pickvance 1976). These services include the provision of housing, health, education, transport, environmental, cultural and social welfares services and in advanced societies it is evident that these services can be effectively provided only by developing sophisticated planning systems. The concept of collective consumption readily maps onto the broad concept of planning that McAuslan had promoted during the 1970s. Since access to, and planning the provision of, such services is determined according to factors that are other than market-based, the concept also covers a broad range of topics falling under the head of administrative law. But most importantly, it offers a sociologically-generated conceptual foundation for the idea of urban law that McAuslan had been advocating since the late-1960s. Does this concept provide the basis for developing a coherent account of urban law?

In his lecture, McAuslan notes that although these processes of collective consumption have 'expanded enormously' in the post-war period, this growth has been 'largely unaccompanied by any general legal perception of the new kind of administrative state coming into being' (McAuslan 1983, p. 3). Instead, the attention of lawyers 'was directed towards the issues of fair hearings for individuals in court-like proceedings, and away from the issues of policy formulation, the allocation of resources and collective decision-making within the processes of collective consumption' (McAuslan 1983, p. 3). The point being made is that administrative law has developed with respect to the protection of the individual against the bureaucracy but hardly at all with respect to the shaping of policy formulation and implementation. And this meant that once these administrative programmes were cut or radically altered, there existed few legal resources that could be called upon to provide guidance or protection mechanisms.

From the late 1970s this is precisely what happened. Public expenditure cutbacks were especially severe in these areas of 'collective consumption', areas in which needs were growing but resources were declining. After 1979, central controls were strengthened for the purpose of privatising public services so far as it seemed possible and setting up surrogate market mechanisms when it was not. Each of these policies had a profound impact on the field of collective consumption. The restructuring of this field caused a breakdown in authority of many of the informal administrative arrangements through which public services had been delivered and the resulting conflicts were transformed into legal disputes. Resort is being made to the courts, noted McAuslan, 'to fight out there disputes which are very different from the traditional fare of the courts' (McAuslan 1983, p. 8). But, he elaborated, 'the courts have been unable or unwilling to handle them satisfactorily because of their over-insistence in individualising issues, and thus misunderstanding the policy conflicts involved in the cases'. Policy conflicts were reduced to disputes between individual rights and the bureaucracy and since this is 'in tune with the ideology of the present government', it simply lends appearance to the view that 'judicial policy is marching alongside government policy at a time when that policy is a matter of acute political controversy' (McAuslan 1983, p. 8). This development caused McAuslan to comment, rather tartly, that 'the only coherent jurisprudence of administrative law that has emerged during the period when the processes and the law have both been evolving is basically antipathetic to collective consumption' (McAuslan 1983, p. 19).

This might have been the moment when McAuslan moved from critical activism to critical scholarship. The germs were there in his use of the concept of collective consumption since this concept, especially by drawing a fundamental distinction between production and consumption, could readily form the basis of a general critique about the restructuring of the state. The privatisation programme, it might be noted, focused on production functions (gas, electricity, telecoms, rail, local public transport etc.) and its overall objective was entirely to remove entrepreneurial activities from the public sector. Contrary to Fabian socialist assumptions, government was no longer to be conceived as an institution that might control and direct economic activity. As a result, the public sector was left mainly with responsibility for 'consumption' services – health, education, welfare and social security – that were costly to deliver and generated no significant revenue. With respect to these services, the policy has been, so far as practicable, to eliminate the collective dimension of these services (by eliminating cross-subsidisation, recouping from the user the costs of many public services, using competitive bidding techniques for agency funding etc.). But rather than using this moment of the 'fiscal crisis of the state' to develop a critical theory of the crisis in urban law, McAuslan's lecture ends with the familiar call-to-arms: 'the time is ripe for a relook, a rethink and a rewrite on the evolution of our modern system of administrative law and its relationship to the state, policy-making and resource allocation within the state including policy-making by the judges' (McAuslan 1983, p. 20).

The end of the road for this comprehensive concept of urban law is most clearly marked by his inaugural lecture, 'Public Law and Public Choice', given after taking up the public law chair at LSE in 1986. McAuslan recognised that public choice analysis had become the primary instrument of justification of the Thatcherite governmental programme. But there is no explicit acknowledgement that public choice theory is the economic and individualistic alternative to – indeed, nemesis of– the sociological concept of collective consumption. And rather than taking further a critical theory of urban law, McAuslan instead engages in a defensive retreat and seeks to rally a consensus around received ideas of democracy, the public interest and the welfare state (McAuslan 1988, pp. 681–705).

He thus seeks to defend an idea of 'the public interest' as something that 'exists over and above the politicians and public servants who manage the welfare state' and claims that it is for the purpose of advancing the public interest that 'we have constructed an enormous administrative superstructure in which lawyers have played an important role: we have argued for public participation and constructed systems of public participation in the planning and housing fields; we have established, through the mechanism of judicial review, a considerable extension of natural justice to embrace, e.g. legitimate expectations of consultation for Trade Unions, environmental pressure groups, local authorities' (McAuslan 1988, p. 688). McAuslan continues: 'What a contrast there is between that approach to government and that of the public "choicists". For them there is no such concept or ideal "out there" as "public interest"' (McAuslan 1988, p. 688).

Indeed. But what a contrast there is also between McAuslan the critic of the ideology of public interest and of the actual achievements of judicial review. Here instead we have the claim that for what he calls 'the old-fashioned democrat', 'the evolution of the planning system in the 20–25 years from 1958 ... was in some respects a model of how government ought to be carried on' (McAuslan 1988, p. 691). And here also he notes how public lawyers 'have praised the onward march of judicial review since *Ridge v. Baldwin* was decided 25 years ago; we consider that government is now more under law than it was' (McAuslan 1988, p. 693). The tide had turned. There was no hope of delivering a radical programme organised around the theme of public participation. The best chance, in the face of privatisation in all its dimensions, was to rally around the cause of the public interest in retaining public goods.

This was a retreat to old-style functionalism, in which faith was to be placed in administrative methods and a professional ethic for delivering the public interest. But had not his strident critique of the 1970s – indicating that the structure of planning law had become a 'positive hindrance' to the realisation of a better urban environment and that the planning profession faced a 'crisis of legitimacy' – actually provided the grounding on which public choice analysis could do its work?

Conclusion

Although told through the development of the work of a single scholar, this is in reality the story of a movement. The story concerns the concerted attempt since the 1960s to rejuvenate the teaching of English law in the universities and, through this innovation in teaching, to map out an agenda about what legal scholarship might become. The Warwick project of teaching law in its social context expressed a general orientation rather than a fixed intellectual programme and within it many distinctions could be drawn between idealists and realists, analysts and activists, social democrats and neo-Marxists. I have tried to show how, with respect to the law of property and land, the pioneering work was undertaken primarily by Patrick McAuslan. McAuslan mapped out an approach to teaching and scholarship of considerable ambition, organised around the theme of urbanisation. That this ambition was not fully realised is scarcely the responsibility of any single individual. What I have tried to do in this paper is to highlight McAuslan's singular achievements in re-orientating approaches to teaching and scholarship. But I have also used the benefit of hindsight to indicate its limitations. What should be emphasised with respect to this latter aspect of the inquiry is that the main reason his agenda for urban law could not be realised was because the structural economic and political changes taking place in the 1970s and 1980s undercut many of the assumptions on which his approach was founded. His agenda for urban law had a collectivist underpinning that has seemed increasingly marginal to the socio-political realities of the last 20 and more years.

This structural factor also explains why the comprehensive approach to the teaching of urban law that he pioneered achieved only partial success. While the teaching of property, housing, land use and environment law was considerably reorientated under the influence of his approach, the overarching (collectivist) planning dimension was lost. If there were an organising factor of the field, then from 1990s this became environment rather than urbanisation. This involved the replacement of the local with the global, the experiential with the abstract, the sociological orientation with the moral-philosophical, and perhaps even the good with the right. Sustainability has replaced participation as the clarion call.

McAuslan's scholarly agenda was subject to similar constraints. His functionalist method treated law merely as a tool to promote certain social objectives. This instrumental method formed part of a more general theory of law that regarded positive law as a vehicle for promoting what Duguit called the 'jural principle'. This jural principle is the principle of social solidarity: 'Do nothing which can possibly infringe upon social interdependence ... [and] do all that is within your power, within your given situation and within your aptitudes, to insure and increase social interdependence' (Duguit 1917, pp. 1–185, 178. See also Duguit 1921). Explicitly advocated by Duguit in his remarkable studies of the early twentieth century, it was implicitly followed by the British functionalist public lawyers and it also underpins McAuslan's scholarly conception of urban law. Consequently, once the social conditions that sustained this theory were eroded during the 1980s, he was obliged to move from his critique of the public interest conception (which was aimed at producing a more authentic conception of the public interest) to a defence of that conception. Ultimately this seemed unrealistic.

It was perhaps because of a growing realisation of future possibilities that during the 1980s McAuslan adjusted the focus of his interests. Always the practical reformer rather than an armchair scholar, from the late 1980s Patrick McAuslan determined to devote his considerable energies to the promotion of the reform of land and planning law abroad, and especially in post-colonial regimes. The period 1968 to 1988 might therefore be characterized as one of the rise and fall of a scholarly project to promote an integrated and collectivistically-orientated urban law. But this is in no way to belittle the ambition and signal achievements of McAuslan's pioneering venture.

References

Alder, John E. 1979. *Development Control.* London: Sweet & Maxwell, Modern Legal Studies Series.

Arden, Andrew. 1977. *Manual of Housing Law.* London: Sweet & Maxwell.

Arden, Andrew and Martin Partington. 1994. *Quiet Enjoyment: A Guide to Remedies for Harassment and Illegal Eviction,* 4th edn. London: Legal Action Group.

Atiyah, P.S. 1971. *Accidents, Compensation and the Law.* London: Weidenfeld & Nicolson, Law in Context Series.

Bailey, Ron. 1973. *The Squatters.* London: Penguin.

Blowers, Andrew. 1980. *Something in the Air: The Politics of Local Planning Policy.* Oxford: Pergamon.

Boddy, Martin. 1980. *The Building Societies.* London: Macmillan.

Bradley, Anthony W. 2004. Sir William Ivor Jennings: A centennial paper. *Modern Law Review* 67: 716–33.

Castells, Manuel. 1977. *The Urban Question.* London: Arnold.

Chapman, Harry and William A. Robson. 1933. *Town and Regional Development: A Guide to the Town and Country Planning Act, 1932.* London: Dent.

Davies, Jon Gower. 1972. *The Evangelistic Bureaucrat.* London: Tavistock.

Davies, Keith. 1978. *The Law of Compulsory Purchase and Compensation,* 3rd edn. London: Butterworth.

Dennis, Norman. 1970. *People and Planning: The sociology of Housing in Sunderland.* London: Faber.

de Smith, S.A. 1959. *Judicial Review of Administrative Action.* London: Stevens.

Duguit, Léon. 1917. The law and the state. *Harvard Law Review* 31: 1–185.

Duguit, Léon. 1921. *Law in the Modern State.* Frida and Harold Laski, trans. London: Allen & Unwin.

Farrier, David. 1980. *Drugs and Intoxication.* London: Sweet & Maxwell, Modern Legal Studies Series.

Grant, Malcolm. 1982. *Urban Planning Law.* London: Sweet & Maxwell.

Griffith, J.A.G. and Harry Street. 1952. *Principles of Administrative Law.* London: Pitmans.

Heap, Desmond. 1987. *An Outline of Planning Law*, 9th edn. London: Sweet & Maxwell.
Hoath, David C. 1978. *Council Housing*. London: Sweet & Maxwell, Modern Legal Studies Series.
Hoath, David C. 1983. *Homelessness*. London: Sweet & Maxwell, Modern Legal Studies Series.
Jennings, W. Ivor. 1933. *The law and the Constitution*. University of London Press.
Jennings, W. Ivor. 1934. *The Law Relating to Local Authorities*. London: Knight.
Jennings, W. Ivor. 1936. *The Law of Public Health*. London: Knight.
Loney, Martin. 1983. *Community Against Government: the British Community Development Project, 1968–78, a Study of Government Incompetence*. London: Heinemann.
Loughlin, Martin. 1980a. Planning control and the property market. *Urban Law and Policy* 3: 1–22.
Loughlin, Martin. 1980b. The scope and importance of 'material considerations'. *Urban Law and Policy* 3: 171–192.
Loughlin, Martin. 1981. Planning gain: law, policy and practice. *Oxford Journal of Legal Studies* 1: 61–97.
Loughlin, Martin. 1985. 'Apportioning the infrastructure costs of urban land development'. In Susan Barrett and Patsy Healey (eds) *Land Policy: Problems and Alternatives*. Aldershot: Gower, pp. 229–248.
Loughlin, Martin. 1986. *Local Government in the Modern State*. London: Sweet & Maxwell, Modern Legal Studies Series.
Loughlin, Martin. 1992. *Public Law and Political Theory*. Oxford: Clarendon Press.
Loughlin, Martin. 2005. The functionalist style in public law. *University of Toronto Law Journal* 55: 361–403.
Loughlin, Martin. 2009. 'Why the history of English administrative law is not written'. In David Dyzenhaus, Grant Huscroft and Murray Hunt (eds) *A Simple Common Lawyer: Essays in Honour of Michael Taggart*. Oxford: Hart.
Macpherson, C.B. 1973. *Democratic Theory: Essays in Retrieval*. Oxford: Clarendon Press.
McAuslan, Patrick. 1975. *Land, Law and Planning*. Weidenfeld and Nicolson.
McAuslan, Patrick. 1980. *The Ideologies of Planning Law*. Oxford: Pergamon Press.
McAuslan, Patrick. 1983. Administrative law, collective consumption and judicial policy. *Modern Law Review* 46: 1–20.
McAuslan, Patrick. 1984. Book review: Urban-planning law – Grant, M. *Town Planning Review* 55(2): 237.
McAuslan, Patrick. 1988. Public law and public choice. *Modern Law Review* 51: 681–705.
McAuslan, J.P.W.B. 1971. The plan, the planners and the lawyers. *Public Law* 247–74.
McAuslan, J.P.W.B. 1974. Planning law's contribution to the problems of an urban society. *Modern Law Review* 37: 134–152.
McAuslan, J.P.W.B. 1977. Planning and the Future: A Review Symposium. *Town Planning Review* 48: 238–240.
O'Riordan, Timothy, Ray Kemp, and Michael Purdue. 1988. *Sizewell B: Anatomy of an Inquiry*. London: Macmillan.
Pahl, Ray. 1970. *Whose City? And Other Essays on Sociology and Planning*. London: Longman.

Partington, Martin. 1975. *Landlord and Tenant: Cases, Materials, and Text.* London: Weidenfeld & Nicolson, Law in Context Series.

Pickvance, C.J. (ed.) 1976. *Urban Sociology: Critical Essays.* London: Tavistock.

Prichard, A.M. 1981. *Squatting.* London: Sweet & Maxwell, Modern Legal Studies Series.

Roberts, Neal A. 1976a. *The Reform of Planning Law: A Study of the Legal, Political And Administrative Reform of the British Land-use Planning System.* London: Macmillan.

Roberts, Neal A. 1976b. Review of McAuslan's 'Land, Law and Planning', *Modern Law Review* 39: 608–610.

Robson, William A. 1941. *The War and the Planning Outlook.* London: Faber and Faber.

Robson, William A. 1943. *Planning and Performance.* J.M. Dent.

Robson, William A. 1948. *Public Administration Today.* London: Stevens and Stevens.

Robson, William A. 1951 [1928]. *Justice and Administrative Law,* 3rd edn. London: Stevens.

Robson, William A. (ed.) 1972 [1954]. *Great Cities of the World: Their Government, Politics and Planning,* 3rd edn with D.E. Regan. London: Allen and Unwin.

Saunders, Peter. 1979. *Urban Politics: A Sociological Interpretation.* London: Hutchinson.

Saunders, Peter. 1981. *Social Theory and the Urban Question.* London: Hutchinson.

Schaffer, Frank. 1970. *The New Town Story.* London: MacGibbon & Kee.

Simmie, James. 1974. *Citizens in Conflict: The Sociology of Town Planning.* London: Hutchinson.

Starkie, David Nicolas Martin. 1982. *The Motorway Age: Road Traffic Policies in Postwar Britain.* Oxford: Pergamon Press.

Stewart, Ann. 1981. *Housing Action in an Industrial Suburb.* London: Academic Press.

Telling, A.E. 1973. *Planning Law and Procedure,* 4th edn. London: Butterworth.

Tyme, John. 1978. *Motorways Versus Democracy: Public Inquiries into Road Proposals snd their Political Significance.* London: Macmillan.

Webb, Sidney and Beatrice Webb. 1975 [1920]. *A Constitution for the Socialist Commonwealth of Great Britain.* Cambridge: Cambridge University Press.

Wilson, Geoffrey. 1976 [1966]. *Cases and Materials on Constitutional and Administrative Law,* 2nd edn 1976. Cambridge: Cambridge University Press.

Wynne, Brian. 1982. *Rationality and Ritual: The Windscale Inquiry and Nuclear Decisions in Britain.* London: British Society for the History of Science.

Chapter 7

Comparative and international urban land law and policy

A celebration of the work of Professor Patrick McAuslan

Leslie A. Stein

The ideologies of Patrick McAuslan

The profound influence that Patrick McAuslan's work has had on the development of planning and land law internationally arises from his particular orientation to the law as well as his personal sensibilities. In true McAuslan spirit, I seek the ideologies behind this orientation. What principles guide him? In what manner does he address the complex issues? The ideologies are not hard to find. He perceives legal rules in relation to property as concealing underlying, value-laden ideologies that are ever present and exist always in conflict with each other. He maintains two conflicting sets of ideologies: one for planning law and one for land law. For planning law, on the one side are values relating to private property as an essential, axiomatic aspect of society, and on the other the need for sublimation of these values by the public interest dimension carried out by government. In terms of land law, on the one side is land tenure as a basic human right and on the other the encroachment from the demands of a market economy.

Loughlin states that McAuslan's work is part of the 'functionalist' style of legal philosophy (2005, p. 361) that indicates that his focus is not on the evolution of legal doctrine but rather on the aims and objectives of laws and therefore he 'adopts an instrumentalist social policy approach' (Loughlin 1992, p. 62). Loughlin indicates that starting from the 1970s, McAuslan adopted 'a more radical and empiricist tone' that appeared in McAuslan's *Ideologies of Planning Law* where: 'his tone is more strident and perhaps less hopeful' (ibid. p. 217). If he saw it as less hopeful, he certainly did not see it as hopeless, as he has maintained this point of view steadfastly for the 50 years that are being celebrated.

What is apparent in a review of his work for this chapter is that McAuslan has not waivered in his insistence that planning and property laws are to be evaluated in terms of the conflicting sets of ideologies upon which they are founded. His ideologies do not jump off the page when reading statutes and regulations or the decisions of courts. They are instead those that are unexpressed and are of a different class than the sentiments expressed in policies or the reasons given for the passage of laws or, in fact, even stated legislative or judicial philosophies (as explained in the Preface to McAuslan, 1980). They can be said, if a definition is possible, to be those formative ideas or unconscious motivations that are left out of the debate but yet are the underlying bases for what is written; they are the archetypes of the rules and policies. An example is the bias towards a market economy, never expressed, but yet the obvious basis for formulation of laws that support development over private property rights.

Whenever he examines a subject matter in his writings, McAuslan consistently identifies ideologies. As an instance, in an unpublished paper he states: 'One thing the Brookings analysis leaves out however is the ideology behind the international community's increasing involvement in post-conflict land administration' (McAuslan 2010b). It is not difficult to find evidence of his search for underlying ideologies; it is explicit. In a 1974 article concerned with planning law in the *Modern Law Review* (McAuslan 1974, p. 134), he was prescient as to the problems facing planning and land in urban society: a constant increase in discretion, the resort to formal procedures in the decision-making process, the complexity of the law in this area and, most importantly, an overemphasis on private property rights. The latter, in 1974, was perhaps the first specific introduction of his perspective in relation to this core ideology. He explained it more specifically in his work on *The Ideologies of Planning Law*: 'it was, almost by definition, the property owners who used the courts and it was in the resolution of their disputes that the common law was formed. So the whole climate and ideology of the law stressed private property, its uses and transactions' (preface to McAuslan 1980, p. 3).

These two simple sentences changed the emphasis as to how planning law is understood so that it could no longer be envisaged as merely a set of statutory controls but instead must be perceived as an ideological struggle between individual claims to private rights and government control of the use of land in the public interest. It was as if the planning community and local government woke from a deep slumber. He then added the additional subtlety, the effect of which was not apparent at that time, that the failure of slum clearance efforts in that period was an inability to allow a human rights orientation to land tenure that might override property interests.

These ideologies created a subtle foreground/background shift in planning and property law so that the socio-legal stratum was the basis and not the result of law. This thinking may now seem to be commonplace in jurisprudence, but there was no writing of this kind in the 1970s about planning and property other than that of McAuslan. In fact, it is argued that ideological analysis generally was dormant in law and economics until its use in this period and McAuslan's book, *Land Law and Planning* is in fact cited as a prime example of its development (Brietzke 1991, pp. 346–347, note 3).

To others at this time, planning law was a regulatory subject concerned with development control, housing standards, compensation issues, and appeals. For this reason, his ideas and ideologies perhaps did not receive immediate acceptance. When McAuslan's work was referenced at that time, it was in the context of the possibility of reform or as interesting ideas.[1] However, due to his industriousness and perhaps sheer force of personality, his approach has now echoed around the world and has become implanted in planning and property regimes. He has been relentless in his insistence of uncovering ideologies and it is reflected in all the work he has done. As just one example, he expresses it in a report he prepared for Syria (2008a):

> These laws however do not exist and are not applied in a vacuum of policy, or of economics or social and historical development. So there is a need to try and set the scene and explain the author's understanding of the socioeconomic context in which urban planning operates in Syria and the wider socioeconomic and legal context in which urban planning and local government generally is developing in the world at large.

His approach has consistently been to look behind the legal regulatory framework and search for these illusive ideologies, examine them in the wider context of the social setting, and to suggest laws that reflect human rights dimensions that override other interests. This is not a common orientation for a lawyer and is especially rare for planning and property law in the United Kingdom and the Commonwealth where the evaluation of planning ideology has been left to planners[2] and not lawyers, and land law is seen as an immovable registration system (see, for instance, Paisley 2004–2005, p. 267). It is recognized in the literature that it is McAuslan that introduced this orientation to planning and property law;[3] he is the source of this commentary that became explicitly or implicitly a part of the subsequent debate on land use and land law.[4]

I can only speak from my own experience as the means by which his views seeped into legal thinking, as such a subtle process in never obvious. My casebook *Urban Legal Problems* in 1974 (Stein 1974) was influenced by

1 As in Ryden, 1999, p. 197 or a review of his case book, *Land, Law and Planning* (1975) in Humphreys, 1976, p. 289.

2 Examples of the main work in this area: Tett and Wolfe 1995, p. 195; Healey 1997; Peel and Lloyd, 2007, p. 396.

3 It is acknowledged that he introduced these concepts: Cowell and Owens 2011, p. 24. See also: Loughlin, 1986, p. 31.

4 See Grove-White 1991, p. 32. Caldwell and Shrader-Frechette 1993 reflects similar dimensions of policy.

early work of McAuslan and Yash Ghai on Kenya (Ghai and McAuslan 1970) where it appeared to me that for the first time there was an ideological analysis of the application of land law. They expressed that, up until their work, legal scholarship was a recital of the rules: cases, statutes, and legal texts. It was extremely novel in 1970 that they examined the law in the context of political power and this was contrary, it has been pointed out (Greenberg 1993, p. 65), to the phenomenon of the 1960s where lawyers were trained to see the law as static and explicable only in terms of an exposition of what was extant. I can say that intimations of this view were perhaps apparent in his earlier book *Aspects of Land Law in Kenya and Tanzania* (1966), but were only incipient at that stage.

McAuslan's influence on my book *Principles of Planning Law* (Stein 2008) is more profound than merely an adoption of his philosophical orientation in that it enabled me to view the entirety of the subject matter, planning law, as other than a series of interconnected statutes, regulations, and cases having some neutral balance of interests. I started and finished the book by regarding planning law as a profound struggle between notions of private property and public interest demands. This is the centerpiece of McAuslan's writing on planning and there is no other model that is similar. Accordingly, I was able to understand that the law revolves around the unarticulated ideologies, perhaps the unconscious motivations and biases that lead to law rather than attempt to find the ideologies by looking at what the law and policy makers say. Thus, the approach to planning law that I adopted was that each case and doctrine, each principle and idea of reform, are all along an axis between the two poles. For that reason, I asked McAuslan to write the *Foreword* to the book, which he generously accepted.

The ideologies he suggested in *Ideologies of Planning Law* also include the public's right to participation and led him to the view that there should be more open government, greater debates about policy underlying planning decisions, and also a recognition of the rights of deprived persons in the community to offer them a voice so that their concerns override the loss of civil liberties required by legal structures. In 1980, this claim of participatory democracy in planning was a harbinger of the so-called 'critical' public law analysis.[5] His work has been continually referenced as a basis for increased calls for participation in planning when that notion is discussed (as in Simpson 1997, p. 907; Gertel and Law-Yone 1991, p. 173; Lloyd 2006) and for 'legitimacy, accountability, equity, transparency, and efficiency leading to certainty and predictability of tenure' (Daryono 2010, p. 419, referencing McAuslan 1997b, p. 34). It can be said that he has quietly cemented these ideas in his writings on planning and local government[6] so that they eventually entered the mainstream.

5 Perhaps best explained by Allan Hutchinson in: Hutchinson 1990, p. 374.

6 As in 'Local Government and Planning Legislation' in McAuslan, Bayless, Cresswell and Mustow 1986, section 3.1.

Perhaps his ideologies have also influenced the critical thinking in respect of climate change issues such as the public participation in schemes that reduce emissions and more relevantly, the complex property issues surrounding future sea-level rise.[7] Although this was not an apparent issue in the 1980s when McAuslan formulated these ideologies and I doubt if he would take credit for his influence, as will be discussed, climate change issues have been absorbed in planning and property law as can be seen by the introduction of the *Planning Policy Statement: Planning and Climate Change (Supplement to Planning Policy Statement 1)* now part of the National Planning Policy Framework. In any event, it is McAuslan's philosophical, value-driven orientation that perceives that the law is a means to implement a wider agenda that is primarily humanitarian and compassionate. To refine an understanding of the influence of his work on planning and land law, it is important to tease out his philosophy, his values, and his humanitarian objectives.

McAuslan's ideologies in relation to land

An analysis of the ideologies in relation to planning law is incomplete without an exploration of his ideologies in relation to land, as land is the subject matter of planning. In English law, the system of registration of title and priorities is so well established that there are no *apparent* conflicts or ideologies to be balanced. The conflict of ideologies between land tenure and market forces are, however, present in systems of land law where there are different forms of land tenure. His ideologies in relation to land law are founded primarily in his work in Africa and other developing countries. His experience ranges over 30 developing countries all with different nuances in respect of security of tenure and political realities. It brings to mind the South African legend called the *Lost Message* (Honey 1910, p. 8):

> The ant has had from time immemorial many enemies. ... Not only were most of the birds their enemies, but Anteater lived almost wholly from them, and Centipede beset them every time and at all places when he had the chance.
>
> So now there were a few among them who thought it would be well to hold council together and see if they could not come to some arrangement whereby they could retreat to some place of safety when attacked by robber birds and animals. But at the gathering their opinions were most discordant, and they could come to no decision.

7 This cross-over of McAuslan's work to climate change issues was foreshadowed in the commentary: Miller, 2001, p. 1899. Some of the legal issues relating to climate change and planning law are summarised in: Cote, 2010.

> There was Red-ant, Rice-ant, Black-ant, Wagtail-ant, Gray-ant, Shining-ant, and many other varieties. The discussion was a true babel of diversity, which continued for a long time and came to nothing.
>
> A part desired that they should all go into a small hole in the ground, and live there; another part wanted to have a large and strong dwelling built on the ground, where nobody could enter but an ant; still another wanted to dwell in trees, so as to get rid of Anteater, forgetting entirely that there they would be the prey of birds; another part seemed inclined to have wings and fly.
>
> And, as has already been said, this deliberation amounted to nothing, and each party resolved to go to work in its own way, and on its own responsibility.
>
> Greater unity than that which existed in each separate faction could be seen nowhere in the world; each had his appointed task, each did his work regularly and well. And all worked together in the same way. From among them they chose a king – that is to say some of the groups did – and they divided the labor so that all went as smoothly as it possibly could. But each group did it in its own way, and not one of them thought of protecting themselves against the onslaught of birds or Anteater.

So it is with land tenure, land rights, and human rights in Africa and other developing countries. These fundamental aspects of society are treated differently throughout the developing world and there was no 'King' before McAuslan that attempted to explain why the differences arise and what is necessary for a synthesis. He has, as a consequence, discovered the secret of unity for land tenure systems: pluralism.

The best explanation of the need for pluralism is his analysis in *Bringing the Law Back In* (McAuslan 2003, p. 6) that the existence of diverse land law systems arises because the concept of land is multidimensional (economic, social, political) and, in addition, following the work of Milton Santos, has two *non-complimentary* 'circuits'. The upper circuit is the official land market regulated by law and the lower circuit consists of the customary land tenure arrangements and the activities of unofficial markets. The two do not fit together naturally and it is McAuslan's analysis that suggests how they both can operate and form a pluralistic arrangement.

McAuslan finds the means to synthesize both circuits because he is equally at home with the familiar laws of land registration, land tenure and regulation, a circuit on which we as lawyers are accustomed to travel, but also is at home with the unfamiliar, idiosyncratic circuit of customary law that, for him, is the more important indicator of the actual intertwining of the relationship of an individual to society and each other. McAuslan's writings operate on the two circuits together, thus allowing him a horizontal view across systems. In fact, he has indicated that this view makes pluralism essential:

> Customary tenure is – and always has been – one of the foundational elements of the land laws of all states in Africa. It is not an add-on to received law; indeed, received or imposed law is the add-on. Received law thus needs to be adapted and adjusted to indigenous law, not vice versa, and proponents of received law should be advancing the case for legal pluralism.
>
> McAuslan 2006

One can speculate as to how he derived his interest in balancing customary arrangements as to land with state regulation. In 1961, after completing the Bar exam, he went to his first teaching job as a lecturer at Dar es Salaam at the time when the law school was being established. In a paper delivered at a conference on land development at Cornell, (McAuslan 2004), he explained that in Africa in the early 1960s, law schools were modelled on the British system but also had the lofty goal of being relevant to the local population. McAuslan credits the influence of Wolfgang Friedman for creating this sentiment. Friedman wrote in the early 1960s that the role of the lawyer in developing countries was specifically to understand the local situation and thus customary law (McAuslan references Friedman 1963, p. 181). McAuslan states that this was the beginning of his long quest for reconciliation of customary and traditional legal concepts:

> The two contrasting approaches to land tenure reform and the use of the law to provide the foundations of it in the 1960s –the one, state control and the nationalisation or repatriation of land rights, the other state facilitation and regulation of private ownership of land – heralded the battleground over land reform and the role of law therein, fighting over which continues to this day.
>
> McAuslan 1980, p. 25

This pluralism has been his abiding interest, as his writings illustrate. As just one example, in a presentation he gave to an International Conference on Forests in Central and West Africa McAuslan (2009), with reference to the Tanzanian Forest Act for which he was a draftsman, he emphasized that both customary tenure and statutory tenure should be of *equal value* and that customary tenure be given recognition under any regime, after investigation as to its substance and history.

There are two philosophical pillars that therefore underpin his work and determine how he integrates the two circuits. The first is that of a search for the heart of the personal, human dimension of land ownership, no matter what the form, to forge some relationship with statutory schemes. The second is to equate land tenure and security with human rights and to view these rights as an aspect of the humanitarian function of the law.

His desire for extracting the ideological gold from the regulatory lead is his *leitmotiv* and can be seen in respect of land law in his book, *Land, Law and Planning* in 1975. This was the first in the *Law in Context* series to bring a policy analysis to planning and land law and set a tone for this series, followed, for example, in 1979 by Geoffrey Robertson's socio-legal analysis on obscenity. McAuslan made his approach even more concrete in *Ideologies of Planning Law* in 1980 where the examination of planning law also explained the ideologies surrounding land, its value and use. In 1980, as mentioned, this was a breakthrough work as prior to that planning law was perceived merely as a regulatory subject relating to control of the user of land and the policy strands were buried in the provisions. To undertake this analysis, as *Ideologies* demonstrated and is apparent in all his writings, it is never enough to set out the case law and statutes for examination but rather it is a process of sinking deeply into the material, reflecting, applying it, and thinking about it some more.

His humanitarian orientation to land law is patent. *Bringing the Law Back In* is a series of essays, thoughts, and musings on land law in Africa, the Caribbean, India and Bangladesh. What stands out in each essay is a direct negation of cultural imperialism as to land tenure and, in its place, a constant reiteration of his respect for traditional or customary law, as well as the rights of the inhabitants of tenuous cities. McAuslan implores policy makers that to see the humanitarian aspects of land tenure they must: 'Get right away from the crude stereotype of squatter settlements as being hotbeds of vice, crime, disease and incipient revolution' (McAuslan 1980, p. 19). There is a strong bias here for governments to face the plight of the urban poor and he exposes those factors of land policy that contribute to urban poverty (ibid. p. 33). One such factor, by way of example, is that governments are oriented towards production of primary products: 'In short, they are locked into a world economic system which sees the Third World as an area for capitalist exploitation rather than a equal partner in equitable development'. As a consultant to these countries, he is not shy of putting his own position on the line in the cause of his goals. He makes this direct and forceful statement: 'But there must be a large question-mark set against many of the multi-volumed studies that thud so often on the desks of bewildered public servants in many Third World countries' (ibid. p. 37).

This capacity to be fearless, outspoken, and to speak candidly of his own failures adds credibility and importance to his stance for the advancement of human rights. The candid revelations make it all the more convincing. This is illustrated in a recent article where McAuslan reveals his problems in drafting laws to improve women's access to land rights (McAuslan

2010a.). Emergent problems in Africa in this respect have been, for example, the inability of women to inherit land, the plight of 'illegal' spouses whose marriages are not recognized by law and thus their land rights are ignored, and the prohibition to hold land through purchase or allocation. McAuslan explains his frustrations and his failures: the draftsman overrode his suggestions for legislative reform in different jurisdictions and he did not, he believed, consult sufficiently with women's groups. He states: 'It is, however, a fallacy to assume that legal drafting can provide a magic wand to ensure women's rights to land. ... But without changed social attitudes, new laws will be difficult to implement, however well drafted they may be' (ibid. p. 117).

The origin of his humanitarian writing is apparent in his earliest works but it is perhaps *Urban Land and Shelter for the Poor* (McAuslan 1985) where McAuslan first elaborates the connection between the insecurity of land tenure to the plight of the urban poor. This book appears to be the first that directly links the plight of the poor to legal structures of property law. Subsequent work (for example, Hardoy and Satterthwaite 1989) has relied upon this pioneering analysis that a source of the problem is a lack of land tenure security. McAuslan has recorded carefully the research on the plight of urban poor living in the shantytowns of Africa and Asia from the 1960s (McAuslan 1998, p. 18). This work, published in the 1990s, gave empirical force to his views that slums are not merely a consequence of urban poverty but are a consequence of land tenure failings. This has led the way for others to view land tenure as a critical element in the need to regularize those illegal settlements.[8]

The ability to jump between jurisdictions leads to an acceptance of his policy suggestions as containing undeniable wisdom. In the last essay of *Bringing Back the Law In*, as an example, the question is addressed as to whether urban policy has the effect of exacerbating the problem of urban poor. He draws on the statutes of India, Nigeria, Lesotho, Botswana, Thailand, Peru, and Barbados, all appearing interrelated. He uses this to illustrate the inability of governments to address traditional land tenure problems, the use of inappropriate development permission requirements, refusal to accept lesser building standards, the failure of urban development authorities, and the resultant socio-political quagmire. The breath of his knowledge makes his argument more than a theory or idea but a solid empirical fact of the effect of law on land.

McAuslan and modern planning law

A participatory culture, suggested by McAuslan in his earliest writings, is now commonplace in word but still not in deed. The 1970's citizen

8 The development of the awareness of this issue is discussed in Fernandes 1998.

participation movement led to planning authorities routinely seeking oral or written submissions after a plan has been drafted but not when the proposal is first put on the table: at its formative stage of development (Brody, Godschalk and Burby 2003). These after-the-fact submissions, usually on a tight time deadline even where the proposal has taken years to develop and involves expert opinion, have been accepted as fulfilling the requirements of involvement of the citizenry in the complex issue of determining a planning application.

More sophisticated models of participatory democracy theorize the public as having greater potential in government decisions: as an interest group, as consumers that need information, voters who are entitled to information, clients of an agency such as a local government, and more generally citizens who have rights (Frederickson 1991). McAuslan's brand of participation spans all of these modalities as evidenced by his work in land tenure in Africa that requires, for example, localism or local participation in land management, as well as access of the citizenry to information. In summarizing papers from a conference in Rome on tenure security for the poor in Africa, McAuslan (2007) noted:

> Localism applied as much to pastoralists as to sedentary farmers, and customary approaches to land management and resolving conflicts between pastoralists and sedentarists were much more likely to be successful than imposed solutions from central government.

It is no surprise that McAuslan's work has been used as the starting point for a submission by a community group on the status of participation in the UK for the 1998 *Aarhus Convention*: 'the United Nations Economic Commission for Europe on Public Participation in Decision Making and Access to Justice in Environmental Matters' (Le-Las 2011). The submission states that the participation situation has deteriorated in the 30 years since McAuslan called for participatory democracy. The Thatcher government, it asserts, biased planning towards developers and the new Labour government in 1998 did little to help as there was always the fear of a planning appeal that threatened costs to the Local Planning Authority. As well, the 2000 Local Government Act concentrated power in the hands of the 'local cabinet', but lead to an imbalance of power as against citizens when Local Strategic Partnerships were established. The 2008 Planning Act introduced fast tracking of infrastructure issues and loss of public participation.

The Localism Act 2011 has been enacted in an attempt to allow communities to play a larger role in the planning process. The essence of that Act is to give local governments a 'competence' to do anything an individual could do and not be constrained by being a creature of statute. The immediate effect will be less accountability, it would appear, as the measure of an action is not the statute but the common law. In my reading of the Act, every large planning proposal will be commenced by developer involvement with the Local Planning Authority (LPA) and community participation by way of submissions will be called for less than three weeks after a complex scheme is put forward, returning participatory democracy in planning to its position in the 1970s. The submission to the *Aarhus Convention* concludes: 'The development of partnership working during this century has led, in McAuslan's terms, to an alliance of the public interest with private interests, making a charade of public participation in the planning system.'

A newsletter report of a talk given by McAuslan (2012) to the Leamington Society on the new Act indicates that he suggested that the Act 'distorted and emasculated the original idea of open source planning as a simple lay-person friendly system of planning that would allow local communities to develop their own futures'.

The difficulty is in the ideology: planning law is governing a market economy and the bias is always in the direction of development and a free market. As McAuslan has stated: 'An agenda which concentrates on the development of a market economy and uses that perspective to advance the cause of good governance is misguided' (1997b p. 34). This bias is unstated and thus the laws and the decisions of the courts do not have a countervailing principle upon which to mediate the market. As an example, the decision in *Watson v Croft Promo-Sport*[9] emphasized that planning permission does not affect private rights in the form of nuisance in any situation, confirming that the balance is firmly in favour of private rights over the public interest.[10]

The only possibility for the balance to be struck in planning law is when there is an obvious issue that overrides that of the market, such as the plight of the poor and disadvantaged. These arguments are successful because they have human rights dimensions that are enshrined in treaties that carry an overriding sentiment. The argument is made that the public interest can only subjugate private property rights in limited instances because land is equated with value; the concept of property as far back as the *Uthwatt Report* is that it includes the value of the land according to its highest and best use. Decisions are therefore made with respect to the value of land and its market. The only change in this might occur in respect of land affected by climate change. This will be in issue when the value of land is lost entirely such as when there is a sea-level rise or where weather conditions render land useless for its purpose, such as a drought in relation to agricultural land or melting snow for tourist resorts.

9 [2009] EWCA Civ 15.

10 The effect of that decision is discussed in Bishop and Jenkins 2011.

McAuslan and the new land issue: climate change

By exposing the deficiencies of the land tenure system in developing countries, McAuslan has pointed to the barriers to effective climate change mitigation and adaptation. He has never addressed that issue specifically and in correspondence he has foresworn any connection but his work is useful as a basis for interlacing the effects of climate change with land tenure (see for example, Adams 2002; Dougill, Fraser, Reed 2010) and decision making. The critical relevance of his work in this respect is twofold. The first is his understanding of how decisions get made in developing countries and the second is the conflation of housing security with human rights.

Local decision making is essential to address local vulnerabilities to climate change. Importantly, local shantytowns and illegal settlements are, in many areas, subject to sea-level rise and are thus the most vulnerable. In an article on the plight of slums in the context of climate change, McAuslan is called in aid by the author for the argument that these settlements are without a voice as the land planning process in developing countries is carried out by central government and those decisions are made without public participation (Crawford 2009, p. 220). The consequence is that those most vulnerable to climate change do not have a say in the method of adaptation or can in any way mediate the consequences of catastrophic sea-level rise.

The only solution that McAuslan comes to in an analysis of granting tenure to the inhabitants of illegal settlements is to equate the right to housing as a human right. This dovetails into a consideration of these settlements in respect of climate change. McAuslan explains his thinking clearly in a book chapter on the place of law in relation to informal land tenure systems (McAuslan 2002). His underlying assumptions, he states, are gathered from the *Istanbul Declaration* that seeks the realization of adequate housing and the *Habitat Agenda* that provides for stability of land tenure and, as well, the *Global Plan of Action* relating to land delivery and land codes. In a lecture given in 2008 to the International Law Association, McAuslan (2008b) indicates that these have been ignored:

> All international and donor pressure on countries in the developing world is to 'modernise' their land laws and modernisation means a land law fit for a market purpose which does not concern itself with matters of equity or pay much regard to the social dimension of land relations.

He proposes instead a 'humanitarian' land law that would go beyond simple land registration and grant rights for women and communities for land tenure to lift them from poverty.[11]

11 Analyzed in report on IASC (Inter-Agency Standing Committee for humanitarian cooperation) 'Governing Land Resources: Connecting Local Experiences to Global Challenges', Cheltenham, England, July 2008.

Adequate housing and climate change

Article 8.1 of the *Pinheiro Principles*,[12] proposes the need for domestic laws in a host country to implement 'adequate housing' for refugees.[13] It explains: 'States should develop a legal framework for protecting the right to housing, land and property restitution which is clear, consistent and, where necessary, consolidated in a single law'.

The *Pinheiro Principles* are based on the premise of a return of refugees to their country of origin. As a consequence, there are no provisions regarding the nature of housing or the form of resettlement or any question of the sanctity of land tenure for those displaced permanently by the effects of climate change or those merely occupying urban slums. In referring to the right to 'adequate housing', The *Handbook on Housing and Property Restitution for Refugees and Displaced Persons to Implement the Pinheiro Principles* states:

> Governmental obligations derived from this right include duties to take measures to confer security of tenure (and consequent protection against arbitrary or forced eviction and/or arbitrary confiscation or expropriation of housing), to prevent discrimination in the housing sphere, to equality of treatment and access vis-à-vis housing and protection against racial discrimination, guaranteeing housing affordability, regulating landlord-tenant relations and securing access to and provision of housing resources suited to the needs of marginalized and/or vulnerable groups, such as women-headed households, persons with disabilities, the chronically ill, migrant workers, the elderly and refugees and internally displaced persons.
>
> (Section IV of the Report, p. 48)

The interlinking of land tenure with housing and other aspects relating to land exist in the *Handbook* because it refers to 'adequate housing' as a

12 2005 UN Principles on Housing and Property Restitution for Refugees and Displaced Persons, endorsed by the UN Sub-Commission on the Promotion and Protection of Human Rights in 2005.

13 Other documents that reinforce the need for 'adequate housing' are: Article 21 of *The International Convention Relating To The Status Of Refugees* (1951), adopted by UNGA resolution 429(V) on 28 July 1951, entered into force on 22 April 1954; Section III(8) of the *Vancouver Declaration On Human Settlements* (1976), adopted by the UN Conference on Human Settlements in 1976; Agenda 21, adopted by the UN World Conference on Environment and Development (UNCED) held in Rio de Janeiro in June 1992; Point 13, Global Strategy For Shelter To The Year 2000.

human right.[14] This is the point McAuslan made five years before. The consequence is that a right, if it is interlaced with other rights, has a profound effect on the overall impact of what is proposed. As an example, Article 21 of the Indian Constitution provides a 'right to life'. The Indian Supreme Court stated that this includes the right to shelter and:

> For a human being [the right to shelter] has to be a suitable accommodation which would allow him to grow in every aspect-physical, mental and intellectual. ... A reasonable residence is an indispensable necessity for fulfilling the constitutional goal in the matter of development of man and should be taken as included in 'life' in article 21.[15]

The relationship of land tenure to human rights has arisen in the area of climate change. The *Report of the Office of the United Nations High Commissioner for Human Rights on the Relationship between Climate Change and Human Rights* in 2009[16] was concerned with the question of whether emissions from developed nations were violations of human rights. The Report addressed a claim by the Republic of Maldives that purported to attribute liability for inundation to North countries. In the analysis of liability, the Report concluded that climate change *may* impact rights related to property, although no further analysis was provided.[17]

As late as the UN Resolution of 26 March 2008[18] the impact of climate change considerations on human rights was only made a subject for further detailed analysis. The March 2009 Resolution[19] reaffirmed that there is a relationship between human rights and climate change but it did not provide reasons. The UN Human Rights Council Report of January 2009 made a specific link between housing, human rights and climate change:

> While the universal human rights treaties do not refer to a specific right to a safe and healthy environment, the United Nations human rights treaty bodies all recognize the intrinsic link between the

14 The EU has considered it a 'fundamental right': Report on Housing and Regional Policy of 28 March 2007 (A6-0090/2007), similar to the right to a decent standard of living in the European Social Charter: CETS No.: 035, in force 26 February 1965. Its terms are interpreted liberally: *European Court of Justice in INPS v. Bruno and Pettini*, C-395/08; C-396-08, 10 June 2010, 31.

15 *Shantstar Builders v. Narayan Khimali Tatome et al* (1) SC 106, Civil Appeal No. 2598 of 1989 (JT 1990); upholding *Olga Tellis v. Bombay Municipal Corporation* 1985 (3)SCC 545.

16 UN Doc A/HRC/10/61 (15 January 2009).

17 The influence of the Report is discussed in Knox 2009.

18 G.A. Res. 7/23, UN Doc. A/HRC/7/78.

19 G.A. Res. 10/4, U.N. Doc. A/HRC/10/L.11 (March 31 2009).

> environment and the realization of a range of human rights, such as the right to life, to health, to food, to water, and to housing.[20]

It can be said that the right to 'adequate housing' is established as the equivalent of other human rights.[21] The barriers to this acceptance are made patent in McAuslan's article. He summarized the 'blockages' to the Habitat Agenda and thus the prevention of adequate housing and security of land tenure as a human right. The first blockage is the inequality of the operation of law, benefiting the elite and leading to corruption. The second is the existence of an exploitive relationship between landlords and tenants leading to what he calls 'commodification' or treating shelter as a scarce good sold to the highest bidder. McAuslan (2002, p. 49) states: 'What this adds up to is a system which if not designed then at least is adapted to facilitate the exploitation of the poor'.

It is thus interesting that adequate housing has not been defined in a more specific manner in the area of climate change or land tenure. The UNHCR states[22] that the standard arising from the right to adequate housing is that of the 'local standard'. No specific guidelines are provided to interpret this standard. The *Handbook on Housing and Property Restitution for Refugees and Displaced Persons to Implement the Pinheiro Principles* addresses whether the right to adequate housing requires a host state to provide housing for all refugees:

> Human rights law does not require States to build housing for everyone who may request it or need it. Rather, housing rights provisions require States to create conditions within society – through law, policy, budgetary allocations and so forth – to ensure that everyone can access housing that is affordable, habitable and fully 'adequate' in accordance with international standards. This can – and should – include the direct financing for the construction of new housing stock and budgetary allocations towards this end, to the maximum of a country's resources, in accordance with international housing rights provisions such as those enshrined in article 11(1) of the Covenant on Economic, Social and Cultural Rights.

McAuslan turns for possible reform to those factors that would lead to openness and transparency for customary law and make tenure security a

20 Human Rights Council, *Report of the Office of the United Nations High Commissioner for Human Rights on the relationship between Climate Change and Human Rights*, 15 January 2009, UN Doc A/HCR/10/61, para 18.

21 The right is conflated with the right to self-determination: idem. at Part 6.

22 Conclusion No. 101 on *Legal Safety Issues in the Context of Voluntary Repatriation of Refugees*, para (j).

consultative process, with local decision making and flexibility in implementation. This will, with other factors, bring the two circuits together. The connection here with climate change is profound. McAuslan (2002, p. 49) indicates that Bangladesh does not confer secure tenure on residents in informal settlements. The Bangladesh *National Adaptation Plan of Action*[23] makes mention of the fact that sea-level rise will displace the poor but no plans are made for their relocation. In fact, the confusion of ownership and management rights in Bangladesh will discourage effective local adaptation and work against effective climate change strategies.[24]

In an essay, 'In the Beginning was the Law ... An Intellectual Odyssey', McAuslan (2004) indicates the problems of land tenure originated from the interplay of various theories of development such as the priority of economic growth, the notion of 'social development' in the 1970s, the 1980's neo-liberal view where the World Bank reasserted the importance of economic growth, and the 1990's emphasis on good governments and solid legal systems for all aspects of development. As to Bangladesh, McAuslan (ibid. p. 63) makes this comment:

> In Bangladesh for instance in 1999, I was advising on the reform of urban land laws with a view to assisting the urban poor to access land. At a workshop to consider the recommendations of my report, while urban NGOs and some lawyers supported the call for reform, a senior official opined that the urban poor would resist reform as they welcomed being exploited; laws which facilitated their being exploited also allowed them to exploit each other. No action followed the report – doubtless to the great relief of the urban poor.

The connection between land tenure, human rights, market economy and participation is presaged by his work. The urban poor are not being answered by climate change mitigation and adaptation efforts. The top down approach of UN climate negotiations proceed on the same ideologies that McAuslan wrote about and foresaw. It would do governments great good to return to an examination of his ideologies and to place them on the table in all negotiations and legislative attempts at the biggest problem facing us.

Conclusion

There is little in life that is constant and less in the law that is tangible and immutable. If McAuslan had spent his career discussing the reported cases and statutes, no matter how clear the analysis or how prolific his writing,

23 Ministry of the Environment and Forest, November 2005.

24 The confusion of rights is discussed in: Ahmed, Deaton, Sarker and Virani 2008, p. 429.

the work would eventually become outdated and would be lost on the shelves in law libraries. Instead, by going beyond the apparent and having a deep, felt conviction for the dignity of individuals, he has created a lasting orientation that is now a bedrock of planning and land law. This exists because he has had the genius to identify that which was unexpressed in the law that is greater than policy underpinnings and that represent the essential values that, like all things, is a set of opposites: the *coincidentia oppositurum* that are the pillars on which the law of property and planning rests. The movement for him is always towards a balance of opposites with the market economy on one side and the human rights of individuals on the other. However, in the tension between the opposites, the law is fully understood and the law can be seen for what it is.

Before McAuslan, these ideologies were hidden below the surface and pushed blindly to achieve ends that were not understood. His consciousness raising, for indeed that is what it is, must have arisen from a quality of his that agitated him and made him look deeper and harder, where most contented themselves with what remained easier. He is therefore a thinker of our time for those of us who know the importance of planning and land tenure to shape our society.

References

Adams, M., R. White, N. Raditloaneng, M. Aliber, G. Stracey, C. McVey, F. Kalabamu, P. McAuslan, N. Kgengwenyane, C. Sharp and B. Egner. 2002. National land policy: Issues report. Republic of Botswana, Ministry of Lands, Housing and Environment, Department of Lands, Natural Resource Services (Pty) Ltd., Gaborone.

Ahmed, I., B.J. Deaton, R. Sarker and T. Virani. 2008. Wetland ownership and management in a common property resource setting: A case study of Hakaluki Haor in Bangladesh. *Ecological Economics* 68: 429.

Bishop, P. and V. Jenkins. 2011. Planning and nuisance: Revisiting the balance of public and private interests in land-use development. *Journal of Environmental Law* 23: 285.

Brietzke, Paul H. 1991. Law, legitimacy and coercion: One view from law and economics. *Valparaiso University Law Review* 25: 343.

Brody, S.D., D.R. Godschalk and R.J. Burby. 2003. Mandating citizen participation in plan making: Six strategic planning choices. *Journal of the American Planning Association* 69: 245.

Caldwell, L. and K. Shrader-Frechette. 1993. *Policy for Land: Law and Ethics.* Lanham, MD: Rowman and Littlefield.

Cote, M. 2010. Climate adaptation planning: Anticipating the legal issues for urban planners. *International Journal of Climate Change: Impacts and Responses* 2: 87.

Cowell, R. and S. Owens. 2011. *Land and Limits: Interpreting Sustainability in the Planning Process,* 2nd edn. Oxon: Routledge.

Crawford, C. 2009. Our bandit future? Cities, shantytowns and climate change governance. *Fordham Urban Law Journal* 36(2): 211.

Daryono. 2010. Transformation of land rights in Indonesia: A mixed private and public law model. *Pacific Rim Land & Policy Journal* 19(3): 417.

Dougill, A.J., E.D.G. Fraser and M.S. Reed. 2010. Anticipating vulnerability to climate change in dryland pastoral systems: Using dynamic systems models for the Kalahari. Centre for Climate Change Economics and Policy, Working Paper No. 32.

Fernandes, E. 1998. The illegal city, in Fernandes, E. and A. Varley (eds) *Illegal Cities: Law and Urban Change in Developing Countries*. London: Zed Books.

Frederickson, G.H. 1991. Toward a theory of the public for public administration. *Administration and Society* 22(4): 395.

Friedman, W. 1963. The role of law and the functions of lawyers in developing countries. *Vanderbilt Law Review* 17: 181.

Gertel S and H. Law-Yone. 1991. Participation ideologies in Israeli planning. *Environment and Planning A: Government and Policy* 9: 173.

Ghai, Y. and P. McAuslan. 1970. *Public Law and Political Change in Kenya: A Study of The Legal Framework of Government from Colonial Times to the Present.* Oxford: Oxford University Press.

Greenberg. D., S.N. Katz, M.B. Oliviero and S.W. Weatley (eds) 1993. *Constitutionalism and Democracy: Transitions in the Contemporary World.* Oxford: Oxford University Press.

Grove-White, R. 1991. Land use and the environment, in Churchill, J., Gibson, J., Warren, L. (eds) Law, policy and the environment. *Journal of Law and Society* 32.

Hardoy, J.E. and D. Satterthwaite. 1989. *Squatter Citizen: Life in the Urban Third World.* London: Earthscan.

Healey, P. 1997. *Collaborative Planning: Shaping Places in Fragmented Societies*. London: Macmillan.

Honey, J.A. 1910. *South African Folk Tales.* Charlotte, NC: Baker & Taylor Co.

Humphreys, H. 1976. Review of McAuslan, P, 'Land, Law and Planning'. *Town Planning Review* 47: 289.

Hutchinson A.C. 1990. Mice under a chair: Democracy, courts and the administrative state. *University of Toronto Law Journal* 40: 374.

Knox, J.H. 2009. Linking human rights and climate change. *Harvard Environmental Law Review* 33: 477.

Le-Las, W. 2011. *Access to Justice: Substantive Review, Outline Paper.* Kent Environment and Community Network, Communication to the Aarhus Convention Compliance Committee.

Loughlin, M. 1986. Planning law through the texts darkly. *Planning Practice and Research* 1: 31.

Loughlin, M. 1992. *Public Law and Political Theory.* Oxford: Oxford University Press.

Loughlin, M. 2005. The functionalist style in public law. *University of Toronto Law Journal* 55: 361.

Lloyd, G. 2006. Planning and the Public Interest in the Modern World. Edinburgh, Sir Patrick Geddes Commemorative Lecture.

McAuslan, P. 1966. *Aspects of Land Law in Kenya and Tanzania.* Dar es Salaam.

McAuslan, P. 1974. Planning law's contribution to the problems of an urban society. *Modern Law Review* 37: 134.

McAuslan, P. 1975. *Land, Law and Planning.* London: Weidenfeld & Nicolson.

McAuslan, P. 1980. *The Ideologies of Planning Law*. Oxford: Pergamon Press.
McAuslan, P. 1985. *Urban Land and Shelter for the Poor*. London: Earthscan.
McAuslan, P. 1997a. Comment: Political mandate and economic reform, in Faundez, J. (ed.) *Good Government and Law: Legal and Institutional Reform in Developing Countries*. London: Macmillan.
McAuslan, P. 1997b. 'Law, governance and the development of the market: Practical problems and possible solutions'. In J. Faundez (ed.) *Good Government and Law: Legal and Institutional Reform in Developing Countries*. London: Macmillan.
McAuslan, P. 1998. 'Urbanization, law and development: A record of research'. In E. Fernandes and A. Varley (eds) *Illegal Cities: Law and Urban Change in Developing Countries*. London: Zed Books.
McAuslan, P. 2002. 'Tenure and the law: The legality of illegality and the illegality of legality'. In Geoffrey Payne (ed.) *Land, Rights and Innovation: Improving Tenure Security for Urban Poor*. London: ITDG Publishing.
McAuslan, P. 2003. *Bringing the Law Back In: Essays in Land, Law and Development*. Aldershot: Ashgate Publishing Limited.
McAuslan, P. 2004. The practice of law & development. Cornell University, 18–20 April 2004, paper no. 2.
McAuslan, P. 2006. 'Legal pluralism as a policy option: Is it desirable? Is it doable?' In E. Mwangi (ed.) *Land Rights for African Development: From Knowledge to Action*, prepared for the Consultative Group on International Agricultural Research's System-wide Program on Collective Action and Property Rights.
McAuslan, P. 2007. *Improving Tenure Security for the Poor in Africa, Synthesis Paper: Deliberation of the Legal Empowerment Workshop – Sub-Saharan Africa*. Rome, Food and Agricultural Organization of the United Nations.
McAuslan, P. 2008a. Positive planning: A new approach to urban planning law in Syria, for Action Plan 9 of the Municipal Administration Modernisation Program.
McAuslan, P. 2008b. Globalisation of Land Markets and the Homogenisation of National Land Laws. Paper presented by Patrick McAuslan at Does International Law Mean Business: A Partnership for Progress? London.
McAuslan, P. 2009. New Opportunities for Central and West Africa. Presentation, International Conference on Forest Tenure, Governance and Enterprise, May 2009, Yaoundé, Cameroon.
McAuslan, P. 2010a. Personal reflections on drafting laws to improve women's access to land: Is there a magic wand? *Journal of Eastern African Studies* 4: 114.
McAuslan, P. 2010b. The liberal peace approach to post-conflict land management and the transformative alternative with special reference to Liberia. Draft, 24 April 2010.
McAuslan, P. 2012. Presentation to Leamington Society, Leamington Spa, UK. http://leamingtonsociety.org.uk/Newsletters/Newsletter%20August%202011.pdf. Accessed 10 December 2011.
McAuslan, J.P.W.B., D. Bayless, R.W. Cresswell and S.N. Mustow. 1986. Local government and planning legislation. In *The Future Role and Organisation of Local Government 3:1*. University of Birmingham: Institute of Local Government Studies.
Miller, C. 2001. Planning and human rights: An inevitable conflict. *Environment and Planning A*. 33(11): 1899.

Peel, D. and M.G. Lloyd. 2007. Neo-traditional planning. Towards a new ethos for land use planning. *Land Use Policy* 24: 396.

Paisley, R.R.M. 2004–2005. Real rights: Practical problems and dogmatic rigidity. *Edinburgh Law Review* 8: 267.

Rydin, Y. 1999. 'Public participation in planning'. In B. Cullingworth (ed.) *British Planning: 50 Years of Urban and Regional Policy.* London: The Athlone Press.

Simpson, B. 1997. Towards the participation of children and young people in urban planning and design. *Urban Studies* 34: 907.

Stein, L.A. 1974. *Urban Legal Problems.* Sydney: Law Book Co.

Stein, L.A. 2008. *Principles of Planning Law.* Melbourne: Oxford University Press.

Tett, A. and. J.M. Wolfe. 1995. Discourse analysis and city plan. *Journal of Planning Education and Research* 10: 195.

Chapter 8

Patrick McAuslan, land law and development

Ambreena Manji

Introduction

Patrick McAuslan published his first paper on land law in East Africa in 1967 (McAuslan 1967). Over the next thirty-five years he also came to occupy a key position in the world of technical legal consultancy. He published extensively on land law and development. I first encountered McAuslan scholarship in Tanzania in the late 1990s where I had begun fieldwork on women's relations to land, carrying out fieldwork in the Kagera region. At that time Tanzania was at the beginning of a difficult land reform process and I found the debates on the purpose and direction of land reform, and in particular of land law reform, compelling. My particular interest at the time was in the question of women's access to land, especially through inheritance, and the first academic paper I published (Manji 1998) was an analysis of the way that gender concerns had been neglected in the Tanzanian process. In the intervening seventeen or so years, my own thinking about some of the main themes in land law and administration has been deeply informed by reading McAuslan's scholarship.

Many of the difficult and controversial topics on which McAuslan wrote, and in which I have shared an interest, are by no means settled: these include, most prominently, debates about styles of legislative drafting, about the desirability and achievement of statutory spousal co-ownership of law, and about the formulation of new mortgage laws. All remain areas of contention for academics and policy makers. In this chapter, I will explore one of the most important themes arising from McAuslan's work on land law reform – the purpose of legislative drafting and the different approaches that might be taken to this exercise. I provide an introduction to the Tanzanian debate on legislative style that took place between McAuslan and Issa Shivji in the late 1990s. The essence of this debate was how law might be used to control administrative discretion. McAuslan (2003, p. 256) argued that the drafting of new land laws is an exercise in 'applied administrative law' because 'it was public officials who were to exercise the relevant powers'. In this chapter, I use this observation to explore the way in which land law in Kenya has been dismantled by bureaucrats who systematically perverted the doctrine that land should be allocated in the public interest. The Ministry of Lands is notorious for its corruption, for the disappearance of title deeds and their forging, for mismanaging, misallocating and 'eating' land. Despite an opportunity to confront this problem when Kenya came to reform its land laws in 2012, little has changed.

In this chapter I explore the rather neglected Report of Kenya's Commission of Inquiry into Illegal/Irregular Allocation of Land (widely known as the Ndung'u report after its chairperson) (2004) which still has a great deal to tell us about the mechanisms by which public land was grabbed in Kenya. I summarise the findings of the Ndung'u report and then discuss the critical issue of control of administrative discretion that has been a long running concern throughout McAuslan's writing in light of what we know about illegal and irregular allocation of public land in Kenya past and present.

Land and the role of law

In his 2003 book, *Bringing the Law Back In*, McAuslan sought to make the case for law in development and especially for the role of law in the process of land reform. He wrote:

> The title of my book sums up my overall stance: there is an important role for law in development generally and in land reform in particular, and it is, in my view, wholly beneficial that after decades of virtually ignoring the role of law in development [...] international financial intuitions, aid agencies and scholars in the West are beginning to appreciate and reaffirm both its centrality to development in practice and its centrality to understanding the process of development and change in societies in developing countries.
>
> McAuslan 2003, p. vii

Explaining the greater emphasis being placed on law, McAuslan describes the changing approach of donors as follows:

> the twin emphasis of donors, led by the World Bank, on 'good governance' and the market economy as the keys to social regeneration in Africa are increasingly seen as necessitating a greater reliance on legal forms and a legal culture similar to those operating in Western, market-orientated economies; conscious moves to adapt legal systems to that end are thus increasingly part of aid programmes.
>
> McAuslan 2003, p. 245

McAuslan's concern was with 'making law work' (2003, p. 245) and, specifically, with how law might be used to restructure land relations. In the late 1990s there was a resurgence of writing and interest in law and development and it is important to place McAuslan's writing of this period in the context of this revival. In *Bringing the Law Back In*, the author was eager to communicate a sense of continuity between his recent work and that of early law and development scholarship (Merryman 1977). It was, he argued, 'wholly beneficial that after three decades of virtually ignoring the role of law in development', it should now be recognised once again that law is central to the development process (McAuslan 2003, p. vii). After all, McAuslan pointed out, despite being sidelined by international donors and scholars, law 'by definition continued to be used' for the purpose of development in the third world (ibid. p. vii). For McAuslan, tales of law and development's demise were both premature and inaccurate.

Tanzania's effort at land reform – beginning in 1991 and culminating (formally at least) in the passing of the Land Act 1998 and the Village Land Act 1998 provides an excellent example of contestation over issues of legal methodology. It was an effort in which McAuslan played a central role. There was considerable disagreement over legal methodology issue in Tanzania when McAuslan was commissioned to draft the new land law. An interesting feature of the Tanzanian debate over land reform was that the two main protagonists who played prominent roles in the formulation of land policy were both legal academics. Issa Shivji, professor of law at the University of Dar es Salaam, chaired the Presidential Commission of Inquiry into Land Matters which reported in 1992 (URT 1994).The recommendations of the commission did not find favour with the government, which failed to issue a white paper in response to its findings and thus sidelined the report (Chachage 1995; Tsikata 2003). The British Overseas Development Agency (since renamed the Department for International Development) then commissioned McAuslan, by that time professor of law at Birkbeck, to draft the new land policy and legislation. The Tanzanian experience of land reform was marked by fierce disagreements between McAuslan and Shivji about the purpose and direction of such reform, the content of the proposed legislation and the legal methodology to be adopted. By virtue of being members of the academy, Shivji and McAuslan both spoke and wrote about their views on land reform - and their differences with each other - in great detail, enabling those studying the politics of land law reform to follow closely the course of the debate (Manji 1998; Sundet 1997).

As regards legal methodology, McAuslan's approach to legislative drafting is described in detail in *Bringing the Law Back In* (2003). It arises out of his view of the role that law plays in development. McAuslan asserted that a detailed legal code was essential for promoting economic certainty and stability and would function as a check on much abused administrative discretion. Rather than land licences and permits that are held at the mercy of administrators, detailed legal provisions could act to guarantee more permanent rights. Describing the impetus behind his work on the 1998 Tanzania Land Bills, McAuslan wrote: '[...] a detailed and inevitably lengthy new land code in which legal rules and checks and balances replace reliance on administrative and political action based on goodwill and common sense, on the evidence, are in short supply where land relations are concerned' (McAuslan 2003, p. 407). McAuslan rejected the proposals of the Presidential Commission of Inquiry into Land Matters (the Shivji Commission), on the grounds that the commission's reliance on broad provisions lacking checks and balances was 'naïve' (2002, p. 11). Shivji had contended that detailed land laws were unworkable in practice, that they would hinder rather than enable change, increase the scope for abuse and potentially undermine the rights of migrant peoples. In Shivji's view, the proposed land bills were unworkable because they set out in intricate detail the powers and responsibilities of bureaucrats in the land administration machinery and sought to exert detailed control over their actions. Shivji was critical of this approach, arguing that it trampled on traditional community methods of controlling the exercise of discretion by public officials (Shivji and Kapinga 1997; Wily 1998).McAuslan disagreed, arguing that 'land reform is pre-eminently land *law* reform: the substitution of a law to facilitate the right of citizens to access and hold land, for a law which had facilitated the state's *administrative control* over the citizens' access to land' (2003, p. 249, author's emphasis).

For McAuslan (2003, p. 256), the South African approach to legislative drafting which favours detailed codes of law was the most workable:

> Administrative law or administrative justice requires that official power be bounded by legal rules, be exercised in accordance with certain principles of fairness, allows for hearings and appeals, and be subject to review. How else can this be done except through statutory provisions which go beyond merely granting powers to officials, to setting out the matter and form of their exercise and control?

Thus, a dual test had to be applied to new Tanzanian legislation (2003, p. 256): did it create a new substantive land law, appropriate to the conditions of Tanzania; and, did it provide a suitable legal framework for the exercise of powers by officials? In the rest of this chapter, I consider these themes in light of Kenya's experiences of illegal and irregular allocation of public land. In order to do this, I provide an account of land grabbing in Kenya in the next section.

Land corruption in Kenya

In 2002, Kenya's ruling political party since independence in 1963, KANU, was defeated in the elections by the National Rainbow Coalition (NARC) headed by Mwai Kibaki. One of NARC's most important commitments, together with the promise of a new constitution to replace Kenya's 1962 independence constitution, was to fight corruption (Cheeseman *et al.* 2010; Prunier 2009; Wrong 2009). In particular, the new government undertook to investigate and ensure the recovery of all public lands illegally allocated by the outgoing government (Kibaki 2003). In exercise of the powers conferred on the President by Section 3 of the Commissions of Inquiry Act 1962 (Cap 102 Laws of Kenya), a Commission of Inquiry into the Illegal/Irregular Allocation of Public Land chaired by the lawyer Paul Ndung'u was appointed to investigate this issue (Kenya Gazette Notice 4559, 4 July 2003).[1] The commission's report (Republic of Kenya 2004, hereinafter 'the Ndung'u report') was presented to President Kibaki in December 2004 and released six months later only after widespread accusations of government censorship in failing to make it public (Africog 2009, p. 11).[2] The 244 page report, which is supported by two annexes of 976 and 797 pages respectively, sets out in forensic detail the illegal land awards made over the years to the families of President Kenyatta and President Moi, to numerous former ministers, members of parliament and civil servants, as well as to individuals in the military and the judiciary. Despite the detail provided in the annexes, it is admitted that the report is incomplete because of the lack of cooperation with which the commission met (Ndung'u 2011 int.; Africog 2009). It provides a snapshot of only a proportion of the illegal and irregular land allocations that have taken place (Aronson 2011 int.; Lamba 2011 int.) The report recommended that a large majority of land titles acquired in this way should be revoked and recommended the rectification of others (Republic of Kenya 2004, pp. 83–85).

1 The commission's terms of reference are set out in Appendix 6, Republic of Kenya 2004, p. 214. It was made up of twenty commissioners: civil servants working in the area of land, lawyers and individual citizens. The commission was asked to investigate the practice of unlawful allocation of public lands; to identify the beneficiaries of land allocations and the public officials involved in illegally or irregularly allocating; to make recommendations for the restoration of illegally allocated land and how this might be prevented in future; and to recommend criminal prosecutions to be brought. The commission sat for a total of 270 days during which it held hearings, considered documents related to land and received memoranda from professional and other bodies and from non-governmental organisations.

2 The government was widely held to be suppressing the report (Yash Ghai 2011 int). Members of Parliament repeatedly requested it be released, but were told this would happen 'once the Cabinet peruses through the contents and deliberates on it' (Hansard 11.11.2004, pp. 4265–4266). In 2005 MPs expressed concern that the report had still not been released and was being ignored (Hansard 05.10.2005, p. 3500). Even after its release, MPs stated the report had not been circulated and was 'impossible' to find (Hansard 14.06.2006, p. 1322). For an account of the difficulties faced in getting a range of inquiry reports released, see Kenya Human Rights Commission 2011.

Although it has been widely discussed in the Kenyan media and its findings taken up by leading human rights groups (see Kenya National Commission on Human Rights (KNCHR) and Kenya Land Alliance (KLA) 2006; and Africa Centre for Open Governance (Africog) 2009), the Ndung'u report has received surprisingly little academic attention (but cf Southall 2005). In addition, although the economic and social costs of widespread land corruption are likely to be far higher than the overall costs of better known corruption scandals such as Anglo-Leasing and Goldenburg (Aronson 2011 int; Africog 2011 int) the findings of the Ndung'u report have not been systematically studied by academic or other commentators. Discussion of the report have tended to focus on its 'juicy findings' (Southall 2005, p. 142),the 'what' and 'whom' of illegal or irregular land allocation – the forests, road reservations, school playgrounds and graveyards that have been misallocated and the individuals and families who acquired them (so far as this can be ascertained) – rather than the 'how' of land grabbing. Nonetheless, the report itself does provide detailed information about the mechanisms by which public land was misallocated and the means by which the doctrine that public land should be administered and allocated 'in the public interest' (Republic of Kenya 2004, pp. 8–9) was consistently perverted. This has been recognised by Southall who has noted that

> it is the chapter and verse which the Report gives concerning the systematic way in which established procedures, designed to protect the public interest, were perverted to serve private and political ends which may well prove to be its most long lasting value.
>
> Southall 2005, p. 143

One of the most significant issues raised by the Ndung'u Commission – the extent to which illegal or irregular transactions in public land in Kenya have been made possible through administrative and professional corruption – has been largely neglected. In his short assessment of the Ndung'u report, Southall remarked that the 'extensive complicity of professionals (lawyers, surveyors, valuers, physical planners, engineers, architects, land registrars, estate agents and bankers) in the land and property market was key to the process of land grabbing' (Southall 2005, p. 146) but did not explore the point in any detail. The Ndung'u Commission, finding that 'public land has been allocated contrary to the substantive and procedural provisions of the relevant laws' (Republic of Kenya 2004, p. 53), made three recommendations: that investigations be conducted and if necessary, prosecutions brought against professionals involved in facilitating illegal or irregular allocation of public land; that professional bodies take disciplinary action under their Codes of Conduct; and that the government recover all money and other proceeds acquired as a result of professionals' involvement (Recommendations 8–10,

Republic of Kenya 2004, pp. 83–85). In so doing, the Ndung'u Commission went further than the earlier Commission of Inquiry into the Land Law Systems of Kenya 2002 (known as the 'Njonjo Commission') which strongly condemned the professions for their role in the irregular allocation of public land (Mwathane 2009) but had to stop short of recommending disciplinary action because this was outside its terms of reference (Ndung'u 2011 int.). To date, despite the report's recommendations, no investigations of professionals' involvement in land corruption have been initiated (Ndung'u 2011 int.). Neither has legal or disciplinary action been taken by the police or by the Law Society of Kenya against lawyers involved in land grabbing (Lamba 2011 int.).

Arguably the most important contribution of the Ndung'u report has been to set out the detailed mechanisms by which public land was illegally or irregularly allocated not for the purposes of development but as political reward. Importantly for our understanding of Kenya's fraught electoral history (Throup and Hornsby 1998), the commission found that illegal allocations of public land escalated significantly before or soon after the multiparty general elections of 1992, 1997 and 2002, evidence that public land was allocated 'as political reward or patronage' (Republic of Kenya 2004, p. 83). For Southall 'even a cursory analysis serves to confirm earlier analyses that corruption and patronage have become thoroughly embedded in Kenya's politics' (Southall 2005, p. 143). This was a critical issue as Kenya prepared for general elections in 2012. Press reports at the time suggested that illegal and irregular allocation of public land to raise electoral finance and to shore up political support, as well as to consolidate personal gain before losing office, was indeed taking place in preparation for the coming contest (*The Standard* 6.7.2011). Politicians continue to use public office to identify profitable land to be grabbed and to sell land they have grabbed in the past. Professor Yash Pal Ghai, the Chairperson of the Kenya Constitutional Review Commission, wrote that:

> Some politicians are busy grabbing land; a few senior ministers have bought hundreds of acres in Lamu, with inside information of plans for the port there. Sometimes the same people who improperly appropriated land in the past are 'laundering' it by selling it to the state at high prices for the 'settlement' of [internally displaced people (following post-election violence in January 2008). Others are conspiring with developers, often foreigners, to evict people from their traditional land, to create the so-called 'conservation' areas, today a major cause of illegalities and the suffering of the people.
>
> *The Star* 15 October 2011

The venality of the political and business elite has long been the focus of academic writing concerned with the nature and working of the African state (Bayart 1993). It is less common to find accounts of corruption amongst bureaucrats, administrators and professionals (Budlender 2004; Ghai and Cottrell 2004). The Ndung'u report is of particular interest in this regard. It makes clear that the professionals, including land administrators, far from upholding the rule of law (Carothers 2006; Harrington and Manji 2003), has played a key role in land corruption in Kenya, using its professional skills and networks to accumulate personal wealth for itself and others. The Ndung'u report's findings on the complicity of professionals in land grabbing have important implications for our understanding of administrative discretion.

According to a report by the African Centre for Global Governance, the Ndung'u report established that 'illegal allocation of public land is one of the most pronounced manifestations of corruption and political patronage in our society' (Africog 2009, p. 11). On a conservative estimate, some 200,000 illegal titles were created between 1962 and 2002. Of these, 98 per cent were issued between 1986 and 2002. The categories of public land affected include forests, settlement schemes, national parks and game reserves, civil service houses, government offices, roads and road reserves, wetlands, research farms, state corporations' lands and Trust lands. The report makes it clear that the illegal allocations took place either on the direct orders of the president or on the orders of prominent, senior public officials and well connected business people and politicians. Those who benefited from the illegal or irregular allocations of grabbed land included ministers, senior civil servants, politicians, business people, churches, temples and mosques.

The report distinguishes between the illegal and the irregular allocation of public land (Republic of Kenya 2004, pp. 48–49). The first category of wrongful allocation, when land is *illegally* issued, occurs when the legal safeguards governing the allocation of land are ignored or subverted. For instance, where a title is issued fora piece of land, which is not legally available for allocation, the title acquired is illegal. The Ndung'u report recommended that such titles should be revoked and stipulated that in certain instances, such as where the land had been sold on to a third party or is being held by a bank as security for a loan, decisions as to revocation should be made on a case-by-case basis by a Land Title Tribunal using clear criteria such as the number and classes of people financially affected and 'the public interest'.[3]

The second category of wrongful allocation is *irregular* allocation of land. According to the Ndung'u report, irregular allocations occurred when administrative procedures for dealing in land were not followed. Here, the

3 A Land Title Tribunal is one of four new institutions the Ndung'u Commission recommended be set up, the other three being a Lands Division of the High Court, a National Land Commission and a Task Force on Land. (Republic of Kenya 2004, pp. 67–70).

land concerned was in fact legally available for allocation but was allocated in such a way that the requisite legal standard was not met or the correct administrative procedure followed. For this second category of cases, the Ndung'u report recommended that irregular titles could be rectified by following the administrative procedures that had been bypassed (Republic of Kenya 2004, pp. 136–137).

The Ndung'u report provides exhaustive details of the processes by which the wrongful allocation of public land was achieved. Although these processes have not been the subject of academic commentary or analysis to date (but cf Southall 2005), they are likely to make a lasting contribution to our understanding of how land law in Kenya has been subverted. According to the Ndung'u report, the abuse of the powers of allocation was central to the plundering of public land (Republic of Kenya 2004, p. 54). It is therefore necessary to understand the allocation process. In order to do this, the report identifies three categories of land in Kenya. The first is government land, which includes both alienated land (that is, land which has been leased to a private individual or company or reserved for use by a government department or corporation or institution, or which has been set aside for another public purpose)and unalienated land (that is, land that has not yet been leased or allocated). Secondly, Trust land is held by County Councils on behalf of local communities under African Customary Law. Once such land is registered according to any of the land registration statutes it becomes private land and is then regarded as the sole property of the individual or group in whose name it is registered (Republic of Kenya, p. 45). Thirdly, land which is registered in accordance with the land registration statutes in the name of an individual or a company is known as private land.[4] This category of land can be created from either government land or Trust land through registration after certain procedures have been adhered to (Republic of Kenya 2004, pp. 44–45; Southall 2005). The Ndung'u Commission investigated the illegal and irregular allocation of government land and, when cases came to its notice, of Trust land where fraudulent practices had affected this

4 'The categories of public land highlighted ... are subject to various laws which prescribe the legal procedures to be followed if they are to be allocated to private individuals or companies. There are several laws the provisions of which must be followed by the Government to create private title to public land. The main laws in this regard are: The Constitution of Kenya, 1963; The Government Lands Act, 1984 (Cap 280); The Registration of Titles Act, 1982 (Cap 281); The Trust Land Act, 1970 (Cap 288); The Land Adjudication Act, 1977 (Cap 284); The Registered Land Act, 1963 (Cap 300); The Forests Act, 1982 (Cap 385); The Physical Planning Act, 1996 (Cap 286); The Wildlife Management and Conservation Act, 1985 (Cap 376); and The Survey Act, 1989 (Cap 299). It is important to note that 'even after these actions have taken by the Minister...the provisions of the Government Lands Act and other Planning and Environmental Legislation would have to be strictly followed before such lands can be legally allocated' (Republic of Kenya 2004, p. 52).

category of land. Taken together, government land and some Trust land go to make up the category of 'public land' into which the Ndung'u Commission inquired.[5]

According to the commission's findings, it was the very individuals entrusted with being custodians of public land who were involved in 'pilfering the public' (Klopp 2000). They did this by subverting or ignoring the legal safeguards in place to protect public land (Republic of Kenya 2004, p. 53). Thus, although the president has the right to allocate unalienated government lands (and can delegate limited powers to the Commissioner of Lands), he cannot exercise his powers without taking into account the public interest. The report describes how in practice the Commissioner of Lands and his officials were given responsibility for public land: under the Government Lands Act 1963 they could allow township plots on unalienated land to be sold by auction if it is not required for public purposes. However, neither the President not the Commissioner of Lands has the authority to allocate alienated government land, that is, land that has been earmarked for a public purpose (such as road reservations) (Republic of Kenya 2004, p. 51).

As well as subjecting the President and the Commissioner of Lands to these legal safeguards, the law also controls the process of allocation itself. A formal offer of sale must be made to an approved purchaser by the Commissioner for Lands. This is known as a letter of allotment. It is only made to the person to whom it is addressed, lapses after 30 days, and has various conditions attached. Significantly, a letter of allotment cannot be legally transferred to another person (Republic of Kenya 2004, p. 48) (the use of letters of allotment is explored in greater detail below). Similarly, land that is categorised as Trust land can only be removed from the communal ownership of local people by a process of adjudication in which local communities are given adequate notice and the opportunity to claim their ownership in accordance with customary law (Republic of Kenya 2004, p. 52).

The commission investigated the illegal allocation of different types of land, including urban land, ministry land, national parks and museums, to mention a few. The process by which land was grabbed can be shown by reference to any one of these. To take urban land as an illustration, the commission found evidence of widespread abuse of presidential discretion with regard to unalienated urban land. Both Presidents Kenyatta and Moi were found to have made grants to individuals without any reference to the public interest. The allocation was therefore done without following the correct legal procedure (Ndung'u 2011 int.). Furthermore, both presidents

5 Included in public land are: urban, state corporations' and ministries' lands; settlement schemes and trust land; and forestlands, national parks, game reserves, wetlands, riparian reserves, protected areas, museums and historical monuments.

also allocated alienated land despite the fact that this is not a category of land which they have any legal power to allocate. The Ndung'u report also found that a number of Commissioners of Lands had made direct grants of government land without any authority from the president. Often, land was quickly sold by grantees at very high prices to third parties without any adherence to the conditions laid down by letters of allotment and despite the fact that such letters only have the status of letters of offer and cannot be sold (Republic of Kenya 2004, p. 13; Aronson 2011 int). Far from being restrained by the principle of public purpose, the Commissioner of Lands and many local authorities completely disregarded it and sold land reserved exclusively for public purposes such as schools, playgrounds, and hospitals. Forged letters and documents were commonly used to allocate land. Records at the Ministry of Lands and Settlements were found to have been deliberately destroyed (Republic of Kenya 2004, p. 38).

The Ndung'u report also provides critical details of what took place in the aftermath of illegal or irregular land allocations. It uncovered in its investigations how those allocated land would move quickly to sell them. In many cases, the land was sold to state corporations at hugely inflated prices. State corporations were in effect exploited as coerced buyers of grabbed land. Pressurised into making illegal purchases of public land, they become 'captive buyers of land from politically connected allottees' (Republic of Kenya 2004, p. 92). As the report makes clear, there is a further injustice in the fact that state corporations had sometimes also been the victims and not just the conduits of land grabbing. They could 'lose their land to grabbers for free, and then be pressured to buy other lands for millions of shillings' (Ndung'u 2006, p. 5). The primary state corporation targeted to purchase land was the Kenyan workers' pension scheme, the National Social Security Fund (NSSF). It spent about 30 billion Kenya shillings (approximately USD 400 million) between 1990 and 1995 on the purchase of illegally acquired property. The NSSF was set up in 1965 and is regulated by the Minister for Labour, to whom a tripartite Advisory Council gives advice and assistance in connection with the implementation of the National Social Security Fund Act 1965 (Mullei 1988, p. 433). This legislation stipulates that the purpose of the NSSF is to provide for contributions to the payment of benefits out of the Fund and to provide 'some form of social protection' (Mullei 1988, p. 433) against old age, death and incapacitating physical or mental disability. Instead, the Ndung'u Commission found that the NSSF and other state corporations were simply abused as a vehicle for off-loading grabbed land: 'State corporations were used as conduits for land grabbing schemes through which the public lost colossal amounts of money' (Republic of Kenya 2004, p. 87). For example, the Ndung'u report found that a former chairman of the Cooperative Bank of Kenya was illegally allocated land in Ngong Forest, which he then sold on to the NSSF (Republic of Kenya 2004, Annexe 2, p. 673).

The human and social costs to the country of this plundering of the NSSF – 'diverting resources away from public use' (KNCHR and KLA 2006, p. 5) – have not been quantified. However, it is clear that the NSSF continues to suffer losses even in the present day. As recently as September 2011, the auditors of the NSSF noted that the corporation's legal bills were in excess of KES 76 million (approximately USD 763,000) and were critical of the fact that significant amounts of money paid in legal fees (amounting to KES 6 million) that had not been approved by its board (*Daily Nation*, 25 September 2011). The majority of the legal costs incurred involve disputes about the status of land that the NSSF still holds on its books. Long after the NSSF was used as a coerced buyer of land it continues to lose money relating to activities outside its core remit to provide social security payments to Kenyans. It is also conceivable that the assets of the NSSF are overvalued as a result of its holding grabbed land, making it difficult to assess its financial health (Cottrell 2011 int.).

More broadly, the likely economic and social costs of widespread land corruption will be borne for many years to come. The misallocation of public land instigates a process by which land that should be available for the public good – for the building of medical clinics and schools, for public parks and public transport facilities such as railways – is transformed into private land. This privatisation deprives the public of significant social goods whilst generating large profits for the private consumption of well connected individuals and families. Two examples of this process can be given. In one prominent case, a questionable change of user enabled 18 acres of land in a suburb of Nairobi that had been reserved to build two state schools to be sold to a diplomatic mission (Aronson 2011 int.; see more generally Republic of Kenya 2004, p. 187). The schools were never built on this or any other site. In another case, land reserved for the development of a public medical clinic and day nursery was, again through a questionable change of user, instead given over to the building of a shopping centre in an exclusive suburb of Nairobi (Cottrell 2011 int.; *The Star* 9 November 2009)

The Ndung'u report remains a valuable source of information on land grabbing in Kenya, providing details of the processes by which the wrongful allocation of public land was achieved.

Land law as 'Applied Administrative Law'

Reading the Ndung'u report on the mechanisms by which a 'grabbed state' (Manji 2013) comes into being, it is clear that this has entailed the systematic dismantling of land law and administration. The abuse of administrative discretion in land matters which is at the crux of the Ndung'u report recalls the wider debates on this theme that took place elsewhere in East Africa in the 1990s. During the drafting of Tanzania's new land legislation (which became the Land Act 1998 and the Village Land Act 1998) the role and control of bureaucratic discretion was vigorously debated (see Manji 1998; Manji 2006; Shivji 1998). The Tanzanian debate on the powers and responsibilities to be vested in bureaucrats can cast light on the illegal or irregular allocation of public land.

According to McAuslan, a dual test had to be applied to new Tanzanian legislation when it was under consideration in the 1990s: 'did it create a new substantive land law, appropriate to the conditions of Tanzania; and, did it provide a suitable legal framework for the exercise of powers by officials?' (McAuslan 2003, p. 256). When Kenya reviewed the legal framework governing land in 2012, I argued that the test to be applied in assessing the powers and responsibilities of public officials should draw on this formulation and should centre on the question whether the proposed changes would have prevented the illegal and irregular allocations of public land on the vast scale identified by the Ndung'u Commission (see Manji 2014). I was at the time a member of a consortium on land research in Kenya, comprising the Katiba (Constitution) Institute headed by Professor Yash Pal Ghai (former Chairperson of the Kenya Constitutional Review Commission) and Kituo cha Sheria (Kenya Legal Aid Office). The consortium gave evidence before the Parliamentary Select Committee on Land and Natural Resources in January and February 2012, providing commentaries on the Land Bill 2012, the Land Registration Bill 2012, and the National Land Commission Bill 2012.

In my submission, I argued that the Ndung'u report demonstrated that bureaucratic control of land matters is a critical issue in Kenya and that its findings should guide us in reviewing the proposed land bills. The consortium noted that many saw the review of land law in 2012 as an opportunity to address the longstanding abuse of control over the allocation of land. According to Boone (2012):

> Unlike land politics in many African countries, which often centers on the use and abuse of ostensibly customary authority (and is thus "repressed" or bottled-up at the local level), the major land disputes in much of Kenya are focused on how the power of the central state has been used to allocate land ... Struggles over land are therefore played out as struggles to capture or retain state power. This makes the national public sphere a prime theater of land conflict. The drafting of a National Land Policy from 2004 to 2008, and the enactment of some of its main provisions in the 2010 Constitution, are the latest acts in an on-going drama over the structuring and use of state power to distribute and redistribute land.

Far from reviewing the proposed land laws in this light, Kenya's reform process in 2012 in fact provided further evidence of the state's determination to maintain a firm hold of its power to distribute land. One way to do this was to hamper as far as possible the proposed new National Land Commission which was widely seen as a new institution that would help to address the corruption of the Ministry of Lands. This response was reminiscent of Uganda's land law reform process which had also been characterised by 'bureaucratic sabotage' (McAuslan 2003, p. 348). In Uganda, McAuslan records how officials sabotaged a project concerned with the timely the implementation of the Land Act. The Directorate of Lands and Environment which stood to lose a significant amount of power over land when its role in land management was devolved (McAuslan 2003, p. 330) was particularly involved in trying to delay and then destroy the project. Similarly, in Kenya, since 2012 underfunding the National Land Commission has been the main way that the Ministry of Lands has responded to the reduction in its powers contained in the National Land Commission Act 2012. Since the new land laws were passed, the ongoing wrangles between Ministry of Lands and the National Land Commission over their respective mandates, staffing and funding have consumed more time and energy than addressing the very real land problems facing the country. This wrangling over powers is taking place despite the widespread acknowledgement that corruption in land matters must be dealt with urgently and distracting from the task of confronting land corruption.

Conclusion

Reflecting on the challenges confronting academic lawyers, McAuslan has written that:

> Academic lawyers face […] the challenge of scholarship to rise above the merely descriptive and analytical approach to writing about land law and adopt a more policy-orientated and innovative approach which offers new models and creative ideas as solutions to practical problems of land management; and, if the opportunity presents itself, to become involved in the challenging business of turning these ideas and models into legislative drafts – a scholarly endeavour, for which creative and not just critical scholarship is needed.
>
> McAuslan 2003, p. 272

In this chapter, I have reviewed an important aspect of McAuslan's work as a technical legal adviser and suggested that his interest in land bureaucracies, their role, effect and control, is of continuing relevance and importance. If the Ndung'u report and its account of the misallocation of public land in Kenya has shown that it is important to investigate the workings of local land grabbing, as well as to the global land rush or investor rush which has received a great deal more academic and media attention, Kenya's 2012 land reform process demonstrated how difficult it will be to hold bureaucrats to account for the systematic perversion of land law.

References

Adar, K. and I. Munyae. 2001. Human rights abuse in Kenya under Daniel Arap Moi, *African Studies Quarterly* 5(1): 1–17.

African Centre for Open Governance (Africog). 2008. *Postponing the Truth: How Commissions of Inquiry are Used to Circumvent Justice in Kenya.* Nairobi: Africog.

African Centre for Open Governance (Africog). 2009. *Mission Impossible? Implementing the Ndung'u Report.* Nairobi: Africog.

Alden Wily, Liz. 2011. *The Tragedy of Public Lands: Understanding the Fate of the Commons Under Global Commercial Pressure.* Rome: International Land Coalition.

Bayart, Jean-Francois. 1993. *The State in Africa: The Politics of the Belly.* Essex: Longman.

Berry, Sara S. 2004. Reinventing the local? Privatization, decentralization and the politics of resource management: examples from Africa, *African Study Monographs* 25(2): 79–101.

Boone, Catherine. 2012. Land conflict and redistributive politics in Kenya, *African Studies Review* 55(1): 75–103.

Borras, Saturnino M. and Jennifer Franco. 2010. *Towards a Broader View of the Politics of Global Land Grab: Rethinking Land Issues, Reframing Resistance.* Amsterdam: ICAS, LDPI and Transparency International (TI).

Borras, Saturnino M., Philip McMichael and Ian Scoones. 2010. The politics of biofuels, land and agrarian change: Editors' introduction, *Journal of Peasant Studies* 37(4): 575–95.

Branch, Daniel, Nic. Cheeseman and Leigh Gardner (eds) 2010. *Our Turn to Eat: Politics in Kenya Since 1950.* Berlin: LIT Verlag.

Budlender, Geoff. 2004. Access to courts, *South African Law Journal* 121: 339–58.

Bush, Ray, Janet Bujra and Gary Littlejohn. 2011. The accumulation of dispossession, *Review of African Political Economy* 38(127): 187–92.

Capital FM. 2011. Available at: www.capitalfm.co.ke/eblog/2011/07/14/orengo-lumumba-graftspat-healthy, accessed 19 October 2015.

Carothers, Thomas (ed.) 2006. *Promoting the Rule of Law Abroad: In Search of Knowledge.* Washington, DC: Carnegie Endowment for International Peace.

Casanelli, Lee. 1995. *Victims and Vulnerable Groups in Southern Somalia.* Ottawa: Immigration and Refugee Board of Canada.

Cheeseman, Nic. 2008. The Kenyan elections of 2007: an introduction, *Journal of Eastern African Studies* 2(2): 166–84.

De Waal, Alex. 1995. *Somalia: Crimes and Blunders.* Oxford: James Currey.

Deininger, Klaus. and Derek Byerlee. 2010. *Rising Global Interest in Farmland: Can it Yield Sustainable and Equitable Benefits?* Washington, DC: World Bank.

Department for International Development (DfID), UK. 2009. *Eliminating World Poverty: Building Our Common Future,* available at: www.official-documents.gov.uk/document/cm76/7656/7656.pdf, accessed 19 October 2015.

Dugdale, Anthony and Keith Stanton. 1982. *Professional Negligence.* London: Butterworths.

Faundez, Julio. 2009. Rule of law or Washington consensus: The evolution of the World Bank's approach to legal and judicial reform, in Amanda Perry-Kessaris (ed.) *Law in the Pursuit of Development: Principles into Practice?* London: Routledge, 180–202.

Furedi, Frank. 1989. *The Mau Mau War in Perspective.* London: James Currey.

German, Laura, George Schoneveld and Esther Mwangi. 2011. Processes of large scale land acquisition by investors: Case studies from sub-Saharan Africa, occasional paper 68, Bogor, Indonesia: CIFOR.

Ghai, Yash. 1981.' Law and lawyers in Kenya and Tanzania: Some political economy considerations'. In C. Dias, R. Luckham, D. Lynch and J. Paul (eds) *Lawyers in the Third World: Comparative and Developmental Perspectives.* Uppsala: SIAS, 144–76.

Ghai, Yash. 1987. Law, development and African scholarship, *Modern Law Review* 50(6): 750–76.

Ghai, Yash. 2011. Land and the criminalised state, *The Star,* Nairobi, 15 October 2011.

Ghai, Yash and Jill Cottrell (eds) 2010. *Marginalized Communities and Access to Justice.* Abingdon: Routledge.

Githongo, John. 2000. Towards an anti-corruption strategy for Kenya: The private sector's role, presentation to the National Anti-Corruption Plan: Private Sector Stakeholder Consultation, Nairobi, 17 October 2000.

Hall, Ruth. 2011. The many faces of the investor rush in southern Africa: towards a typology of commercial land deals, ICAS Review Paper Series 2, ICAS and TNI.

Harrington, John and Ambreena Manji. 2003. 'Mind with mind and spirit with spirit': Lord Denning and African legal education, *Journal of Law and Society* 30(3): 376–99.

Harrington, John and Ambreena Manji. 2011. Alimentary satire and the politics of corruption in Kenya, British Institute in Eastern Africa annual lecture, British Academy, London, November 2011.

Hunt, Diana. 1984. *The Impending Crisis in Kenya: The Case for Land Reform.* London: Ashgate.

ICC Kenya Monitor. 2011. Available at: www.icckenya.org/for-all-to-see-and-hear-part-ii, accessed 19 October 2015.

Kagwanja, Peter. 2005. 'Power to Uhuru': Youth identity and generational politics in Kenya's 2002 elections, *African Affairs* 105, 418: 51–78.

Kanyinga, Karuti. 2000. *Redistribution from Above: The Politics of Land Rights and Squatting in Coastal Kenya.* Uppsala: Nordiska Afrika Institutet.

Kanyinga, Karuti. 2005. 'Speaking to the past and the present: The land question in the draft constitution of Kenya'. In K. Kindiki and A. Osogo (eds) *The Anatomy of Bomas: Selected Analysis of the 2004 Draft Constitution of Kenya.* Nairobi: Claripress, 25–6.

Kenya Human Rights Commission (KHRC). 2010. Available at: www.khrc.or.ke/media-centre/pressreleases/-kptj-press-statement-on-petition-to-parliament-on-keriako-tobikos-nomination.html, accessed 19 October 2015.

KHRC. 2011. *Lest We Forget: The Faces of Impunity in Kenya.* Nairobi: KHRC.

Kenya Law Reports. 2006. *Mureithi & 2 others v. Attorney General & 4 others.* High Court Miscellaneous Civil Application no. 158 of 2005: 707–38.

Kenya National Commission on Human Rights (KNCHR) and Kenya Land Alliance (KLA). 2006. *Unjust Enrichment: The Making of Land Grabbing Millionaires.* Nairobi: KNCHR & KLA.

Kibaki, Mwai. 2003. President Mwai Kibaki's speech during the state opening of the 9th parliament, 18 February 2003, Nairobi: State House.

Kituo, cha Sheria *et al.* 2012. The land bills 2012: proposals for a framework chapter and review of the published version of the bills, presented to the parliamentary committee on land and natural resources and the technical drafting committee on the land bills, March 2012 (on file with the author).

Klopp, Jacqueline M. 2000. Pilfering the public: The problem of land grabbing in contemporary Kenya, *Africa Today* 47(1): 7–26.

Klopp, Jacqueline M. 2001. Electoral despotism in Kenya: Land patronage and resistance in the multi-party context, PhD thesis, McGill University.

Klopp, Jacqueline M. 2008. Remembering the destruction of Muoroto: Slum demolitions, land and democratisation in Kenya, *African Studies* 67(3): 295–314.

Kohnert, Dirk. 2010. Democratization via elections in an African 'narco-state'? The case of Guinea-Bissau, working paper 3, German Institute of Global and Area Studies.

Law Society of Kenya. 2012. *Objectives,* available at: www.lsk.or.ke/index.php/about-lsk, accessed 19 October 2015.

Loughlin, Martin. 1992. *Public Law and Political Theory.* Oxford: Clarendon Press.

Lynch, Gabrielle. 2010. 'Histories of association and difference: The construction and negotiation of Kenya's conscious communities'. In D. Branch, N. Cheeseman, L. Gardner (eds) *Our Turn to Eat: Politics in Kenya Since 1950,* LIT Verlag, 177–97.

Manji, Ambreena. 1998. Gender and the politics of the land reform process in Tanzania, *Journal of Modern African Studies* 36(4): 645–668.

Manji, Ambreena. 2006. *The Politics of Land Reform in Africa: From Communal Tenure to Free Markets.* London: Zed Books.

Manji, Ambreena. 2010. Eliminating poverty? 'Financial inclusion', Access to land, and gender equality in international development, *Modern Law Review* 73(6): 985–1025.

Matondi, Prosper B., Kjell Havnevik and Atakilte Beyene. 2011. *Biofuels, Land Grabbing and Food Security in Africa.* London: Zed Books.

McAuslan, Patrick. 1967. 'Control of land and agricultural development in Kenya and Tanzania'. In G.F.A. Sawyerr (ed.) *East African Law and Social Change.* East Africa Institute of Social and Cultural Affairs.

McAuslan, Patrick. 2003. *Bringing the Law Back In: Essays in Land, Law and Development.* Aldershot: Ashgate.

Merryman, J.H. 1977. Comparative law and social change: on the origins, style, decline and revival of the law and development movement, *American Journal of Comparative Law* 25 (3): 457–91.

Mueller, Susanne. 2008. The political economy of Kenya's crisis, *Journal of Eastern African Studies* 2(2): 185–210.

Mullei, P. 1988. Social security in Kenya, *International Social Security Review* 41(4): 433–7.

Mutua, Makau. 2008. *Kenya's Quest for Democracy: Taming the Leviathan.* London: L. Rienner.

Mwangi, Paul. 2001. *The Black Bar: Corruption and Political Intrigue within Kenya's Legal Fraternity.* Nairobi: Oakland Media Services.

Mwathane, Ibrahim. 2009. The role of professionals in the irregular/illegal allocations of public land: What professional associations can do! Unpublished speech to a public forum on implementing the recommendations of the Ndung'u report, delivered at the Hilton Hotel, Nairobi 14 July 2009.

Ndung'u, Paul. 2006. Tackling land related corruption in Kenya, available at: http://siteresources.worldbank.org/RPDLPROGRAM/Resources/459596-1161903702549/S2_Ndungu.pdf, accessed 19 October 2015.

Okoth-Ogendo, H.WO. 1991. *Tenants of the Crown: Evolution of Agrarian Law and Institutions in Kenya.* Nairobi: ACTS press.

Olima, W.H.A. 1997. The conflicts, shortcomings, and implications of the urban land management system in Kenya, *Habitat International* 21(3): 319–31.

Onoma, Ato Kwamenta. 2010. *The Politics of Property Rights Institutions in Africa.* Oxford: Oxford University Press.

Republic of Kenya (RoK). 2002. Report of the Commission of Inquiry into the Land Law Systems of Kenya. Nairobi: Government Printers.

Republic of Kenya (RoK). 2004 Report of the Commission of Inquiry into Illegal/Irregular Allocation of Land. Nairobi: Government Printers.

Republic of Kenya (RoK). 2010. *Constitution of Kenya.* Nairobi: Government Printers.

Ross, Stanley D. 1992. The rule of law and lawyers in Kenya, *Journal of Modern African Studies* 30(3): 421–42.

Shivji, I. 1998. *Not Yet Democracy; Reforming Land Tenure in Tanzania.* International Institute for Environment and Development (IIED).

Shivji, Issa and W. Kapinga. 1997. Implications of the Draft Bill for the Land Act. Proceedings of the Consultative Conference of NGOs and Interested Persons on Land Tenure Reform, 15–7 May, Dar es Salaam, LARRRI/HAKIARDHI.

Society for International Development (SID). 2011. *Public Land, Historical Land Injustices and the New Constitution.* Nairobi: SID.

Southall, Roger. 2005. The Ndung'u report: Land and graft in Kenya, *Review of African Political Economy* 32(103): 142–51.

Throup, David and Charles Hornsby. 1998. *Multi-party Politics in Kenya: The Kenyatta & Moi States & the Triumph of the System in the 1992 Election.* Oxford: James Currey.

Transparency International (TI). 2011 *Bribe Payers Index 2011.* Berlin: TI.

Trubek, David M. and Alvaro Santos (eds) 2006. *The New Law and Economic Development: A Critical Appraisal.* Cambridge: Cambridge University Press.

Widner, Jennifer. 1992. *The Rise of a Party-state in Kenya: From 'Harambee!' to 'Nyayo!'* Berkeley, CA: University of California Press.

World Justice Project. 2011. Available at: http://worldjusticeproject.org/about, accessed 19 October 2015.

Wrong, Michela. 2009. *It's Our Turn to Eat: The Story of a Kenyan Whistle-Blower.* New York: Harper.

Zagema, Bertram. 2011. Land and power: The growing scandal surrounding the new wave of investments in land, Oxfam briefing paper 151. Oxford: Oxfam GB.

Chapter 9

Policy and development

Perspectives from public law and political thought – a twenty-first century odyssey

John McEldowney

Introduction

Patrick McAuslan's distinctive contribution to the field of public law scholarship is assessed in this chapter. McAuslan's approach was to explore the interactions between law and other disciplines. A major focus of his work on urban planning law exposed many of the boundaries of the UK's Constitution, particularly its political and institutional structures in urban planning. McAuslan was sensitive to the political exercise of power, often cloaked in legal language, and its potential abuse, for the advancement of powerful interests at the expense of ordinary citizens. It is important to put McAuslan's work in the context at the time it was written. Even in the late-twentieth century, public law scholars in Britain had to overcome some serious hurdles to move outside the traditional boundaries of law that defined legal scholarship of the period. Public law was narrowly defined at this time but it was becoming clear that areas of government, economics, political and social change were increasingly relevant to facilitating a true understanding of law. Even so such issues were not fully considered by many lawyers. The Diceyan conservatism of the nineteenth century expressed in his *Law of the Constitution* (Dicey, 1959) had rigidly defined the boundaries of public law, even though many of Dicey's ideas on administrative law were robustly and successfully challenged by Jennings (Jennings 1933) in 1933, Dicey's legacy remained. Many legal academics and practitioners accepted Dicey's understanding of legal sovereignty though doubting that the rule of law was capable of holding parliamentary sovereignty to account against the excess of executive power. As Ernest Barker famously observed, few lawyers had turned their attention to 'the fundamental questions of politics'. As public law engaged with the system of government, how the country was governed was often ignored leaving political studies to engage with government and how it related to administration or even law (see von Gneist 1886; Johnson 1977). Many lawyers versed in the discipline of law feared to step outside the close and empirically driven confines of the legal profession. One reason for such inhibition came from the way lawyers tended to a technical and instrumental approach to their subject that was not always appropriate for a deeper understanding of government and administration. There was also considerable caution among the legal profession in entering into the world of political science which was occupied by 'politicians with a philosophic gift or philosophers with a practical interest' (Barker Introduction to Gierke 1934, p. xix; and also Barker 1947. Both sources quoted in Collini 2011, p. 251). Separating party politics from the academic study of law was a skill facilitated greatly by the adoption of a scientific methodology for legal case law analysis. It was 'objective' in focus and practical/professional in nature. Studying law in the broader context of its relevance to society was not easily achieved or appreciated. Setting boundaries between law and social science disciplines such as philosophy, economics and political studies (see Johnson 1977) proved to be excessively demanding and time consuming.

McAuslan readily understood the many obstacles facing the exploration of the boundaries between law and other disciplines. His overall curiosity and inquiry into the working of urban planning law had made him well prepared to understand the boundaries of the UK's Constitution especially in matters of the law reform of land tenure and urban planning. In fact, McAuslan's work as a consultant extended to the technical and skilled art of law drafting particularly in East Africa and this added to his understanding of the challenges facing public law. It also explains his interest in societal problems rather than remaining within the confines of abstract or academic law. Undoubtedly this led to a questioning of basic assumptions and legal doctrines and provided his interest in societal problems rather than remaining within the confines of abstract or academic law. His practical sense of engagement with real social problems allowed him to be better informed about the practical operation of the law. It was also the result of numerous consultancies for many international organisations such as the United Nations.

He also brought other benefits to the subject as his approach to public law came with the perspective and accuracy of a technical property lawyer, skilled in the art of case law dissection and statutory interpretation. Few public lawyers took their perspective from an expertise in land and property law though many had begun their career as planning lawyers. McAuslan's analysis of planning law was distinctive from many others of that time realising that the politics of the day and ideology of the period influenced outcomes more than was perhaps accepted or understood. McAuslan was also part of a new radical intellectualism that in the United Kingdom informed the development of administrative law from the 1980s (see Arthurs 1985). Academic dissatisfaction with what many saw was a narrowly defined legalistic approach to legal scholarship had given way to a broader curriculum and retreat from orthodox law teaching. Legal education in the United States was influential. There was also the experience of many law teachers who returned from abroad with an enthusiasm for developing the curriculum. Empirical and social legal research was in fashion and this was taken up through various research centres[1] but also through individuals who were pioneering in their efforts in the discipline of their study. Experience from abroad included the fast emerging study of law and development. This contributed to a different pedagogy than the orthodox that drew on overseas experience where law was often ineffective and authoritarian. A common methodology is evident – scientific, analytical and requiring comparative and evaluative study that focused on new boundaries beyond traditional 'comparative law'.

McAuslan also benefitted from the writings of John Griffith (McEldowney 2014, pp. 85–99; Gee 2008, pp. 20–45), who had come to the question of the role of law from a sociological approach believing that law was 'one of the forms of which the social control effort' related to the political life of a state as well as the idea of being a security against misrule and a central element in accountability. Drawing on the ideas of Bentham the rule of law emerges as a key element in the checks and balances on parliamentary government. J.S. Mill[2] in 1857 identified that one of the key elements to the legitimacy of the state lay in a 'sufficiently popular constitution'. Dicey's influence had down-graded administrative law. In Griffith's view, especially striking is the reliance on political processes and the empowerment that law gave to interests groups, professionals and others.

In contrast to Griffith, McAuslan adopts a formally legalistic methodology that gives prominence to law being essential in establishing structures, procedures and mechanisms that delivers fairness, and democratic and accountable government (McAuslan 2003. Also see McAuslan 2004/08). This is recognition of law being at the centre of defining the state and its economic foundations and being integral to market and social reform. Governance reform at different levels of central and local government, the role of the judiciary and the recognition of land ownership are all within a legal remit. Constitutional drafting in the aftermath of the collapse of the Communist state, the grant of independence to former colonies and in the creation of new democracies are examples of its dynamic form and relevance.

McAuslan's distinctive contribution to public law came from his knowledge and experience of the role of public bodies and institutions in urban planning. His work was instrumental in redrawing the boundaries of the subject and considering the role of political thought, the administrative state and its impact on the citizen. Finding the materials for the inquiry was only one challenge; locating a role for law amidst the plethora of discretionary decision-makers another and more challenging enterprise. The

1 The Centre for Socio-Legal Studies was established in Oxford in 1972.

2 J.S. Mill (1806–1873). English philosopher and a leading social reformer.

broader inquiry involving law and other disciplines was influenced by similar debates about the role of law within the field of law and development. Questions were easy to pose but more difficult to find satisfactory answers to, or to achieve a consensus among academics.

This chapter begins with the historical context where the formative ideas that are present in McAuslan's approach to public law may be examined. Particular attention is given to the legacy of legal scientific methodology found in the discussions of public morality and ethics that informed much of the 19th century's approach to law and law reform. The next section considers the changing role of public law in the 1960s, the increasing centralising influence of Thatcher's government from 1979 and the complaint of ineffective controls on the executive, particularly in the aftermath of privatisation and increased consumerism. The shift to government as enabling rather than providing public services through state-owned entities is also important. The critical delegation of providing public services to private entities leaves considerable uncertainty as to the adequacy of accountability. The legality of the changes is not in doubt but the nature of the changes is such as to raise fundamental questions about their desirability. Doubts and uncertainties about their potential destabilising effect raised many questions that are unanswered by the legality of the changes. Many of the values underpinning McAuslan's analysis of constitutional legitimacy and his arguments for public participation in urban planning law are fundamental requirements of democratic constitutionalism. Such values are required on occasions to act as a limitation on the executive or administration behaving unreasonably or unfairly. Setting constraints on the executive is essential even when acting legally as it goes to the fundamentals of accountability and democratic legitimacy.

Historical legacies: public law and political thought, scientific legal methodology and legal altruism

The nineteenth century sets the scene for unprecedented administrative growth, the expansion of government and, through broadening the franchise, the creation of greater local autonomy in local government. Social reform legislation was extensive covering public health, the poor law and factory inspections. Economic matters were distinguished from social policy. On economic affairs laissez-faire ideology was much in evidence while social policy was influenced by the public good, the incipient fear of social revolution and the necessity of public order. Pertinent to this analysis is Bentham's utilitarian theory, but also Adam Smith[3] and Ricardo.[4]

3 Adam Smith (1723–1790). *Wealth of Nations* 1776.

4 David Ricardo (1772–1823). Political economist, *Principles of Political Economy and Taxation* (1817).

Conflicting accounts are available over the degrees of influence that were attributable to utilitarianism (see MacDonagh 1958, p. 52; and Parris 1960, p. 17).

Particularly relevant to the nineteenth-century history of public law and intellectual thought are two foundational influences – that of scientific legal methodology and legal altruism. Scientific methodology is linked to empirical inquires focused on social problems and their legal redress from the middle of the nineteenth century in Britain, as industrialisation and urbanisation began to have its effects on the lives of many families. Transformational in its impact, legislative reform resulted that laid the foundations of what was later to be called the welfare state. In such endeavours, legal expertise and know-how became integral to the state's relationship with the citizen.

Legal altruism is a term used to describe the ideas and ideologies that informed many of the actions and motivations of the legal and social reformers of the Victorian period. Stefan Collini defines the emerging culture of altruism as stemming from J.S. Mill's 'self-conscious moral theorising', defined as the opposite of selfish by placing 'benevolence' at the heart of the project of addressing social evils, particularly poverty and distress. Altruism was far-reaching in its influence in 'English and Scottish moral philosophy since the time of Hobbes and certainly since Mandeville' (Collini 2011, p. 67). Concerns about poverty, social deprivation and ill-health as well as crime and social disorder created a common cause. Placing law in the context of social concern was primarily legislative in focus and instrumental in outcome by seeking to achieve improvement in the lives and social conditions of ordinary citizens. Property and succession, wills and intestacies, land law and its protection, the traditional areas of legal expertise were being expanded to meet new legislative challenges. English case law had relatively little to contribute and judicial thinking struggled to meet new developments through improvisations in tort and land law. Even the law of contract had to adjust to new developments and challenges.

Leslie Stephen[5] in his *Science of Ethics* categorised 'moral health' as an element of social responsibility and ethical training as a means of building a 'moral being' necessary to provide 'enduring motives to noble action' set the moral spirit and optimism of the age. Linking law to political thought was the work of many jurists notably – Austin,[6] Bryce,[7] Dicey,[8] Maitland[9] and

5 Leslie Stephen (1789–1859). Published the *Science of Ethics* in 1882.

6 John Austin (1790–1859). *English jurisprudence.* See Austin 1832 and 1863.

7 James Bryce (1838–1922). Bryce 1901.

8 Albert Venn Dicey (1835–1922). English jurist and author of *Law and the Constitution,* 1885.

9 Frederic Maitland (1850–1906). Downing Professor of the Laws of England and author of *History of English Law before Edward I,* 1895.

Maine.[10] Victorian political thought enveloped many lawyers and their works, though their defining ambition – social and economic reform – was subsumed into the study of political economy as a rival jurisprudence to legal scholarship. The underlying pre-occupation with law reform helps explain why legal methodology was important.

Scientific legal methodology defines an approach to legal study that counter-acted many of the shortcomings in the common law. This was particularly true of the lack of any coherent structure of legal classification that could be derived from a constitutional foundation. The existing civil and criminal law could be broken down into legal classifications that covered an array of legal problems. These were defined by legislative reforms and ranged from public health to factory inspectorates, local government to railways and utilities. A pragmatic, rather than a dogmatic approach was adopted (Frazer 1950; Lewis 1952; Flinn 1968; Evans 1983, p. 12; Mokyr 1985; Usher 1920). This was shaped by practical experiences and solutions that were strongly influenced by the prevailing political ideology of the time towards social reform. The influence[11] of statistical thinking was at its greatest. It was linked to many of the innovations that accompanied mathematical and statistical study being applied to social problems, including public health, pollution and waste.[12]

Studies on smallpox (Black 1830), insanity and the causes of poverty were undertaken. Local statistical surveys identified inadequate poor law provisions and Boards of Public Health were formed to fill the gaps. Water and sanitation systems proved inadequate in the face of the growth of new towns and cities and lead to a variety of health problems including the 1831–32 cholera outbreak, which claimed 32,000 lives (McManus 1994, p. 4). The poor sanitary conditions were identified in the 1842 parliamentary report on the *Sanitary Condition of the Labouring Population of Great Britain*, which perhaps marks the beginning of environmental legislation. The House of Commons became a focal point for the collection of statistics on societal concerns from poverty and crime to unemployment. A series of Nuisance Removal Acts and the Public Health Act 1848 were introduced on the basis of this theory. Powers were given to local authorities to construct sewers, licence slaughterhouses and lodgings, and remove nuisances. The General Board of Health, a central government department, received default powers to regulate and enforce local authority powers and duties. The Public Health Act 1872 divided the country into sanitary areas and gave local authority enforcement powers. The Public Health Act 1875 consolidated the law on all aspects of public health[13] and formed the

10 Henry Maine (1822–1888). *Ancient Law* 1861, and *Early Law and Custom* 1883.

11 A general historical analysis may be found in Bell and Bell 1972; Flinn 1969.

12 On science see Gribbin 2003; Wohl 1984; and also Ponting 1991.

13 In Scotland see the Public Health (Scotland) Act 1897.

foundation of the modern law on public health. There were major changes in housing law as well, with local authorities given powers to demolish unfit housing and erect buildings for working class tenants.[14] Similarly, environmental health considerations became a major focus of the legislation on food standards and health. The Housing, Town and Country Planning etc. Act 1876 created in embryo the development of a system of town and country planning[15] in Britain and came from concern that the problems of unregulated housing and overcrowding risked outbreaks of typhoid and cholera. Standards were also set for the manufacture, sale and consumption of food and drink under the Adulteration of Food and Drugs Act 1872 and the Sale of Food and Drugs Act 1875. Even a cursory glance at the extent of legislation of the nineteenth century revealed state engagement in nearly every aspect of life and society. This was taken forward in the period from 1906–1911 with the National Insurance Act 1911 and the accompanying administrative arrangements of a new welfare state. The nationalisation legislation of the 1940s also confirmed the state's role that challenged many of the principles of private property as well as land ownership. Defining the past was complicated, often contradictory but certainly necessary. As Boyd Hilton observed when considering the mid-nineteenth century:

> a two party system without coherent parties: attempts to find national solutions to social problems while reducing the size of the State and allowing scope for greater local independence; a determination to export British freedom by extending Britain's control over more and more of the world.
>
> Boyd Hilton 2008, p. 627

Located in local government, since 1835, were many of the provisions of the delivery of the welfare state including housing and poor law as well as policing, education and planning. A myriad of local government Acts provided functions associated with municipal corporations combined with local magistrates' courts. In the late 1880s county councils, parishes and various county boroughs all elected with their own electoral mandate but operating under party-political policy making substantially delivered the welfare state.

Tensions between local and central government endemic to the relationship did not prevent major delegated powers being allocated to local government from the 1888 Local Government Act which gave local government autonomy and tax raising powers. Electoral choices between

14 See the Housing of the Working Classes Act 1885 and 1890. Also see the Shaftesbury Act 1851 and the Torrens Act 32 & 32 Vict.c.130.

15 See The Town and Country Planning Act 1947.

local and central government underpinned the legitimacy of allocated powers within a single sovereign Parliament at Westminster. Private Bills could be applied for and used to ensure that local government received any additional powers it required. The Westminster model of majoritarian government with little practical restraints on legal powers had been gradually fashioned into a democracy. Three electoral reform Acts, 1829, 1832, 1884, ensured a secret ballot, male franchise and a broadening of the social composition of Parliament. The Married Women's Property Act 1870 gave women property rights culminating in the vote in 1918, just after the First World War. On a wider canvass Britain's Empire abroad represented some of the worst excesses of executive power, mitigated at times through proper administration and administrative systems often paternal in approach (Ruskin 1989, p. 77). One of the other aspects of the diversity of the common law experience was its variability found with geographical location. In Ireland and Scotland and to some extent Wales there was inequality but under the legacy of the rule of law there was optimism that law reform might result in improvement. Due process, fairness and procedural correctness defined the technical way law could be manipulated and used to advance social causes as well as redress grievances. Viewed from lands distant from the British Union, the results seemed less benign. Independence granted in many African countries had not been kind, and economic and social malaise was common in many of the poorest regions. Colonialisation and the educative values of Empire questioned assumptions about law and the state that were often underestimated by the establishment.

The experiences of Empire and the fragility of what was termed 'the rule of law' had lessons in the limitations of restraints on abuse. The theory of government that was representative and democratic, in practice often lacked substantial legal protection. Decision making was dominated by an elite on behalf of the many. Dicey (Walters 2012) greatly facilitated discussion at the end of the 19th century as to the values of the rule of law, borrowing a scientific legal methodology from Austin and many of the values found in the rule of law in the public morality and altruism that motivated the public good from Bentham (Collini 2011, p. 293). Methodology appeared a more holistic way of engaging with social problems. Reasoning by analogy, the skilful use of precedent or re-definition, either through legal fiction or pretence, the skilful avoidance of eighteenth-century revolution and the building of an Empire through advanced industrialisation, all came together as the 'triumph of the common law'. Those with power, prestige and status were accepted through land law, and property law, and that legacy survived remarkably intact. The tools of 'the science of law' as the common law was often compared to civil law systems and gave room for remarkable optimism to those law reformers who believed that given persistence, reform might triumph, equality might be achieved and social growth and economic prosperity might bring forward a new society.

Taking account of the historical legacy of government in a modern context sees the aftermath of the Second World War as a great opportunity with rising expectations in the rebuilding of the fabric of the state. The significance of law as part of an ideological conflict in which law played a significant role in defining the state is relevant. Prosser (1995, p. 507) has pointed out the reluctance to engage in a theory of the state or an overarching theory of public law. There were debates about the role of social reform and the application of economic theory with lawyers forming a central role. Two elements may be detected – the redress of social problems through legislation and improvement; the creation of substantial regulatory systems to address the reach of the regulatory state and administrative reform. McAuslan's altruism is most marked (see McAuslan 1975, Preface p. xxv) as is his approach to law studies that followed Lipset's definition focused on the 'capacity of a political system to engender and maintain the belief that existing political institutions are the most appropriate or proper ones for society' (Lipset 1959, p. 8). That said, he went on to question not the legality of government decision making but the values and morality that underpinned decisions.

Public law in transition: democratic constitutionalism

Public law has undergone considerable changes since the 1960s. Most notable is the rising self-confidence of the judiciary, illustrated in several landmark cases.[16] The breadth and depth of judicial oversight offers a tangible way to ensure that the benefits of the rule of law should extend to most citizens.[17] The striking down of government decisions on the grounds of their legality reinforces, in a substantive way, many of the values and principles that underline and define the rule of law. The pathway of change outlined below illustrates the dynamics of the rule of law and the articulation of core values. Defining such values and identifying their limitations sets the scene for the undeniable truth of the UK's constitution that there is considerable uncertainty as to when such values might apply against the executive. Are there circumstances when legally enacted laws, with the exception of EU law, are not enforceable under constitutional arrangements, with judicial authority able to disapply primary legislation? What values are these and according to what principles may their moral authority be applied?

16 *Ridge v Baldwin* [1964] AC 40; *Padfield v Minister of Agriculture, Fisheries and Food* [1968] AC 997; *Wednesbury* [1948] 1 KB 233; *O' Reilly v Mackman* [1983] 2 AC 237. *Council of Civil Service Unions (CCSU) v Minister for the Civil Service* [1985] AC 374.

17 *R v Secretary of State for the Home Department ex parte Daly* [2001] 2WLR 1622.

McAuslan's interests in ideologies of planning law and in constitutional legitimacy are considered in this context and in his broad approach to studying and writing public law. McAuslan's thinking is particularly relevant today, even though his writing was before the coming into force of the Human Rights Act 1998. The act incorporated the main provisions of the European Convention of Human Rights into domestic law including fair trials and prohibitions against retrospective law. Decisions of public administrators, courts and government are required to conform to Convention rights but this stops short of the courts being able to strike down legislation that is incompatible with Convention rights. The need to articulate the values and ethics underlying democratic constitutionalism is pertinent in setting the boundaries of good behaviour and propriety. Human rights jurisprudence provides considerable assistance in explaining relevant values and ethics.

Public law drew much from the work of Sidney and Beatrice Webb, while de Smith's influential *Judicial Review of Administrative Action* (de Smith, 1973) set the direction of a new approach to administrative law. Coinciding with the early period of McAuslan's career was the publication of B. Abel-Smith and R. B. Stevens, *Lawyers and the Courts* in 1967. A flurry of titles mapping different aspects of a new found context for law came with works by Street (1963); Borrie and Diamond (1966); and Wedderburn (1965). McAuslan's first foray into this genre of writing came with *Land, Law and Planning* (1975). This was an early cases and materials collection very much modelled on the US case book format. The work begins with discussion of the reform agenda and the continuous challenges that beset the planning system. Chapter 1 was titled *Prolegomena to Planning: The Continuity of Problems and Laws*. The book is populist in tone and engages in the rhetoric, of 'people being affected by the planning, development and control of the use of land in the United Kingdom and increasingly people wish to play some part in the planning decisions that affect their lives'. Drawing on McAuslan's experience of being a locally elected councillor and having worked in East Africa and Canada, the orientation of the work is towards a 'broader base' to legal studies than in the past.

Chapters 5 and 6 are particularly relevant to public lawyers in their discussion of central and local government in terms of planning control. The emergence of judicial controls gives rise to an analysis of judicial review and the role of public inquiries, particularly the influence of natural justice. Leading cases such as *Franklin v Ministry of Town and Country Planning*[18] became influential in the discussion of ministerial discretion and judicial control. The book also captures a recurring interest in local government. Seen as part of the planning system, local government encompassed approaches to social justice in terms of infrastructure,

18 *Franklin v Ministry of Town and Country Planning* [1947] 2 All ER 289.

housing and landlord and tenant responsibilities, including housing the homeless. McAuslan worked with the Institute of Local Government studies and participated in many seminars and discussions. He participated in evidence giving to the Widdicombe Committee on Local Government Business (Widdicombe 1986) and envisaged a participative and pro-active role for local government in the allocation of public sector powers (Cresswell, Bayliss and McAuslan 1986).

Five years later, after the success of *Land, Law and Planning* and sharing the optimism of the age and the self-criticism of the time, came McAuslan's *The Ideologies of Planning Law* in 1980. It represented a refreshing shift in the traditional scholarship of the period in planning law. The period examined in the book spanned from the 1968 to 1978, a watershed in town and country planning as well as in judicial review. Particularly important is McAuslan's influence on administrative law. Here the role of public participation, often overlooked by lawyers, is present in the use of inquiries and marked a seminal shift in attention from the traditional legal interest in tribunals. The link between public participation and the underlying ideology is well drawn out in McAuslan's writing and acknowledged by Paul Craig (Craig 1989, p. 146) as requiring 'more diverse types of institutional mechanism' to ensure adequate consultation, and appropriate levels of good decision making.

The approach McAuslan took was to evaluate the 'ideas, beliefs and assumptions of the laws and the administration of planning and housing'. The audience was not narrowly defined by legal inquiry but broadly addressed through connections made with the writings and frustrations of professional planners and key policy making. Although the main work has an English perspective, it reveals much about the author as well as the law, in terms of McAuslan's wider perspectives. Public law thought has benefitted from a broadening of the inquiry and the engagement with many different disciplines. Paramount is the acceptance of democratic systems linked to adequate forms of accountability. McAuslan's Warwick years had a major influence in shaping the work and direction of his career. Undoubtedly the flexibility of the syllabus, the generous study-leave arrangements and the collegiality of many colleagues contributed to make Warwick an ideal place. Many colleagues shared 'the Dar' experience, referring to the time spent in the University of Dar es Salaam in Tanzania, East Africa and still more believed in the contextual approach to legal studies. McAuslan's own predilections for land law and planning law found a focus in the running of one of the most successful planning modules in the country. Few could rival his passion combining practical with theoretical and class room experience. It was clear that the components of the subject were not just the interpretation of the law but its underlying social, moral and economic purpose. The strong thread running through his course was the belief that public lawyers of the future should engage not only with the legal rules and statutory forms of interpretation but with an understanding of normative rules and values. This went beyond court cases to inform the parliamentary discussion of constitutionality and its moral values in the context of a House of Commons, largely subservient to the executive, even, within Coalition arrangements.

The Thatcher legacy and the parameters of the constitution

The Thatcher period has defined remarkable changes in Britain, more profound than perhaps any other decade. Taking office in 1979, Britain was transformed by Thatcher's vision of a more urbanised society, less power to trade unions, the privatisation of state assets and the creation of an entrepreneurialism that reshaped many declining industries including coal, gas, railways, car and ship manufacturing. It was also an opportunity to redefine relations between local and central government. The mix of ideology and law proved a strong political agenda for change. Contract relations were frequently used to replace the state and contracting out public services defined the era that brought private and public actors closer together.

Reactions to these changes varied. Daintith (1982, p. 191), identified the various ways the government of the day exercises command of the law and the resources of government. The formal use of law as a command, normally through legislation supported by sanctions, is commonplace. The other aspect of government power is in the use of various economic techniques. This allows the distribution of various benefits as well as grants, taxes and incentives. Daintith classified the two types of government intervention as respectively either *imperium or dominium*. The former is used to describe the government's use of the command of law in aid of its policy objectives, while the latter is used to describe the employment of the wealth of the government for this purpose.

The government's preference to shift the role of the state from *imperium* to *dominium* was also a departure from the formal legal regulation of government to one that is harder to constrain through the traditional constitutional forms of accountability. It requires more detailed scrutiny of the policy and the factual basis on which it is being applied. Daintith concluded that this ran the 'risk of impairment of values which our constitutional law and practice ought to protect' (1989, p. 218).

Aligned to the use of central government powers was one of the most controversial changes of the period namely the relationship between local and central government, both elected but accountable to different electorates. Local government had grown considerably since the Second World War, with increasing autonomy and was a major deliverer of public services within the public sector. Planning and municipal control gave local authorities considerable influence under the planning system. Local authorities could raise a large proportion of their own revenue through local taxes while remaining subservient to parliamentary authority. There were political and ideological differences and this may explain the conflict that ensued between the Conservative government under Thatcher and local government, often dominated by Labour. Central government Conservative monetarism was in opposition to a form of Labour neo-Keynesianism.

The constitutional dimension to the debate on local government led to considerable differences in opinion as well as the passion with which it was engaged in. Legal scholarship defined by conscientious research and dispassionate publications found the political agenda too difficult to engage. Academic opinion[19] was divided between those that favoured constitutional protection to local government supporting its autonomy, the legitimacy of its elected mandate and its revenue raising powers. In constitutional terms it was thought that some form of entrenchment might be achieved through a Bill of Rights or statutory enactment. The Council of Europe made a similar suggestion through a Europe-wide mechanism for protecting local government (Grant 1989).

Opposed to local autonomy and its protection was the view that local government (see Elliott 1981) should be subsumed to legislative supremacy and the constitutional position further clarified to ensure that local government was re-subordinated to central government authority. This may not necessarily involve a coercive mechanism of control but simply a re-affirmation of the prevailing legislative sovereignty of central government. The Thatcher government embarked on fundamental changes including the introduction of a new and controversial local tax, the abolition of the Greater London Council and of the Metropolitan Authorities. McAuslan was opposed to the emasculation of local government by increased centralisation with consequent loss of political and financial autonomy (McAuslan 1987, pp. 154–161).

Privatisation, with the sale of state assets to the private sector and the end of the nationalised industries, created new legal frameworks and a growth in public law. Nationalised monopolies were in need of change through increased competition and action on consumer protection, and there was a need for the discontinuation of the cross subsidies that came from public ownership. Privatisation legislation resolved many of these issues through a new framework of pricing controls and economic and competition regulation. All offering some form of protection to vulnerable customers. At first the rise of the independent regulator was often *ad hoc* and sectoral specific, centred around a single regulator as Director General. The Ofdog culture linked accountability with independence and expertise in the

19 Particularly see Professors Stewart and Jones and many members of the Layfield Committee: Jones and Stewart 1982, p. 251.

specific sector. The Thatcher legacy remains a dominant influence today. Market driven in contrast to legal altruism, ideological and dogmatic rather than evidenced through an appropriate scientific legal methodology, its influence has extended beyond its decade.

The ideologies of planning law and the legitimacy of the constitution

The Thatcher period (see Young 1998 and 1989) questioned the underlying values of public law and challenged the methodological assumptions of a tradition of evidence-based policy making by prioritising the government's ideological preferences. In the areas of planning law and constitutional law ideological debates were at their most fierce and McAuslan (1989) contributed to that debate. McAuslan analyses planning law and identifies three different 'ideologies' at work in this area. There are some public law perspectives emerging from his analysis that show conflicting ideologies at work. His starting point was to recognise the traditional common law influence of property law intended to protect private property. This had a long and unbroken history and dominated the way lawyers considered their role which became strongly entrenched in legal thinking and methodology. The second influence was broadly defined as 'protecting the public interest' and found favour as part of a traditional public administration approach to law and legal rules. The third influence was the role of public participation with strong links to the underpinnings of democratic accountability and control. In many instances the public participation approach was virtually in opposition to the other two approaches. When public participation dominated, it challenged the protection of private property and the public interest, which had been largely dominant because of the influence of public administrators, planners and lawyers. Paul Craig explains:

> The argument that a public participation approach should be adopted came from a view that public opinion especially at a local level should be given a strong voice. The essence of the argument he advanced is that the first two approaches towards planning are dominant, albeit in varying degrees, that participation is much genuflected in theory but pushed very much into third place in practice.
>
> Craig 1989, p. 143

In theory planning legislation since 1947 had encouraged public participation, and the then Town and Country Planning Act 1990[20] required local

20 Now replaced by the Planning and Compulsory Purchase Act 2004 and the Planning Act 2008.

surveys: identification of population needs and the creation of a development plan for the area. Approved by the Secretary of State, the plan represented a compromise between local voices and planners; with public participation encouraged before and after the plan was agreed. In practice much of the decision making vested in the Secretary of State was largely driven by centralised control and direction. This is clear from the procedures and processes that surrounded submissions to the various forms of the plans. The democratic element was deputed to the Secretary of State but this offered a different form of public interest linked to the government of the day with a shift to accountability to Parliament rather than local planning responding to public opinion. McAuslan traces how over many years the theory of public participation was being eroded through codes of practice that steered public consultation towards a professional process largely driven by the Secretary of State. Partly this came from planning professionals who identified planning as a long-term strategic part of governing and partly from administrators who found that policy making through the Secretary of State offered a more coherent form of public management than unpredictable and variable responses from the public. Elected representatives managed through parliamentary processes also fitted with the overarching direction of strong government and a managerial approach to the delivery of public service favoured by the Thatcher government.

Paul Craig makes clear how McAuslan's ideologies have more general lessons for planning law and also administrative law. In both cases public participation may better inform mechanisms to control the discretion of government with potentially far-reaching consequences:

> A real commitment to the public participation ideology would entail an increase in the rights of the participator and a corresponding diminution in the control and discretion of the government. In some areas the procedure would cease to be either inquisitorial or adversarial, but be more in the nature of consultation, discussion, with broader community involvement.
>
> Craig 1989, p. 146

The role of the public local inquiry is particularly relevant to the debate over conflicting planning ideologies. A public inquiry may come about because of a refusal of planning permission. McAuslan traces the public inquiry as an example of the principle of protecting private property but also the protection of the public interest. Judicial in form and procedural in substance, the inquiry had long historical association to the parliamentary form of adjudication and debate. Its role was to consider the competing interests of different views through a combination of techniques. It gave priority to adjudicatory principles but at the same time allowed inquisitorial powers through the inspector. This combination of form and substance let public participation have a voice. In practical terms this opened up the way for third-parties interest groups and pressure groups to participate in the planning system. This, however, has had limited impact as in many instances there are restrictions on the opportunities for third-party participation.

It is clear that the way competing ideologies are resolved in terms of procedure and substance can influence the outcomes that affect the lives of many citizens. Resolving competing ideologies is difficult, leaving it hard to reconcile appropriate procedures and their use. The tensions between state, private property rights, accountability and public participation are difficult to resolve particularly in the area of public/private partnerships. Such partnerships arose in land development projects. Local government was encouraged to engage with developers that would foster new developments through joint schemes, private and public, being granted preferential treatment. Bargaining planning permission is an extension of market forces with a mixture of ideologies present. Private property is being advanced; the public interest is upheld and the local authority provides a test of the public benefit. McAuslan showed that in such examples the role of public participation was diminished. Many of the bargains resulting in planning agreements lacked public debate. Their legality was not in doubt but the legitimacy of their purpose was open to debate. Public participation was greatly diminished.

Craig (2012, p. 274) has also considered how each of McAuslan's different ideologies – private property, public interest and public participation – have significance for public lawyers. Private property ideology favours adversarial procedure familiar to a common law model of adjudication with judicial-style procedures including cross-examination and rights being legally protected. The protection of private property would thereby enjoy substantive rights and the main focus of the inquiry was to ensure that their protection was adequate. The public interest ideology engages with a less formal inquisitorial procedure. Substantive rights are more limited under this model and the government of the day is seen as the 'guardian of the public interest' through its overarching role as policy maker. Complimentary to the government's role is the doctrine of ministerial responsibility which ensures that policy making falls under parliamentary scrutiny. Conflicts between private property and the public interest are more likely to be resolved in favour of the views of those representing the public interest which may override private property. In many instances, the public interest may be given ultimate authority even if it is at the expense of some limitations being placed on substantive rights of individuals, including their private property rights.

The public participation approach requires the most adjustment to the decision-making process. The inquiry procedure would have to be re-adjusted to take account of public views, openly expressed and considered. This requires adjustment at each stage of the inquiry at both pre- and post-submission. Delegated to local government, such responsibilities are undertaken in the form of consultation and discussion rather than through legal procedures that are either adversarial or inquisitorial. The outcome would of necessity result in greater rights for all participants with no priority given to one over the other. Public participation, however, often takes longer, is more expensive and requires more resources. This is highly problematic in times of financial crisis such as the present.

McAuslan's preference for public participation arises from several influences. It is altruistic, and provides a convenient methodology that moves the agenda set by professionals – administrators, planners and lawyers – to the public. The benefit of the discussion is summarised by Craig:

> The portrayal of these different ideologies is of course somewhat stark. A system of planning may well balance between them. Yet this is not to deny the formative influence that each can have on the type of procedures adopted and the nature of the rights granted to those entitled to participate.
>
> Craig 2012, p. 274

One of the virtues of the United Kingdom's unwritten constitution is that it is dynamic. This characteristic enables political change to be accommodated very readily within the constitutional arrangements. The government of the day can be expected to claim that when it undertakes changes, these are constitutional in the sense that they were legally enacted and passed into law in accordance with existing constitutional rules. Legality is claimed on the basis of a democratic mandate often through manifesto approval. This raises the question of whether there are circumstances where the government, while acting legally, is in breach of a subsisting constitutional arrangement. This leads to a question of what is unconstitutional? What are the criteria that should be applied? Grant explains how such a question is problematic:

> there is very little consensus as to what criteria apply in the normative sense of the word. It is a term of art rather than of science, of policy rather than of law. It is an expression of unease; a code word indicating disquiet with a destabilizing intervention. Under the British constitution it needs to be distinguished from validity or legality. An illegal act by government is not necessarily unconstitutional; an unconstitutional act not necessarily illegal.
>
> 1989, p. 253

In *Law, Legitimacy and the Constitution,* (McAuslan and McEldowney, 1985) a collection of essays to celebrate the centenary of the publication of Dicey's *Law of the Constitution*, the main focus shifted to the behaviour of the government of the day and the question of how it may have morally infringed the constitutional checks and balances while legally entitled to do so. The concept of legitimacy was adopted to express ethical concerns about the propriety of the government's actions. The inherent weakness of parliamentary accountability was revealed when Parliament itself was controlled by an elected government, a manifesto mandate and the strength of a parliamentary majority. The absence of a rights culture and the tensions between the 'norms' of constitutional government, including the rule of law, were said to be interpreted too favourably towards the legal authority of the government of the day. Legitimacy as a concept provided a convenient label. As Carol Harlow (2010) has pointed out, public lawyers at first found it difficult to adopt the concept of legitimacy, commonly found in political science scholarship rather than law. The quest for setting limitations on legislative sovereignty fits uneasily in the formal doctrine of parliamentary sovereignty and the underlying principles of elected and democratic government. Additionally, the UK's unwritten constitution, while acknowledging the importance of the rule of law as a restraint on discretionary power, operated for many centuries under limited powers of judicial review.

It is important to view legitimacy as engaging with a number of aspects of law in society as part of the social context of law. Legitimacy is an important analytical tool that poses many challenges for legal theorists and transposes discussions of public law to be informed by political science. Legitimacy may be defined in a variety of ways. It stretches beyond legality, which is a core concept relating to both procedural and substantive aspects of the control of power that insist law should be clear and not retrospective. Additionally the adoption of fair procedures and equality of access to justice are pre-requisites of power. Legitimacy seeks to inform the moral underpinnings of the rule of law, particularly that democracy is important and that representativeness and fairness are enshrined in consent and respect for the law. Concepts of legitimacy inform discussion of public law today, particularly in the context of the appropriate boundaries of judicial review as well as the democratic accountability of the EU, and the influences of increased globalisation. For example, de Burca, mostly influenced by the experience of EU law, notes:

> the power of the state is legitimised through the democratic process, in that government is supposedly based in the consent of the governed, who broadly support the values on which the state is founded. Thus legitimacy has a social aspect in terms of being mooted in popular consent, with a normative aspect in terms of the underlying values on which such consent is based.

Legitimacy finds favour as a means of considering the boundaries of judicial review and the authority of democratic government. It also provides a recognition of the ethics of governing.

Democratic constitutionalism: A twenty-first century odyssey

How far has public law and the administrative state progressed in addressing the legitimacy of constitutional actors and citizen participation through fairness and the values of good government? In Laski's (1925, p. 578) famous construction constitutional law is unintelligible except as an expression of an economic system for which it was designed 'as a rampart'. The pre-eminence of law is often recognised by non-lawyers. By informing us about the legitimacy of the constitution and the state, interpreting the law may be critical in achieving fairness and addressing the shortcomings of the administration. As McAuslan acknowledged, law may transcend vested interests and provide a constraint on arbitrary power. It is possible to demarcate areas of constitutional law that give rise to concern, exposing the values and justifications for the changes and considering the normative values underpinning political choices and appropriate accountability.

There are signs that the judiciary are becoming more sensitive to public expectations in precisely the way that McAuslan had suggested in his writing in *Ideologies of Planning Law* (1989, chapter 9). In the *Coughlan* case[21] the doctrine of legitimate expectation was expanded into a substantive right to a fair hearing when a local authority 'promised' a claimant who was chronically ill, a 'home for life'. Building on expectations is guided, partly by moral principle, but also by fairness and its application in an individual case. The influence of EU and human rights law is evident. This is evident in the application of proportionality principles as a means of interpretation in administrative law.[22] This offers an evaluative tool over policy and its social and economic consequences of statutory rights.[23] This falls short of a full 'merits review', but proportionality offers a judicial inspection of the formulation of legal duties and responsibilities that rest on the government. This may not always result in a judicial intervention due to the specialist nature of the subject matter or the nature of the decision itself. Lord Bingham made clear in *R. v Secretary of State for the Environment, Transport and Regions ex parte Spath Homes Ltd.*,[24] that the 'allocation of public resources is a matter for ministers, not courts'. Similarly there are

21 *R. v North and East Devon Health Authority ex p. Coughlan* [2001] QB 213.

22 *R. v Cambridge Health Authority: Ex p. B* [1995] 2 All ER 129, *R.(Aquilar Quila) v Secretary of State for the Home Department* [2011] UKSC 45.

23 *R v Secretary of State for the Home Department ex parte Daly* [2001] 2WLR 1622.

24 [2001] 2 AC 349 at p. 395.

boundaries on judicial oversight over national security and public order[25] as well as immigration policy.[26] This may act as a restraint on merits review but it does not diminish the necessity for underlying values to act as a moral guide to the propriety of decisions rather than their legality.

In the UK, as we have seen, the overriding influence of parliamentary supremacy leaves considerable uncertainty in the effective accountability of the government of the day. This makes the underlying moral values of the constitution important even though such values are often vulnerable. In the *Jackson* case,[27] where the House of Lords rejected the claim that the Hunting Act 2004 (banning the hunting of wild mammals with dogs) was invalid, Lord Steyn observed in some *obiter dictum* comments of the existence of some 'constitutional fundamentals' which could not be abolished by the House of Commons. The question of what constitutes a constitutional fundamental is vague and is not easily defined, but a threat or policy to abolish judicial review might be an example. Lady Hale linked the 'rule of law' as fundamental and that the court would treat with 'suspicion and might even reject' any attempt 'to subvert the rule of law by removing governmental action affecting the rights of the individual from all judicial powers'.

In *Thoburn v Sunderland City Council*[28] Laws L.J., suggested that the European Communities Act 1972 was a 'constitutional statute', thus elevating its status to protection by the courts if there was any attempt at repeal or amendment. Statutes which have the potential to affect the legal relationship between the citizen and the state or enlarge or diminish the scope of fundamental constitutional rights may only be amended or repealed by unambiguous words. The courts have to balance the interests of democratically elected government accountable to Parliament and the fundamentals of the unwritten constitution. This may not always guarantee that the values and moral principles will always be observed.

In the *Corner* case,[29] involving serious allegations regarding corruption by BAE Systems, a major British company, the Director of the Serious Fraud Office decided to abandon the corruption investigation. Even though the investigation was detailed and substantial the decision to bring it to an end was controversial. It emerged from the judicial review proceedings, that the decision to end the prosecution was based on advice from the British Ambassador amidst concerns that there was a public interest for no prosecution to be taken. The overriding concern of the government was that if the prosecution went forward, there would be a threat to the

25 *Secretary of State for the Home Department v Rehman* [2003] 1 AC 153.

26 *R(Farrakhan) v Secretary of State for the Home Department* [2002] QB 1391.

27 *Jackson v Attorney General* [2005] UKHL 56.

28 *Thoburn v Sunderland City Council* [2002] EWHC 195.

29 *R. (on the application of Corner House) v Director of the Serious Fraud Office* [2007] EWHC 311.

national security of the state. It was claimed that British lives would be at stake. The Divisional Court held that the Director of the Serious Fraud Office had paid too little attention to the paramount importance of the rule of law. The House of Lords did not accept this view and took a narrower interpretation regarding the issues as standing outside the jurisdiction of the courts. It was not a judicial function to encroach on the role of the Director when the national interest was involved. The case is helpful in providing a useful chronology of the process of consultation involving the Prime Minister, the Attorney General and also the Foreign Secretary. The information provided by the court case is also revealing of how legal advice is interpreted. The case is disappointing if it is expected that the courts will penetrate the 'veil of secrecy' offered by national security, but it is also clear that moral doubts and uncertainties about the propriety of the decision are explained in the case.

There are examples where the courts are prepared to interpret the law in a broader way. In *Ghaidan v Godin Mendoza*[30] it was agreed that same-sex couples could enjoy inheritance rights as heterosexual couples. This was achieved through a 'purposeful' approach to interpretation rather than using the express words of a statutory enactment. Judicial discretion is pragmatic and this may not always result in consistency.

Jowell has noted (2011) that the rule of law contains important values that cover aspects of legality, certainty, accountability, efficiency, due process and access to justice. But the rule of law covers much more. It has a role as an effective inhibitor of arbitrary power. In that regard, scientific legal methodology and legal altruism are important values that are worth cultivating. Together they encourage inquiring into the facts and recognising public concern as pivotal in holding government to account but also setting standards in public life. Underlying constitutional values provide an important check on abuse and in the advancement of good governance. Its importance is emphasised as a means of addressing scandals or allaying public concerns. Recent examples of finding facts include the Leveson Inquiry[31] into press freedom following the phone tapping scandal, and the Chilcot inquiry[32] into the going to war, hopefully, to be published in 2016. Contemporary public lawyers are familiar with the importance of the Scott Inquiry,[33] and inquiries into the banking crisis (see Scott 2010, pp. 15–34; Black 2012, pp. 1037–1063) as well as the role of

30 *Ghaidan v Godin Mendoza* [2004]UKHL30 [2004] 2AC 557.

31 The Leveson Inquiry: *Culture, Practices and Ethics of the Press* Vols 1–4 London House of Commons 780-1-4 (29 November 2012).

32 Sir John Chilcott. See: House of Commons Library, *Chilcot Inquiry: an update* SNIA/6215 (22 October 2014).

33 See Scott 1996. Hereinafter the Scott Report. Para D4.63. See McEldowney 1997, pp. 135–56.

parliamentary select committees and reports of the National Audit Office.[34] Responses to the parliamentary expenses crisis since 2007 have involved a combination of techniques from codes of practice to new statutory forms of regulation often putting into written form the underlying values of public service and stewardship. Originally, it will be remembered that the Nolan Commission[35] made an important contribution by laying out how ethics are relevant in setting standards for public life which are broadly reminiscent of the public ethics of altruism discussed above:

- selflessness: holders of public office should act not solely in terms of the public interest but also in a way that avoids financial gain or other material benefits for themselves or their families;
- integrity: holders of public office should not put themselves in a position that permits others to exercise an outside influence on behalf of individuals or organisations that may seek to influence how they perform their public duty;
- objectivity: holders of public office should seek to make choices on merit and not on other criteria;
- accountability: holders of public office should hold themselves accountable for their decisions and their actions;
- openness: reasons for decisions should be given and information only restricted when the wider public interest demands such restrictions;
- honesty: holders of public office should declare any private interest relating to their public duties;
- leadership: leadership should be provided by example, and these principles should be applied.

Statutory regulation through the creation of the Independent Parliamentary Standards Authority (IPSA) Act 2009 is the result of public pressure, parliamentary debate and the shift from self-regulation to an external form of regulation providing oversight of MPs' pay and pensions. It also reinforces the importance of the work of the Committee on Standards in Public Life. The work of IPSA in particular is a good example of public participation. They undertake wide public consultation and monitor public opinion. IPSA has replaced the self-interested regulation by MPs of their own salaries and expenses with an external and statutorily independent regulator. Standard setting is also to be found in the creation of a statutory basis for the Civil Service under the Constitutional Reform and Governance Act 2010. This is in response to parliamentary and public pressure. Equally important are the plethora of codes and informal

34 House of Commons Library: *The Budget and the Annual Finance Bill* Standard Note SN00813 (14th November 2012).

35 Also see HM Government, *Modernising Government*, Cm 4310, 1999.

working manuals that are part of the Treasury's approach to holding government departments to account for public spending. Probity, value for money, and public stewardship are all underlying values.

The interface between public and private bodies has also required attention as it illustrates the mix of both *dominium* and *imperium* forms of government intervention today. It is the ethics of such an interface that is at the heart of the government's desire for improvements in the PFI (Private Finance Initiative) system. This is highlighted in HM Treasury's report in March 2006, *Strengthening Long-term Partnerships* and also in the analysis of PFI projects undertaken by KPMG. The aim is to develop the working relations between private sector project managers and their public service counterparts.[36] It is intended to provide a greater integration between the private and public sectors including recruitment policies and the use of technical advisers common to each sector. Many operational contracts appear to be on budget and on time. It was estimated that 94 per cent of contracts are meeting their service level agreements and in many cases, this gives rise to deductions in costs because targets are met. The benchmarking of PFI contracts also appears to be successful, though it is premature to suggest that this area has yet been reliably assessed. The wording of contracts has improved and in many instances, there are high returns on the contracts, over 90 per cent of projects make a profit for the contractors. KPMG also noted that risk management analysis had improved. Risk assessment is seen as a key element for the future. Equally there is some evidence from the KPMG study that the infusion of the private sector into public sector bodies has brought about a re-alignment of practices, processes and procedures.

Numerous value-for-money examinations have been undertaken by the National Audit Office on behalf of the Public Accounts Committee. The Treasury has provided strong support for PFI projects. Its estimation is that over 88 per cent of PFI projects were delivered on time and within budget. In contrast only 70 per cent of publicly funded projects are delivered later than their contract date and 73 per cent cost more than are expected.[37] Some question such claims, and there are serious doubts about whether technically complex PFI arrangements are being properly scrutinised. The recent findings of the National Audit Office (NAO) study, *PFI Improving the Tendering Process*,[38] provides an evaluation of best practice. The value of this type of NAO report is that it provides a useful analytical framework for deciding how effective different ways of regulating PFI are in practice. This helps to highlight instances of weakness and how arrangements might be

36 Executive Summary, KPMG, *Effectiveness of operational contracts in PFI* London, KPMG, 2007.

37 *The Independent* 20 September 2007.

38 NAO, *PFI Improving the Tendering Process*, London: Stationery Office, 2007.

improved for the future. In fact, from the start of PFI projects there has been a never-ending number of measures taken by the government to tackle procurement issues.

Underlying values and ethics are at issue when it comes to bankers' pay and conditions and the tax liabilities of the very wealthy. In a period of financial crisis and limits on financial markets there is a paradox worth noticing that freeing the markets from government requires increasing regulation of the rules and responsibilities of markers to protect the public interest. The recent LIBOR (London inter-bank lending rate) scandal is indicative of this need[39] where conventional approaches to law and regulation fail or are ineffective. There are dangers of legislating without regard to the prevailing moral, social and political culture (Prosser 2006, pp. 364–87) of the time and this is clearly illustrated. As Awry, Blair and Kershaw have pointed out, private law constructions of corporate responsibilities, directors' duties and policies for remuneration, and sanctioned-based oversight by regulatory authorities have proved inadequate and unsuccessful. Relations between shareholders, government and other stakeholders are not sufficiently underpinned by a moral compass, making existing arrangements inadequate. Providing an ethical dimension in the discussion of the governance of financial services is seen as an important step forward in pursuit of broader social objectives (see Awry, Blair and Kershaw 2012).

Ethical interests also arise in terms of the adequacy of legal aid, and reducing the availability of legal advice raises serious concerns about access to justice. In *R (on the application of Edwards and Pallikaropoulos) v The Environment Agency*[40] the Advocate General of the European Court of Justice (ECJ) expressed concerns about the rule that environmental campaigners should be required to pay the other side's legal costs if they are unable to show that they had an extensive economic interest in the outcome. Articulating this concern, the Advocate General considered the public interest at stake in environmental cases. Assessing the costs and gauging the ability to pay may impede ordinary citizens from litigating. These examples of recent developments in public law serve to remind us of how McAuslan's writing was in advance of his times and how it provides lessons for us all.

Conclusions

The main focus of this chapter is to provide an assessment of McAuslan's contribution to public law. Primarily, this is to be made through his claims about the ideology of public participation as a way of ensuring a link

39 House of Commons Library: *LIBOR, Public Inquiries and FSA Disciplinary Powers* SN/BT/6376 (14 November 2012).

40 C-260/11 (2012) New Law Journal 1332 (26 October 2012).

between public opinion and the government. Planning law, through this mixture of rules and procedures, becomes an important evaluative device on how government decisions are made, and the legal framework that is used to achieve this makes a difference to the outcomes. There are many variations on how to develop a discourse between public or private law that includes a 'quasi-public' jurisprudence among property lawyers (see Gray and Gray 1999, p. 18). McAuslan was one of the first public lawyers to realise with some certainty that some areas of private property are affected by the public interest. This is in essence recognition that the modern state has many ways of finding its way into the lives of the citizen. McAuslan saw the dangers of allowing the state unfettered powers, and that vigilance was achievable through different levels of public participation. This is clear from his work on *Ideologies of Planning Law* (McAuslan 1989; McAuslan 1975) and in his edited collection on *Law, Legitimacy and the Constitution* (McAuslan and McEldowney 1985). McAuslan forewarned that the absence of systems for public participation would put in jeopardy the legitimacy of government. This had echoes of previous concerns such as Hewart's *New Despotism*.[41]

Another important aspect of McAuslan's contribution to public law was in the area of local government. His interest in planning law took him to the role of local authorities as an interested party in the legitimate and elected alternative to the power of central government. McAuslan's assessment of the significance of local government arose because local authorities provided the main delivery of various aspects of the welfare state including homes, social care and education; even though this role was perceptively changing, as delivery of local services was being changed to the local authority which was becoming the regulator of the service. McAuslan viewed accountable and effective local government as essential and conceded that many of the existing mechanisms of accountability in the 1980s that allowed the public challenge of local government decisions were ineffective (McAuslan and McEldowney 1988, pp. 89–102). Alternatives included introducing a cabinet-style formulation of accountability that would ensure that elected members and officials would each have their lines of accountability designated and clarified. This was mainly intended to separate political decision making based on party-political choices from administrative decisions. Undoubtedly the value of political choices made at the level of local government required some protection and electoral accountability rather than legal challenge, which McAuslan regarded as the most appropriate mechanism of control (see McAuslan 1987, pp. 154–161).

Planning, the environment and, more generally, public law provided an important link with his many consultancies abroad and his teaching

41 Lord Hewart 1929. More recently see Hennessy 1995. Bogdanor 2011.

interests at Birkbeck College, University College London and Warwick. Integrating research, teaching and consultancy work provided a distinctive education pedagogy that provided powerful and often unique insights into a vast gambit of legal understanding and systems of decision making. It also provided a point of reference for cross-disciplinary co-operation that crossed many fields of study. It was particularly the case with the issue of planners and planning law, an area in which McAuslan worked overseas on many important projects.[42]

Evaluating McAuslan's contribution to public law goes beyond understanding his analysis of the role of law as an instrument of social control. His work provides insights on the legitimacy of governance, the allocation of power and the control of unfettered discretion. His prescription of open and accountable government enabled through appropriate mechanisms for public participation remains unfulfilled. This defines his legacy that builds on constitutional fundamentals that define the accountability of the government, which are no less important today than when there was a more general political consensus over the state's involvement with welfare provision. The state's role has changed remarkably today in its relationship with the citizen and its partnership with the private sector, engaging in marketization and privatisation strategies.

McAuslan also contributed to the overall pedagogical contribution of public law to legal scholarship. This involves migrating the methods of case law analysis familiar to private lawyers and the protection of private property, a common feature of land law, to the arena of government and the legal authority of the state. The building blocks common in the 19th century foundations of scientific legal methodology and legal altruism are evident in McAuslan's thinking and correspond to the values and beliefs that he felt should inform our understanding of the role of law. Democratic constitutionalism provides 'principles of morality' that are inherent in any dynamic democracy and are a product of a number of influences including history, culture and legal tradition. It is also offers a conceptual framework with which to assess the underlying values supporting social justice and community-based principles of public trust and stewardship. This operates beyond national legal systems towards global governance and recognises the stages of law in development. It is pivotal to constitutional building in the development of democratic states and engages questions of legitimacy, the right to govern, as well as the legal authority to exercise power. Regulatory agencies as well as the traditional forms of government fall within its auspices. Democratic constitutionalism also allows cross-boundary and transnational issues to be examined and can engage both private sector and

42 This included the Department for International Development (DFID) project on Ethiopia, for the Lands, Survey and Physical Planning Department of the Ministry of Local Government 1998–2000. Payne 2012.

public sector entities. It also encompasses different constituencies and communities, local and central, specialist and non-specialist as well as non-governmental. Extending juridical discourse beyond a narrow construction of the rule of law engages with issues at the boundaries between law, justice and political accountability. This inevitably advances inquiries within the legal system into what is fair within the context of the politics of elected government and democratic control. Political adaptation and change has to be more than accounted for by juridical responses in setting the limits of power (see Gee 2008, pp. 20–45. Tomkins 2005). In his analysis of land law and reform in Eastern Africa, (McAuslan, 2013), he returns to his original analysis that political considerations are often uppermost in determining the success of urban reforms. Too often political power elites dominate and re-cast the implementation process in their own interests, even if reforms are well drafted and well considered. This is not cynicism but an experienced voice based on the realisation that powerful influences opposing change may dominate. Winning the hearts and minds of government to support a more broadly framed public law agenda is essential to overcome vested interests. McAuslan's odyssey had really only begun to realise his goals of social, political and economic justice.

References

Arthurs, Harry. 1985. *Without the Law.* Toronto: University of Toronto.

Austin, John. 1998 [1863]. Province of Jurisprudence Determined (1832). In *Lectures on Jurisprudence.* Indianapolis, Cambridge: Hackett Publishing Company.

Awry, Dan, William Blair, and David J. Kershaw. 2012. Between law and markets: Is there a role for culture and ethics in financial regulation? *LSE Working Papers* 14.

Barker, Ernest. 1934. Introduction to *Otto Gierke, Natural Law and the Theory of Society 1500–1800.* Cambridge: Cambridge University Press.

Barker, Ernest. 1947. *Political Thought in England 1848–1914.* Oxford: Oxford University Press.

Bell, Colin. and Rose Bell. 1972. *City Fathers: The Early History of Town Planning in Britain.* Harmondsworth: Penguin.

Black, Julia. 2012. Paradoxes and failures: 'New Governance' techniques and the financial crisis, *Modern Law Review* 75(6): 1037–1063.

Black, William. 1830. *Observations Medical and Political on the Smallpox.* London.

Borrie, Gordon and Aubrey L. Diamond. 1966. *The Consumer, Society and the Law.* London: Penguin.

Bogdanor,Vernon. 2011. *The New British Constitution.* Oxford: Hart.

Boyd Hilton, A.J. 2008. *A Mad, Bad and Dangerous People? England 1783–184.* Oxford: Oxford University Press.

Bryce, James. 1901. *Studies in History and Jurisprudence.* New York: Oxford University Press.

Collini, Stefan. 2011. *Public Moralists: Political Thought and Intellectual Life in Britain 1850–1930.* Oxford: Clarendon Press.

Craig, Paul. 1989. *Administrative Law* 2nd edition. London: Sweet & Maxwell.

Craig, Paul. 2012. *Administrative Law* 7th edition. London: Sweet & Maxwell.
Cresswell, Roy W., D. Bayliss and Patrick McAuslan. 1986. *The Future Role and Organisation of Local Government.* Birmingham: INLOGOV.
Daintith, Terence. 1982. Legal analysis of economic policy, *Journal of Law and Society* 9: 191.
Daintith, Terence. 1989. 'The executive power today: Bargaining and economic control'. In Jeffrey Jowell and Dawn Oliver (eds) *The Changing Constitution,* 2nd edition. Oxford: Oxford University Press.
De Smith, 1973. *Judicial Review of Administrative Action* 3rd edition. London: Stevens.
Dicey, A.V. 1959. *The Law of the Constitution* 10th edition. E.C.S. Wade. London: Macmillan.
DIFID. 1998–2000. Project on Ethiopia, for the Lands, Survey and Physical Planning, Department of the Ministry of Local Government.
Elliott, Michael. 1981. *The Role of Law in Local Central Relations.* London: Social Science Research Council.
Evans, Eric J. 1983. *The Forging of the Modern State: Early Industrial Britain 1783–1870.* London: Routledge.
Flinn, Michael W. 1968. *Public Health Reform in Britain.* London: Macmillan.
Flinn, Michael W. (ed.) 1969. Introduction to *The Medical And Legal Aspects of Sanitary Reform.* Stewart, Alexander P. and Edward Jenkins. Leicester University Press/New York: Humanities Press.
Frazer, William M. 1950. *A History of English Public Health 1834–1939.* London: Bailliere, Tindall & Cox.
Gee, Graham. 2008. The political constitutionalism of J.A.G. Griffith, *Legal Studies* 28(1) March: 20–45.
Grant, Malcolm. 1989. 'Central-local relations'. In Jeffrey Jowell and Dawn Oliver (eds) *The Changing Constitution* 2nd edition. Oxford: Oxford University Press, 1989.
Gray, Kevin and Susan Gray. 1999. 'Private property and public propriety'. In Janet McLean (ed.) *Property and the Constitution.* Oxford: Hart Publishing.
Gribbin, John. 2003. *Science: A History.* Penguin.
Harlow, Carol. 2010. The concepts and methods of reasoning of the new public law: legitimacy. *LSE Working Papers* 19.
Hennessy, Peter. 1995. *The Hidden Wiring: Unearthing the British Constitution.* London: Gollancz.
Hewart, Lord. 1929. *The New Despotism.* London: Benn.
House of Commons Library. 2012. *The Budget and the Annual Finance Bill* Standard Note SN00813 (14 November 2012).
House of Commons Library. 2012. *LIBOR, Public Inquiries and FSA Disciplinary Powers* SN/BT/6376 (14 November 2012).
HM Government, *Modernising Government,* Cm 4310, 1999.
Jennings, Ivor. 1933. *Law of the Constitution.* London: London University Press.
Johnson, Nevil. 1977. *In Search of the Constitution: Reflections of State and Society in Britain.* Oxford: Pergamon Press.
Jones, G. and J. Stewart. 1982. 'Defending local government. Local Government Chronicle 75'. In Grant, Malcolm. 1989. Central-local relations in Jeffrey Jowell and D. Oliver (eds) *The Changing Constitution* 2nd edition. Oxford: Oxford University Press.

Jowell, Jeffrey. 2011. 'The rule of law and its underlying values'. In Jeffrey Jowell and D. Oliver (eds) *The Changing Constitution* 2nd edition. Oxford: Oxford University Press.

KPMG, Executive Summary, *Effectiveness of Operational Contracts in PFI.* London, KPMG, 2007.

Laski, Harold. 1925. *A Grammar of Politics.* Allen and Unwin, p. 578. Quoted in Carol Harlow and Richard Rawlings. 2009. *Law and Administration.* Cambridge: Cambridge University Press, p. 1.

Leveson Inquiry: *Culture, Practices and Ethics of the Press* Vols 1–4. London: House of Commons 780-1-4 (29 November 2012).

Lewis, Richard Albert. 1952. *Edwin Chadwick and the Public Health Movement 1832–1854.* London: Longman.

Lijphart, Arend. 1984. *Democracies: Patterns of Majoritarian and Consensus Government in Twenty-one Countries.* New Haven, CT: Yale University Press.

Lipset, Seymour M. 1959. Some social requisites of democracy: Economic development and political legitimacy, *American Political Science Review* 53, p. 86.

MacDonagh, O. 1958. The nineteenth-century revolution in government: A reappraisal, *Historical Journal* 1: 52.

McAuslan, Patrick. 1975. *Land, Law and Planning.* London: Weidenfeld & Nicolson, Preface p. xxv.

McAuslan, Patrick and John McEldowney (eds) 1985. *Law, Legitimacy and the Constitution.* London: Sweet & Maxwell.

McAuslan, J. Patrick and John F. McEldowney. 1988. Public challenge and local government, *Coexistence* 25: 89–102.

McAuslan, Patrick. 1987. The Widdicombe Report: Local government business on politics? *Public Law* pp. 154–161.

McAuslan, Patrick. 1989. *Ideologies of Planning Law.* Oxford: Pergamon Press.

McAuslan, Patrick. 2003. *Bringing the Law Back In: Essays in Land, Law and Development.* Aldershot: Ashgate.

McAuslan, Patrick. 2004–08. In the Beginning was the Law – An Intellectual Odyssey. Unpublished paper.

McAuslan, Patrick. 2013, *Land Law Reform in Eastern Africa.* London: Routledge.

McEldowney, John F. 1997. The Scott Report: Inquiries, parliamentary accountability and government control in Britain, *Democratization* 4:4 Winter, 135–56.

McEldowney, John F. 2013. One-party dominance and democratic constitutionalism in South Africa, *Journal of South African Law* 269–291.

McEldowney, John F. 2014. A.G. Griffith: Parliament and legislation, *Public Law* 85–99.

McManus, Francis. 1994. *Environmental Health Law.* London: Blackstone Press.

Maine, Henry. 1861 *Ancient Law.* London: John Murray.

Maine, Henry. 1883. *Early Law and Custom.* London: John Murray.

Mokyr, Joel (ed.) 1985. *The Economics of the Industrial Revolution.* USA: Rowman & Littlefield Publishers.

National Audit Office. 2007. *PFI Improving the Tendering Process.* London: Stationery Office, 2007.

Parris, Henry. 1960. A nineteenth-century revolution in government: A reappraisal reappraised, *Historical Journal* 3: 17.

Payne, Geoffrey. 2012. *Putting the Law into Context: An Appreciation of Patrick McAuslan and His Influence.* Geoffrey Payne & Associates.

Pempel, T.J. (ed.) 1990. *Uncommon Democracies: The One-Party Dominant Regimes.* Ithaca, NY: Cornell University Press.

Ponting, Clive. 1991. *A Green History of the World.* London: Sinclair-Stevenson.

Prosser, Tony. 1995. The state, constitutions and implementing economic policy: Privatization and regulation in the UK, France and the USA, *Social and Legal Studies* 4: 507.

Prosser, Tony. 2006. Regulation and social solidarity, *Journal of Law and Society* 33: 364–87.

Ruskin, John. 1989. *Praeterita 1885–89.* Oxford: Oxford University Press.

Scott, Colin. 2010. 'Regulatory governance and the challenge of constitutionalism'. In Dawn Oliver, Tony Prosser and Richard Rawlings (eds) *The Regulatory State.* Oxford: Oxford University Press.

Scott, The Rt. Hon Sir Richard, The Vice-Chancellor. 1996. Return to an Address of the Honourable House of Commons dated 15 February 1996. Report of the Inquiry into the Export of Defence Equipment and Dual-use Goods to Iraq and related Prosecutions, HC 115 London: HMSO, 1996.

Smith, Adam. 1904. *Wealth of Nations.* London: Methuen and Co.

Stephen, Leslie. 1899. *Science of Ethics.* Cambridge: Cambridge University Press.

Street, Henry. 1963. *Freedom the Individual and the Law.* London: Penguin.

Tomkins, Adam. 2005. *Our Republican Constitution.* Oxford: Hart.

Usher, Abbott Payson.1920. *An Introduction to the Industrial History of England.* Boston, MA: Houghton Mifflin Company.

von Gneist, Rudolf. 1886. *History of the English Constitution.* London: Clowes.

Walters, Mark D. 2012. Dicey on writing the 'Law of the Constitution', *Oxford Journal of Legal Studies* 21.

Wedderburn, K.W. 1965. *The Worker and the Law.* London: Penguin.

Widdicombe, David. 1986. The Committee of Inquiry into the Conduct of Local Authority Business Cmnd. 9797, London.

Wohl, Anthony. 1984. *Endangered Lives: Public health in Victorian Britain.* London: Methuen.

Young, Hugo. 1989. *One of Us.* London: Macmillan.

Young, Hugo. 1998. *This Blessed Plot: Britain and Europe from Churchill to Blair.* London: Macmillan.

Cases

Council of Civil Service Unions (CCSU) v. Minister for the Civil Service [1985] AC 374.

Ghaidan v. Godin Mendoza. [2004] UKHL 30.

Jackson v. Attorney General [2005] UKHL 56.

O'Reilly v. Mackman [1983] 2 AC 237.

Padfield v. Minister of Agriculture, Fisheries and Food [1968] AC 997.

R (Farrakhan) v. Secretary of State for the Home Department [2002] QB 1391.

R. v. North and East Devon Health Authority ex parte Coughlan [2001] QB 213.

R (on the application of Corner House) v. Director of the Serious Fraud Office [2007] EWHC 311.

R (on the application of Edwards and Pallikaropoulos) v. The Environment Agency C-260/11 (2012) New Law Journal 1332 (26 October 2012).
R v Secretary of State for the Home Department ex parte Daly [2001] 2WLR 1622.
Ranklin v. Ministry of Town and Country Planning [1947] 2 All ER 289.
Ridge v. Baldwin [1964] AC 40.
Secretary of State for the Home Department v. Rehman [2003] 1 AC 153.
Thoburn v. Sunderland City Council [2002] EWHC 195.
Wednesbury [1948] 1 KB 233.

Statutes

The Public Health (Scotland) Act 1897.
The Housing of the Working Classes Act 1885 and 1890.
The Shaftesbury Act 1851 and the Torrens Act 32 & 32 Vict.c.130.
The Town and Country Planning Act 1947.
The Planning and Compulsory Purchase Act 2004 and the Planning Act 2008.

Chapter 10

Public participation and legal standing

Mexican high courts and environmental conflicts

Antonio Azuela

Introduction

One of the most insightful contributions of Professor Patrick McAuslan, during his time at Warwick, was his analysis of the three ideologies that compete in the field of planning and environmental law (McAuslan 1979 and 1980). Private property, the public interest (as seen from state agencies) and public participation, are indeed the three points of view from which any decision that transforms cities and the environment can be considered. Often, when one of them prevails, it is at the expense of the other two. It would not be an exaggeration to assert that legal practices in this field are nothing less than the result of the ever changing balance between those points of view. This chapter describes a shift of balance between those three ideologies in the case of Mexico, as a result of changes in the rules that recognise standing before the courts to members of the community that oppose projects that damage the environment. In particular, we will analyse how in the last three decades high courts abandoned traditional notions of legal interest, in order to give access to the courtroom to members of the community that claim their right to an adequate environment – a process that empowered citizens as much as it empowers judges themselves.

Our subject matter lies at the intersection of two issues that are usually debated in separate contexts. On the one hand, since the nineties many Latin American countries, like Mexico, have experienced deep constitutional transformations as part of what has been called the 'democratic transitions' (Woldemberg 2012). The consolidation of a strong judiciary, committed to the protection of fundamental rights, has been at the centre of expectations towards the law in the region. Neo-constitutionalism is the name of the doctrine that translates these expectations into the realm of legal scholarship. On the other hand, the problem of standing, i.e. the question of who is entitled to mobilize the judiciary, is a central issue in planning and environmental law. Organisations that defend environmental rights have been demanding the recognition of standing in order to enforce environmental regulations through the courts when governments fail to do so (Almagro-Nosete 1982; Landi 1991; Aguirrezabal-Grünstein 2006; Cafferatta 2005). Both issues have become salient in Mexican legal practice and there is no doubt that this way public participation has gained power *vis à vis* the ideologies of private property and administrative power.

In July 2011 the Mexican Constitution[1] was amended in order to introduce class actions as well as a profound reform of the *amparo* suit, which is the main remedy that Mexican law provides for the protection of fundamental rights. One of the main features of that reform was the broadening of the possibilities for having access to the *amparo*. The rigid rules of the 'legal interest' that was necessary to show in order to file an *amparo* are being replaced with the recognition of a 'legitimate interest' (also called 'diffuse interest').[2] This was seen by progressive legal scholars as a great innovation and, not surprisingly, private businesses' organisations declared their fears that this would open the door for opportunistic litigation that would jeopardize economic development. However, and this is the main point in this chapter, the fact is that the widening of the concept of legal interest had begun many years before, when urban (and later environmental) legislation granted neighbours a right to oppose developments that damaged their environment, which paved the way for a change in judges' attitudes towards the question of standing in urban and environmental disputes. As will be seen, even if McAuslan was at that time engaged mostly in Africa and had not even visited Mexico, he was part of that process.

In the first section of this chapter I briefly review the legislative changes that in 1983 and 1996 granted neighbours what the courts would describe as a 'right to preserve the residential environment' and then as a mechanism to defend the environment as a 'common good'. In the second section I analyse the way federal courts interpreted those legislative changes through *tesis de jurisprudencia*, which represent the main form of judicial interpretation in Mexico. These 'theses' are the centre of this chapter because our intention is to present the recognition of standing rights as a process of cultural change. As we will see, the process had at least two salient features. First it took a long time, almost three decades, for the federal high courts to recognise the full legal consequences of something that enacted legislation had laid down quite clearly since the early eighties. And second, it looks like a straightforward process of making explicit what

1 *Constitución Política de los Estados Unidos Mexicanos*, as amended, Diario Oficial de la Federación [DO], 5 February 1917.

2 Most authors equate 'legitimate interest' with 'diffuse interest' (Schmill 2011). For us, the latter indicates more clearly the collective nature of the grievances that are at stake. Of course there is a doctrinal debate around these categories which falls outside the scope of this chapter.

legislation already says. Whereas most public interest lawyers in Mexico would say that this has been a painful process, in which proving an environmental damage has been at times an impossible mission, when one reads the Mexican *jurisprudencia* on the subject it seems like a natural, even painless, process. We will come back to this paradox in the conclusion.

Now it is important to clarify the meaning of the word *jurisprudencia* in the Mexican context. Legal dictionaries authorize the use of the English word 'jurisprudence' to refer to 'judicial precedents considered collectively' (*Black's Law Dictionary* 2000), so we will use the Spanish and the English word as synonymous. In any case, it is important to bear in mind that *jurisprudencia* is recognised as a 'source of law'. There is a widespread belief that in legal systems where the Romano-Germanic element predominates, as in the case of Mexico, the judiciary does not have a meaningful role in the creation of the law. Indeed, one of the criticisms that young legal scholars direct towards courts is that they are too loyal to the texts of enacted legislation (Concha and Caballero 2004). However, the truth is that judges are far from being automats that apply the law in a consistent way and we will try to illustrate this throughout the chapter.

Let us start by pointing to one of the most relevant features of Mexican *jurisprudencia*, i.e. the fact that it appears as a collection of legal formulae, called '*tesis*' (or *tesis*), that bear no clear relationship to the cases that prompted them. As opposed to the doctrine of precedent in the Common Law tradition, our *jurisprudencia* appears under the guise of abstract formulations, entirely de-contextualized. That is one of the reasons why it is frequently argued that it does not work as precedent, i. e. because it is impossible to compare a current case with the one that motivated a previous judicial decision (Zertuche-García 1992; Carmona-Tinoco 1995; Magallón-Ibarra 2004; Vázquez-Robles 2012). On the other hand, there are clear rules, established in enacted legislation as to when a *tesis* is compulsory for the judiciary as a whole – typically, it takes five cases in which a *tesis* is sustained in order for it to be compulsory.[3] However, the fact is that judges at all levels refer to all sorts of *tesis* in order to uphold their arguments. And they invoke *jurisprudencia* as if it was enacted legislation. I will try to show that, in spite of its abstract and de-contextualized character, reading *jurisprudencia* is full of surprises.

Standing as public participation in urban and environmental legislation: from quiet changes to prominence

Let us see how the question of standing in urban and environmental conflicts in Mexico entered the legal system. In May 1976 Congress passed

3 See *Ley de Amparo*, section 172.

the Human Settlements General Act (HSGA, or *Ley General de Asentamientos Humanos*).[4] This was the first time that urban problems were the subject of a comprehensive law at national level.[5] Its title reveals the intention of the Mexican government to be in tune with the international debate. In fact it was enacted just before the first UN World Conference on Human Settlements. It included public participation as one of the aspects that should be present in the planning process. Somehow, those who drafted it had the idea that the expertise of planners and other civil servants was not enough to give legitimacy to urban plans – a widespread view, in fact, in planning circles around the world. However, there were no precise mechanisms to make public participation compulsory or to guarantee that the affected populations were taken into account.

In 1983 it was necessary to revise the HSGA as a result of a constitutional amendment that had just included new provisions to give way to a 'municipal reform'. Local governments were granted explicit powers and became the main actors in the urban planning process. Since then, section 115 of the Constitution became the symbol of the most ambitious decentralization programme in modern Mexico. Thus the government prepared a bill amending the HSGA in order to get the planning process in tune with the new municipal regime. At that time, the dominant political party in the country the Institutional Revolutionary Party (PRI) had such an ample majority in Congress that it did not need to convince or negotiate with other political forces to pass almost any legislation. Thus in November 1983 upon the initiative of President Miguel de la Madrid Congress passed the bill to amend the HSGA and three months later the new version was in force. Apart from changes in the planning process that fall outside the scope of this paper, the new act included a provision written by a team of lawyers of the Ministry of Urban Development and Ecology – which included a former student of McAuslan. There was no public debate around the bill, but everyone who took part in the process thought that it was a good idea to strengthen public participation by granting citizens a right to oppose developments that would infringe the rules of an urban plan and would bring with it a loss in the quality of life in the neighbourhood. The result was a section 47 that read as follows:

> When constructions, subdivisions, changes of land use, or other developments that contravene laws, regulations, or urban development plans are taking place and they originate a deterioration of the quality of life in human settlements, the residents of the area that are directly affected will have the right to demand the corresponding suspensions,

4 *Diario Oficial de la Federación*, 26 May 1976.

5 There have been planning laws at state level since the thirties, but they referred mostly to the opening of new roads for urban expansion. See, generally, Azuela 1989.

> demolitions or necessary modifications, so that the rules in force are complied with. Permits that contravene legislation, regulations, and urban development plans will be null and void and the responsible civil servants will be punished according to the law.
>
> This right will be made effective before the corresponding authorities or their immediate superiors, who will listen to the neighbours and the affected parties, and will resolve in no less than thirty days after the complaint was filed.[6]

In the next section we will see how federal judges interpreted this rule in the following decades. For the moment suffice to say that its adoption was neither the product of a social demand nor the subject of a public deliberation. It emerged from federal bureaucracy, almost as a prank of low-level civil servants, and did not attract the attention of the media or even the specialised literature. It was only years later that neighbours' organisations began to use it in order to oppose developments.

During the next decade the Mexican political environment changed radically. After the earthquake of 1985, social mobilization coalesced in the formation of a wide variety of organisations. An environmental movement began to emerge and in 1987 new environmental legislation was being discussed in Congress. This time the government had to listen to several social organisations in order to give legitimacy to the legislative process. As a result, the Ecological Balance and Environmental Protection General Act (EBEPGA or *Ley General del Equilibrio Ecológico y la Protección al Ambiente*) came into force in February 1988. No doubt the most ambitious piece of legislation in Mexican environmental law; in its first version it included some instruments for social participation, such as the right of access to information of projects in the process of being subject to an environmental impact assessment. This attracted the involvement of many organizations throughout the country that demanded changes in development projects and sometimes their cancellation.

Nevertheless, the new environmental legislation did not provide for a remedy that would make compulsory for the government to reconsider projects that had already been authorized. Thus, lawyers representing affected communities kept using article 47 of the HSGA. A few years later, with the creation of a new Ministry for the Environment, Natural Resources and Fisheries in late 1994, new spaces for public participation were opened up and environmental NGOs began having an unprecedented voice in the crafting of public policies. In this context, a public consultation process was started in March 1995 in order to revise the EBEPGA. One of the demands

6 Section 47, Human Settlements General Act. *Diario Oficial de la Federación*, 7 February 1984.

of the NGOs was the introduction of judicial procedures to carry out class actions, so that every person could have the right to challenge in court projects or government decisions that affected the environment. The consultation process was so intense and conflictive, that it took almost eighteen months to get the bill through Congress. On several occasions, the process was halted because there was no consensus about several issues, the most difficult being the recognition of diffuse interests and the involvement of courts in environmental conflicts. Although the original demand of the organizations was not fully achieved, in the end a consensus was reached in order to include a rule similar to article 47 of the HSGA. Through an apparently innocent twist, it became explicit that citizens' complaints would start a process of administrative review in which they were formally recognized as plaintiffs. The legal consequence of this is that the conclusion of such a procedure can be challenged in courts. This became section 180 of the EBEPGA:

> Whenever works or activities that contravene this Act, land-use plans, the regulations of natural protected areas, or any regulation derived from the same Act, individual and collective persons of the affected communities will have the right to challenge the corresponding administrative acts, as well as the right to demand that the authorities take the necessary actions in order to comply with the applicable rules, provided that such persons demonstrate that those works or activities originate or may originate a damage to natural resources, wildlife, public health or the quality of life. To this effect, they must file the procedure of administrative review as established in this chapter.

Once the government accepted this text, environmental NGOs saw this as a victory and the bill became law by a unanimous vote in both the Senate and the House of Representatives (*Cámara de Diputados*). Much could be said about this unanimity, which at that time was a symptom of the influence of environmental NGOs in Mexico's public life (Azuela 2006). For the purpose of this chapter, what matters is to stress the contrast between the amendment of the HSGA in 1983, that passed largely unnoticed, and that of the environmental legislation one decade later, in an episode that attracted the participation of social organizations that exerted an unprecedented influence in the crafting of a piece of legislation.

These legislative changes did not create new judicial procedures such as those that recent constitutional amendments established in 2011. However, even if they can be seen as 'backdoor' adjustments of established procedures, they opened the way to what urban and environmental litigation is today in Mexico: dozens of cases throughout the country in which judges are granting injunctions that halt projects while they consider whether they infringe or not urban or environmental legislation. The novelty is, of course, that they have been mobilized by social organizations. Unfortunately, there is no statistical record of this activity, but to any observer it is obvious that this is a new, and very relevant, area of litigation in contemporary Mexico.[7]

The jurisprudence parade

There can be no doubt that, since the early eighties, reforms in the statute book granted rights to members of a community to demand the compliance of urban regulations and plans. However, the actual recognition of those rights by the judiciary required a change in the way judges saw legal standing. Public interest lawyers who tried to use the new legal devices in the 1990s complained that judges were reluctant to recognise what in continental Europe is known as 'diffuse interests'. Judges who come from the private law tradition required the existence of an individual holding a right that has been violated by another individual. In turn, administrative judges depended on another simplified dichotomy, i.e. the conflict between someone who governs in the public interest and a 'governed' person, both linked by an 'administrative act' by which the former affected the latter. In environmental conflicts, both were quite strict as to the need to prove the damage to the environment. As a result, it took almost three decades for the Judiciary to recognise the full implications of what the statute established with seemingly obvious clarity. Such recognition did not take place with one single decision, but as a result of a long and cumulative process. In what follows we will examine fourteen theses of *jurisprudencia* through which federal courts made sense of the issue of legal standing for the protection of the environment and the quality of life in urban areas.

A 'good' *tesis de jurisprudencia* consists of a rule plus an explanation. It usually makes a reference to a legal norm (be it a general principle of law, a provision in the Constitution or in a piece of legislation), then it offers an argument about the correct way of interpreting it. Between 1993 and 2011, federal courts issued fourteen jurisprudence theses that refer directly to the rights of neighbours to oppose a project that affects their environment. We will see that although they did not do so in an outright way, ultimately they did not find it difficult to sustain such a right, as it was clearly granted, first by the legislation on Human Settlements, and then by the environmental legislation.

The first time this happened was in 1993, nine years after the inclusion of section 47 into the HSGA. The *tesis* reads:

> Section 47 of the Human Settlements General Act *protects a legal interest* to demand the suspensions, demolitions or necessary modifications, in

7 For a first statistical account, see Azuela, Saavedra and Herrera, 2014.

> order for the applicable rules to be complied with, when constructions, subdivisions, changes of land use, or other developments that contravene laws, regulations, or urban development plans and programmes are being carried out and they originate a deterioration of the quality of life of human settlements. This *right* can be exercised by residents that are directly affected before the corresponding authorities, who will be obliged to resolve in less than thirty days... (mphasis added).[8]

At first sight, this *tesis* simply reproduces (and quite literally) the text of the HSGA. But it also explains that, by saying what it says, the HSGA is *protecting a legal interest.* There is neither mystery nor hard reasoning, only a doctrinal explanation of the legal implication of a text that the Congress had approved ten years before. That was how the Supreme Court recognised for the first time that neighbours are entitled to legal standing to demand that the administrative authorities protect their quality of life. It is true that such recognition was rather limited, as it required that neighbours were *directly* affected by the works in progress. But it was nonetheless the first step in a clear direction; and our point here is that the Supreme Court was just making explicit the procedural implications of a substantive rule that was part of the statute book. It is interesting to note that the justice responsible for drafting the opinion, Miguel Montes, was not a judge by career, but a 'political appointee' – something that has never pleased the 'judicial family'.[9] Years before, he had served as the first Attorney for Consumers' Protection in the Federal Government,[10] so it is easy to assume that he had been exposed to arguments in favour of widening legal standing in that area, something that would be difficult to expect from more traditional judges.

The second *tesis* came in 1994 and was issued by a Circuit Tribunal, the same year in which a Constitutional amendment transformed the Supreme Court in such a profound way that most legal scholars say that since then it became a real Constitutional Court, following the trend of other Latin American countries in the post-authoritarian era. However, that *tesis* simply followed the line that the previous one had established. It just added that the law recognises a right of neighbours 'in front of inadequate planning or erroneous decision making in urban development issues and admits ... [their] ability to defend the environment where they live'. Also, it removes procedural obstacles by asserting that the recognition of a legal interest in

8 Registro 206750. 8a. Época; 3a. Sala; Semanario Judicial de la Federación; Tomo XI, Febrero de 1993; p. 6.

9 In fact, judicial functionaries in Mexico use that expression to refer to those who have made their careers within the judiciary.

10 Or *Procurador Federal de Protección al Consumidor.*

the cases defined by the HSGA only requires that 'the plaintiffs demonstrate they reside in the place where the change of land use is to take place'.[11]

Two aspects of this *tesis* are worth mentioning. On the one hand, as we have said, most *tesis de jurisprudencia* in Mexico are quite hermetic as to the conflict that gave rise to them. But it is possible to locate what was at stake. The case involved a plot of approximately 1,000 square meters in a low-income residential area in Mexico City, in which the owner wanted to establish a small workshop, so he obtained a zoning change that was challenged by a group of neighbours. It is disappointing to learn that, in the end, the change of land use was authorized because the neighbours did not show up at the meeting that was organised to hear them.[12] This allows us to see that a relevant *tesis* may not necessarily have an obvious impact upon the conflicts that prompted them in the first place.

On the other hand, the *tesis* does not mention a previous one, i.e. that of Justice Miguel Montes, which would have helped as a source of authority because it was also issued by the Supreme Court. This may seem strange in the context of Mexican legal culture, in which lower courts are particularly deferential[13] towards the Supreme Court's *jurisprudencia*. Most probably, the authors of this new *tesis* were not aware of an earlier one as the electronic system called IUS that some years later made access so easy to jurisprudence theses had yet to be created.

Two years later, in 1996, a new *tesis* appeared, but it went in the opposite direction. A Circuit Tribunal, also located in Mexico City, bluntly ruled that

> residents of a neighbourhood in which someone tries to establish a business lack legal interest to challenge any act regarding such [commercial] land use, because the law does not recognize to them any right to protection for the simple fact of residing in the same area; therefore, closing down a business or cancelling a permit are powers that are vested in the [administrative] authority, who in every case is responsible for any behaviour against the law in force.[14]

This *tesis* appeared the same year in which the reform of environmental legislation (see section 1 *supra*) had included an expanded version of the

11 Registro 210188 8a. Época; T.C.C. Semanario Judicial de la Federación; Tomo XIV, October 1994; p. 282.

12 Acuerdo del Secretario de Desarrollo Urbano y Vivienda, Juan Gil Elizondo, 23 January 1996.

13 As Ansolabehere (2007) has shown in an insightful comparative study of the Argentinian and the Mexican judiciary, in the latter there is a much greater 'discipline' of lower judges and courts *vis à vis* the Supreme Court.

14 Tesis Aislada, I.4o.A.146 A, Semanario de la Suprema Corte de Justicia y su Gaceta, novena época, tribunales colegiados de circuito, IV, September 1996, p. 661.

right originally established by the HSGA, a process that was widely reported by the media. What is remarkable is that this new *tesis* ignored not only the two previous ones but also the very existence of section 47 of the HSGA. This may be due to the fact that litigants did not invoke the HSGA, which at least would have forced the judges to explain their position towards that piece of legislation. At any rate, by ignoring the HSGA they were expressing a widely held position of Mexican judges in relation to standing.

The fourth tesis, this time from the Supreme Court, recognized that the HSGA grants a legal interest to neighbours in the same way as the two first theses. But it also made clear that, before they could file a writ of *amparo* before a federal judge, the plaintiffs should seek an administrative review before the corresponding government agency. However, the interesting turn in this tesis is that it gives a name to the right established in section 47, by stating that it 'grants a *right to preserve the residential environment* to the neighbors of the residential area affected by works that originated a deterioration in the quality of life of human settlements ...' (emphasis added).[15]

Although this was still far from a full recognition of the right to an adequate environment, it is interesting to note that the Supreme Court had decided to use the language of rights for something that had begun as a simple procedural device – i. e. having access to courts. Only two weeks before that *tesis* was approved by the plenary of the Supreme Court, the Mexican Congress had passed, with a unanimous vote in both houses,[16] the amendments to the environmental legislation that had been debated for more than eighteen months. As we explained in the previous section, those reforms expanded the right that had been originally established by the HSGA. Such an unusual situation (a unanimous vote in a context of political pluralism) was possible only because both environmental NGOs and entrepreneurial organizations had expressed their satisfaction with the bill. And the most debated issues of that legislative reform were precisely the new instruments for public participation in environmental governance, i.e. public hearings for major development projects, public access to environmental information, and of course, legal standing to oppose projects that infringe environmental regulations. If it is worth noticing that our *tesis* did not mention the environmental legislation, it is remarkable that the next *tesis* in our saga goes in the opposite direction.

It was in 1999 when a Circuit Tribunal, based in the highly industrialized northern State of Nuevo León, issued a *tesis* that restricted neighbors legal standing in these matters. The Tribunal ruled that neighbors had to demonstrate that a direct and personal offence (or *agravio*) had been

15 Registro: 199493 9a. Época; Pleno; Semanario Judicial de la Federación y su Gaceta; Tomo V, January 1997; p. 6.

16 The jurisprudence *tesis* was issued on 26 November and the sessions of the Senate and the House of Representatives took place on the 26 and 30 October, respectively.

inflicted upon them. Also, it implied that there was no law that granted such rights to neighbors.[17] Like the *tesis* of 1996, it offered neither a new interpretation of enacted legislation nor reference to the other three jurisprudence theses that had recognized those rights. It simply did not mention them; a clear indication that there was still a resistance within the judiciary to recognize legal standing beyond traditional notions of legal interest. However, that was the last time that a jurisprudence *tesis* overtly denied the rights of citizens to object projects in their communities.

Beyond the apparently inconsistent behavior of Mexican federal courts around this issue, we begin to see a pattern: when a court chooses to deny legal standing to neighbours it simply refrains from making any reference to the legislation and the jurisprudence that grants such standing – it remains to be determined whether that is the result of authentic 'ignorance' of the law or of a deliberate strategy. On the other hand, theses that recognize standing always make an explicit reference to legislation. This confirms with what socio-legal scholars have been saying about judicial culture in Mexico during the last years: the main source of legal authority is '*la ley*', i.e. statutory legislation. Sometimes this deference to the legislative extends to by-regulations passed by the Executive (or *reglamentos administrativos*). That is the case with our sixth *tesis* which was issued in 2001 by a Circuit Tribunal in the northeastern state of Tamaulipas. This new *tesis* does not mention previous theses or urban or environmental legislation. It only quotes the state Building Code (*Reglamento de Construcciones*) and points out that, according to it, in order to authorize a land-use change 'it is necessary to notify the neighbours that might be affected with such change', so that they can challenge the permit through an administrative review.[18] Like other theses, this one does not enter into a grand debate about 'diffuse interests'; it only repeats what an administrative by-law already says: neighbours must be notified of land-use changes.

Indeed, one may wonder why justices in that Tribunal imagined that their reasoning in the case deserved to become *jurisprudencia*, i.e. that 'source of law' that emerges from judicial wisdom in hard cases or when obscure legal texts demand a special interpretive effort. In fact, there are many jurisprudence theses that simply repeat what a piece of legislation establishes. According to several sources, there was a huge increase in their numbers after the Judiciary Council (or *Consejo de la Judicatura*), a body created in 1994 to professionalize the judiciary, established certain 'indicators' to measure the performance of federal judges. One such indicator was the number of jurisprudence theses that came out of each court. Very

17 Instancia: Tribunales Colegiados de Circuito; Semanario Judicial de la Federación y su Gaceta Tomo: X, September 1999 Tesis: IV.3o.A.T.23. p. 816.

18 Registro: 188059, 9a. Época; T.C.C.; S.J.F. y su Gaceta; Tomo XIV, December 2001; p. 1827.

much like academics suffering the 'publish or perish' syndrome, judges began to present as theses pieces of legal arguments even if they added nothing to the clarification of the law.[19] This may look like an irrelevant episode, but it allows us to be aware of the changing institutional conditions under which *jurisprudencia* as a source of law is created. Moreover, the case leads us to two further points: one is that the idea of public participation has got as far as the realm of by-laws at state level. The other is that not all judges were hostile to citizens' involvement in governmental decisions with urban and environmental impacts; for some of them a local by-law was enough and they needed neither national legislation nor *jurisprudencia* coming from the Supreme Court in order to protect neighbors' rights.

A new *tesis* appeared in 2003. This time the author was the Circuit Tribunal based in the State of Colima on the pacific coast. There was nothing new in this *tesis* as it follows the one of 1997 in which the Supreme Court declared that there was a 'right to preserve the residential environment'. It is interesting only because it reproduces, *verbatim*, the Supreme Court *tesis* without making any reference to it. And then it adds some rather obvious procedural implications applicable to the State of Colima.[20] It goes without saying that these are not academic texts in which plagiarism could be a problem. But it is difficult to understand why a Circuit Tribunal, instead of appealing to the *jurisprudencia* of the Supreme Court as a source of authority, simply reproduces the very same text as if it was of its own inspiration. Maybe the law clerk who drafted it never imagined that IUS, the electronic data base of Mexican *jurisprudencia*, would become so popular that anyone would notice his own little prank; one only hopes that his or her superiors, i.e. the justices that signed the 'new' *tesis*, did so without realizing what they were doing.

Tesis number eight in our list is just one more in the same line: it declares as unconstitutional the amendment of a transit by-law in the State of Nuevo León because the public enquiry did not follow certain procedures. This is another indication that the idea of public participation began to take hold in Mexican legal culture. In contrast, *tesis* number nine, from a Circuit Tribunal in Mexico City in 2007, brought with it an interesting innovation. Eight years before, the Constitution had been amended in order to recognize an 'adequate environment' as a fundamental right.[21] It is worth

19 Personal communication of a former member of the Judiciary Council (Consejo de la Judicatura) who asked to remain anonymous.

20 Registro: 183918. 9a. Época; T.C.C.; S.J.F. y su Gaceta; Tomo XVIII, July 2003; p. 1030.

21 Section 4 of the Mexican Constitution, amendment published in the *Diario Oficial de la Federación*, 28 June 1999.

reading the *tesis* in full because it links the question of standing to the existence of a right to the environment:

> The legal interest that makes possible to proceed with the *amparo* suit can be identified with a right that derives from a legal norm and becomes real in a certain person, giving that person the power to make a legal claim to a public authority. In this context, there is a legally protected right to preserve the residential environment that derives from Article 4 of the Constitution, which guarantees an adequate environment for the development and welfare of persons as a *fundamental right erga omnes.* Such right *implies a collective action* both in a substantive and a procedural aspect, related to section 57[22] of the Human Settlements General Act, which grants affected neighbors a right to demand from the administrative authority the adoption of security measures as well as sanctions, when building activities, land subdivisions or other forms of developments infringe urban development regulations. Therefore, there is a legal interest of a residents' association to promote an *amparo* against the permit to install a station for gas distribution, provided that such association demonstrates that it has sought remedy from the administrative authority, without having obtained a clear, coherent, and categorical resolution to its demand; (emphasis added).[23]

Even if the practical consequences appear to be the same as in other cases (the cancellation of a project), the way it is defined by the judge introduces a wholly different legal dimension to the case. In times when neo-constitutionalism as a dominant legal doctrine proclaims an evident superiority of human rights law over statutory legislation, this is an important step. It is not only that some 'secondary' legislation grants rights to a certain social category (neighbours); such legislation is also an instrument of a fundamental right which is explicitly recognized in the constitutional text. Also, it is interesting to note the use of the expression 'collective action', which shows a clear intention to overcome the individualist perspective that is so deeply ingrained in the Mexican judicial tradition.

There is, further, another interesting aspect of this *tesis.* Even if it was issued in the context of a growing public presence of environmental NGOs, that ten years before obtained the victory of Article 180 of the environmental legislation, the latter is not mentioned in the *tesis.* The legal reference is still the good old Human Settlements General Act – the same

22 The enactment of a new Human Settlements Act in 1993 had moved our provision from section 47 to section 57.

23 This is a free, rather than a literal, translation. Registro: 173002 9a. Época; T.C.C.; Semanario Judicial de la Federación y su Gaceta; Tomo XXV, March 2007; p. 1694.

piece of legislation that many environmental activists have blamed for subordinating environmental causes to the needs of urban development (Azuela 2006).

It should be noted that there is a *tesis* in 2010 that we will not examine here. It does no harm to our subject, but it does not add anything interesting either. The fact is that its text is wholly incomprehensible; indeed, even impossible to translate.[24] This takes us to the four theses that, in 2011, finally recognized the full effect of what had begun in 1983 with section 47 of HSGA and had acquired momentum with the 1996 reforms to the environmental legislation.

The case that prompted these theses was typical of the current public interest litigation in Mexico: the most important environmental NGO devoted to the legal defence of the environment, i.e. the Mexican Center of Environmental Law (CEMDA),[25] had won an administrative procedure as a result of which the federal Secretary of the Environment and Natural Resources invalidated a permit to carry out a tourist resort in the State of Quintana Roo, on the Caribbean coast. The private corporation that was affected by that administrative decision filed an *amparo*. There was, at last, an opportunity to establish a connection between a relevant case in the public space and jurisprudence as a 'source of law'. The Supreme Court did not miss the opportunity to deliver not one but four theses. José R. Cossío, one of the Court's justices that had been striving for innovative practices in such a conservative environment, stated the *tesis* that reads as follows:

> it can be seen that ... [the intention behind section 180 was to] recognize standing to seek for administrative review to any person of the concerned communities; such concern must consist of a current or imminent harm to natural resources, wildlife, public health, or the quality of life. In this way, the inclusion of such right into the legislation represents a step forward in the recognition of the legal interest of persons to challenge administrative acts even if they are not addressed to them, ... this is about the implementation of a defense mechanism for the protection of *diffuse interests* that constitute a component of the vertical efficacy of a fundamental right, that amounts to the constitutional obligation of the availability of authorities and mechanisms that guarantee the sustainability of the environment, which in turn would

24 Legibility of judicial rulings is something that only the elite of the legal field recognizes as a problem. As a result, in recent years, judges have been subject to training in legal argumentation.

25 The *Centro Mexicano de Derecho Ambiental* was created in 1993, in the context of the negotiations leading to the NAFTA and it is the most important public interest litigation NGO in environmental issues in the country.

> lead to the indirect protection of the right to an adequate environment that is established in the Constitution…and consequently to the preservation of the ecosystems as common goods, the protection of which is of public interest (Emphasis added).[26]

This way, fifteen years after section 180 of EBEPGA, and almost three decades after section 47 of the HSGA, the Supreme Court acknowledged that there was a legislative recognition of diffuse interests. The innovation of this *tesis* resides in that it establishes a clear link between two legal concepts: one is the concept of *diffuse interest* that is used as the foundation for expanding the subjects that can mobilize the judicial apparatus. The other is the right to an adequate environment that had been included in the text of the Constitution. The result is that the environment as a fundamental right becomes enforceable by the courts at the requirement of concerned citizens. Moreover, what in previous theses had been a right to 'preserve a residential environment' is expanded to a more ambitious concept of ecosystems as 'common goods'. The second *tesis* that justice Cossío drew from the same case dealt with the problem of demonstrating the damages to the environment, and it established that

> … the damage to natural resources, the wildlife, public health of the quality of life, has to be proven during the administrative review, and therefore it is not a requirement to start such review… the existence of such damage is part of the matter of the case. [27]

If this *tesis* is taken seriously, it makes illegal for governmental authorities to refuse to substantiate an administrative review on the grounds that the environmental damage has not been proven.

The third *tesis* in the same case states that the justification for the compulsory character of the administrative review is clear in the 'statement of purpose' (or *exposición de motivos*[28]) of the 1996 reform to the Ley General del Equilibrio Ecológico y la Protección al Ambiente (LGEEPA) that introduced section 180:

> As it can be read in the statement of purpose, the fact that the affected communities resort to an administrative review is closely related to the good that is protected by the law (the environment …), as there is a

26 Registro: 160160. 10a. Época; 1a. Sala; S.J.F. y su Gaceta; Libro VII, April 2012, Tomo 1; p. 874.

27 Registro: 160161. 10a. Época; 1a. Sala; S.J.F. y su Gaceta; Libro VII, April 2012, Tomo 1; p. 873.

28 *Exposición de motivos* is the document that accompanies a bill in Congress and explains its purposes.

> public interest in its protection ... [therefore] the legislator provided an adequate justification of the reasons and motives that led him to establish the right [to be heard in administrative review]. [29]

It is important to keep in mind that having access to an administrative review automatically makes the involvement of a federal judge possible, because regardless of the content of the decision that comes out of the review, it is an administrative act that can be challenged in court by the person who started it. Finally, the fourth *tesis* in this case (fourteenth in our general account) makes clear that 'section 180 does not violate the right to legal security established in [...] the Constitution'.[30] This was the first time that the Court made a special reference to the status of section 180 in relation to constitutional principles of due process. This was a clear answer to allegations against the widening of the rules of standing made by lawyers working for investors. Against every regulation that limits economic activity they usually argue that legal security (or *seguridad jurídica*) should be paramount to any other consideration. This time, private interests were restricted not by strengthening government power but by means of a combination of citizens' rights and judicial intervention. McAuslan's triangle of state/community/property had adopted a new and unpredicted configuration.

One of the most salient aspects of these four theses is not their content but their context. Whereas the previous theses passed unnoticed beyond those directly concerned with the conflict, this time the media reported what the Supreme Court had just done. Notably, the Mexican Green Party[31] proudly announced that this *jurisprudencia* was the direct result of their initiative, as some years before one of its members had been part of a congressional committee that suggested minor changes to section 180, as if it were completely new! The fact is that by 2011, there was a 'public' for whom this was relevant news. However small that public may be, its presence in the public agenda means something. What we want to stress here is the sharp contrast between this relatively wide publicity and the almost secret way in which section 47 of HSGA was enacted three decades later.

As we have already pointed out, in 2011 there was also a constitutional amendment that recognised a wide definition of legal interest for the *amparo* suit, which was presented as a completely new issue in the life of the

29 Registro: 160162. 10a. Época; 1a. Sala; S.J.F. y su Gaceta; Libro VII, April 2012, Tomo 1; p. 873.

30 Registro: 160163. 10a. Época; 1a. Sala; S.J.F. y su Gaceta; Libro VII, April 2012, Tomo 1; p. 872.

31 A political party that has been condemned by many Green Parties over the world because of its support of the death penalty.

judiciary. We have seen that judicial practice had been recognising this at least since 1993. The last four theses of the same year that we have just described may be seen as the 'dress rehearsal' of a new era in the capacity of citizens to mobilize judges to defend their environment.

Conclusion

Let us summarise our analysis by addressing three questions: what was the main outcome of the Mexican *jurisprudencia* on standing in urban and environmental conflicts? how did that happen? and what are its probable social consequences? It should be clear that, by means of their '*tesis*', Mexican high courts have recognised new forms of standing that allow residents to participate actively in the enforcement of urban and environmental law. What started in the early 1990s as a mechanism for the protection of the quality of life in the narrow world of neighbourhoods, in 2011 had became the subject of a much wider definition in terms of environmental rights as collective interests. Whereas it would be a mistake to assume that *all* judges will follow that *jurisprudencia*, the fact is that the higher levels of the judiciary have recognised diffuse interests as part of the law. At least formally, that stands as the 'last word' in the legal system.

The main implication of this development is a change in the balance between the three ideologies that, according to McAuslan, compete in planning and environmental law. The ideology of public participation gets stronger at the expense of the ideology of private property that is the main justification of developers. This is relevant because it occurs in times of an alleged pre-eminence of the interests of private investors. In this chapter we have not analyzed the difficulties that social organisations have encountered in the exercising of their new rights. However, no one working in the field would say the legislative and jurisprudential changes we have described are irrelevant for the advancement of environmental causes in Mexico.

Before looking at the possible impacts of these developments, it is interesting to summarise the conditions under which they took place – i.e. 'how did this happen'? When seen from the broader question of the Mexican 'transition to democracy', it is clear that, at least since the early 1990s of the last century, courts began to behave in a more independent way. Political scientists have explained that there is a clear relationship between political pluralism and judicial independence (Ríos-Figueroa 2007). Our fourteen *tesis de jurisprudencia* are a clear expression of this general condition, since they have often meant not only putting limits to economic activity but also to the government actions that make it possible; thus it is also a shift in the balance between public participation and state power. Having said that, we can ask ourselves whether this is one form of 'judicial activism' that would represent a profound change in legal culture. The question calls for a nuanced answer.

It is true that by recognising new forms of standing judges were abandoning their own restricted and individualist definition of the capacity of persons to set the judiciary in motion. However, this happened through the deployment of a very traditional mechanism, i.e. by following the provisions of enacted legislation. It was there, in the realm of the legislative branch, that it all began; first as the initiative of obscure civil servants (in the 1983 amendment of the Human Settlements Act) and then with the participation of social organisations as remarkably central actors in the legislative process (in the 1996 amendment of the environmental legislation). By recognising diffuse interests under different labels, judges were not adding anything substantial to what was clearly established in the statute book. This does not mean to minimize the relevance of the whole process, but simply to acknowledge that it was possible, thanks to the fundamental ambivalence of legal culture: a new element came into existence thanks to the working of an old one. In other words, breaking a tradition was possible because another tradition was alive and well.

For many environmental lawyers the opening of new spaces for collective claims is the result of the mobilization of civil society, a category that since the mid-1980sappears in the public sphere as an unquestionable source of legitimacy (Escalante 2006). While it is true that in the 1996 reform of environmental legislation NGOs played a fundamental role, the process had started more than one decade before as an idea within the bureaucracy.[32]

When one looks at the most relevant environmental conflicts of the last decades, none of them was the subject of a *tesis de jurisprudencia*. The cases that prompted our fourteen theses were indeed minor in comparison to those that involved relevant social mobilizations or at least the attention of the media. Beyond the visibility of two or three NGOs the truth is that there are very few lawyers that practice public interest litigation in Mexico. This is part of the explanation of the fact that the whole process took almost three decades. Of course, another explanation for this delay is that it was hard for the judiciary to break with its own traditional way of defining standing. However, the way the theses were written suggests that there was something else: social organisations and their lawyers took too long to realise that there was in the law a mechanism they could use to protect the environment. To the extent courts were not pressed by lawyers invoking urban and then environmental legislation, they could arrive at judgements

32 This is the place for a personal note that would not be acceptable in a regular academic book. It was the author of this essay who was the one who suggested the inclusion of section 47 in the Human Settlements Act in 1983. I was not only lucky enough to be 'at the right place and the right moment' to do it. I was able to do it because years before I had the privilege of being a student of McAuslan at Warwick. Under his mentorship, it was impossible not to embrace strong ideas about public participation in urban affairs.

and write theses that denied standing to them. If judges themselves were frequently unaware of the Supreme Court's theses, it is reasonable to assume that 'society at large' was even less aware of them. We have seen that it was only when the courts made an explicit reference to the enacted legislation that they recognised standing rights. As a hypo*tesis* for future research, it can be said that judges are able to ignore the law when litigants do not point out the relevant legal texts.

The last element in our description of the conditions under which this happened is the fact that it was the result of an interaction between branches of government. Long before a constitutional amendment included class actions and 'legitimate interests' in the *amparo* suit, planning and environmental law had established the question of standing and collective claims at the centre of its practice, as part of the apparently modest realm of administrative procedures.[33] One may wonder why constitutional law scholars, as much as judges themselves, have taken so long in registering these developments. But this demands a deeper inquiry into the ways in which legal innovations circulate throughout the legal field. As much as we have seen circuit courts using verbatim whole paragraphs from Supreme Court's theses as if they were their own, exposing themselves to the scorn of the profession, we can also imagine lawyers who, in trying to defend neighbours, are ignorant of the fact that there are specific devices that they could use. Another hypo*tesis* here is that the advent of electronic access to the *jurisprudencia* represented an important change in the way the law circulates.

Finally, it is interesting to reflect upon the long term social effects of the recognition of diffuse interests in planning an environmental law. In the Latin American context this is a relevant question since democratic transitions has brought with it new expectations regarding the possibility that courts' activities may bring relevant social changes (Rodriguez-Garavito & Rodríguez-Franco 2010). Not surprisingly, there is at the same time a debate about whether judges are going too far.[34] However, that debate tends to be of a normative character and led by legal philosophers. The contribution of socio-legal studies here lies in the ability to register the sort of changes that are actually taking place. In our subject the current situation is certainly different from that of three decades ago: social organisations are now being able to halt projects that affect their environment. Although it is impossible to have a precise idea of the size of this phenomenon, those who participate actively in the environmental field are aware that for many projects there is such possibility. That means nothing less

33 Gargarella (2011, 1552) makes a similar point. But Article 47 was initially a substantive reform, although not verbalized with the grandeur of rights discourse.

34 For a recent debate on the subject in Latin America, see *Texas Law Review*, Volume 89, number 7, 2011.

than a change in the expectations of relevant actors in relation to urban and environmental law. What is more difficult to assess is the future of this process. It is too soon to tell whether this will reach large corporate interests, such as those represented by open pit mining, who are at the source of many of the most acute environmental conflicts in contemporary Mexico. On a deeper level, it also remains to be seen whether preventing projects is going to be the only, or even the main, way of giving content to the right to the environment.

References

Aguirrezabal-Grünstein, Maite. 2006. Algunas precisiones en torno a los intereses supra individuales (colectivos y difusos), in *Revista Chilena de Derecho* 33(1): 69–91.

Almagro-Nosete, José. 1982–3. Tutela procesal ordinaria y privilegiada (jurisdicción constitucional) de los intereses difusos, *Revista de Derecho Político* 16 Winter.

Ansolabehere, Karina. 2007. *La política desde la justicia. Cortes supremas, gobierno y democracia en Argentina y México.* Mexico City: FLACSO/Fontamara.

Azuela, Antonio. 1989. *La ciudad, la propiedad privada y el derecho.* Mexico City: El Colegio de México.

Azuela, Antonio. 2006. *Visionarios y pragmáticos. Una aproximación sociológica al derecho ambiental.* Mexico City: UNAM/Fontamara.

Azuela, Antonio, Camilo Saavedra and Carlos Herrera. 2014. A tumult of rulings. A quantitative exploration of the legal outcomes of urban litigation in two judicial contexts in Mexico. Working paper. Cambridge, MA: Lincoln Institute of Land Policy.

Cafferatta, Nestor. 2005. Breves reflexiones sobre la naturaleza del daño ambiental colectivo, *Revista CEJ.*

Carmona-Tinoco, Jorge. 1995. La jurisprudencia obligatoria de los Tribunales del Poder Judicial de la Federación, in *Boletín Mexicano de Derecho Comparado* 2008, 83, May–August.

Concha, Hugo and José-Antonio Caballero. 2004. *Diagnóstico sobre la administración de justicia en las entidades federativas. Un estudio institucional sobre la justicia local en México.* Mexico City: National Center for State Courts/Instituto de Investigaciones Jurídicas, UNAM.

Escalante, Fernando. 2004. Los años amargos. Pensamiento político en México a fines del siglo veinte, *Historia y Política. Ideas, procesos y movimientos sociales,* 11, Madrid.

Gargarella, Roberto. 2011. Grafting social rights onto hostile constitutions, *Texas Law Review,* 89(7) June.

Landi, Pasquale. 1991. *La tutela processuale dell'ambiente (art. 18 della lege 8 luglio 1986, N°349),* Padova: Cedam.

Magallón-Ibarra, Jorge-Mario. 2004. *Los sonidos y el silencio de la jurisprudencia mexicana.* México: UNAM.

McAuslan, Patrick. 1979. The ideologies of planning law, *Urban Law and Policy* 2: 1–23.

McAuslan, Patrick. 1980. *The Ideologies of Planning Law.* London: Pergamon Press.

Ricciardi, Victoria and Alejandro Sehtman. 2015. La cuestión villera ante los tribunales: descripción y análisis de la intervención judicial en la política de villas del Gobierno de la Ciudad de Buenos Aires, in Roberto Gargarella and Lucas Arrimada (eds) *La Constitución en discusión. Derechos humanos, justicia social y política democrática.* Buenos Aires: Eudeba (forthcoming).

Ríos-Figueroa, Julio. 2007. Fragmentation of power and the emergence of an effective judiciary in Mexico, 1994–200, *Latin American Politics and Society* 49(1): Spring.

Rodriguez-Garavito, César and Diana Rodríguez-Franco. 2010. *Cortes y cambio social. Cómo la Corte Constitucional transformó el desplazamiento forzado en Colombia.* Bogota: Colección De Justicia.

Vázquez-Robles, Guillermo-Gabino. 2012. *Artesanos de certezas. Un modelo teórico sobre el discurso jurisprudencial.* Tesis de Doctorado en Derecho. México: Facultad de Derecho, UNAM.

Woldemberg, José. 2012. *Historia mínima de la transición democrática en México.* Mexico: El Colegio de Mexico.

Zertuche-García, Héctor-Gerardo. 1992. *La jurisprudencia en el sistema jurídico mexicano.* México: Porrúa.

Index

For Product Safety Concerns and Information please contact our EU representative GPSR@taylorandfrancis.com
Taylor & Francis Verlag GmbH, Kaufingerstraße 24, 80331 München, Germany

www.ingramcontent.com/pod-product-compliance
Ingram Content Group UK Ltd.
Pitfield, Milton Keynes, MK11 3LW, UK
UKHW011000180926
475701UK00004B/471
9781138590823